INSIGHT GUIDE

MALLORCA & IBIZA
MENORCA & FORMENTERA

APA PUBLICATIONS

Part of the Langenscheidt Publishing Group

ABOUT THIS BOOK

Editorial

Project Editor
Melissa de Villiers
Managing Editor
Emily Hatchwell
Editorial Director
Brian Bell

Distribution

UK & Ireland
GeoCenter International Ltd
The Viables Centre , Harrow Way
Basingstoke, Hants RG22 4BJ
Fax: (44) 1256-817988

United States
Langenscheidt Publishers, Inc.
46–35 54th Road, Maspeth, NY 11378
Fax: (718) 784-0640

Australia & New Zealand
Hema Maps Pty. Ltd.
24 Allgas Street, Slacks Creek 4127
Brisbane, Australia
Tel: (61) 7 3290 0322
Fax: (61) 7 3290 0478

Worldwide
APA Publications GmbH & Co.
Verlag KG (Singapore branch)
38 Joo Koon Road, Singapore 628990
Tel: (65) 865-1600
Fax: (65) 861-6438

Printing

Insight Print Services (Pte) Ltd
38 Joo Koon Road, Singapore 628990
Tel: (65) 865-1600
Fax: (65) 861-6438

©1999 APA Publications GmbH & Co.
Verlag KG (Singapore branch)
All Rights Reserved
First Edition 1989
Fourth Edition 1999

This guidebook combines the interests and enthusiasms of two of the world's best known information providers: Insight Guides, whose titles have set the standard for visual travel guides since 1970, and Discovery Channel, the world's premier source of nonfiction television programming.

The editors of Insight Guides provide practical advice and general understanding about a destination's history, culture, institutions and people. Discovery Channel and its extensive web site, www. discovery.com, help millions of viewers explore their world from the comfort of home and also encourage them to explore it firsthand.

How to use this book

This book is carefully structured both to convey an understanding of Mallorca, Ibiza, Menorca and Formentera – known collectively as the Balearics – and to guide readers through their sights and activities:

◆ The first section, with a yellow colour bar, focuses on the islands' History and Culture in **Features** written by experts.

◆ The main **Places** section, with a blue bar, is a complete guide to all the sights and areas worth visiting. Places of particular interest are cross-referenced by numbers or letters to specially commissioned full-colour maps.

◆ The **Travel Tips** section gives information on travel, hotels, restaurants, shops and so on. A Travel Tips index is printed on the back cover flap, which can also serve as a bookmark.

The Contributors

The task of assembling this latest edition of *Insight Guide: Mallorca and Ibiza* fell to **Melissa de Villiers**, a travel journalist and editor based in London. Completely revised and updated, this book builds on the original edition produced by long-time Insight contributor, **Andrew Eames**.

Tony Kelly, a UK-based travel journalist with a formidable knowledge of the Balearics, covered Mallorca, Menorca and Cabrera, and also revised many of the chapters in the Features section.

Robin Neillands wrote the chapters on Pollença and expatriate life for the first edition, and updated them this time around. Fellow-freelance **Teresa Fisher** revised the essays on architecture, jet-setters, birdwatching and the Mallorcan village of Deià.

Text retained from previous editions contains material from many experts on the Balearics, including **Felipe Fernandez-Armesto**, **Gil Carbajal**, **Ray Fleming**, **Vicky Hayward**, **John Matthews**, **Mike Mockler**, **Pedro de Montaner**, **Don Murray**, **Bob Norris**, **Anna Pascual**, **Ben Roth**, **Pol Ferguson-Thompson** and **Dr William Waldren**.

Many of the photographs are by **Bill Wassman**, who has produced the pictures for numerous Insight Guides. Others came from **Glyn Genin**, who returned to photography after many years as a newspaper picture editor.

Travel Tips were updated by **Sarah Raphael** and edited by **Sue Platt**. The book was proof-read by **Rachael Vermont** and indexed by **Penny Phenix**. Many thanks go also to **Natalia Farran Graves** for checking the Catalan spellings in the text.

Map Legend

●—●—●	National Park/Reserve
– – – –	Ferry Route
✈ ✈	Airport: International/Regional
🚌	Bus Station
P	Parking
❶	Tourist Information
✉	Post Office
╪ † ✝	Church/Ruins
†	Monastery
☾	Mosque
✡	Synagogue
⚔ ▨	Castle/Ruins
∴	Archaeological Site
∩	Cave
⚑	Statue/Monument
★	Place of Interest

The main places of interest in the Places section are coordinated by number with a full-colour map (e.g. ❶), and a symbol at the top of every right-hand page tells you where to find the map.

CONTENTS

The colours
of the islands
captured by
Betty White

Insight on ...

Information panels

Places

Travel Tips

A CLOSER LOOK

Tour brochures deluge you with images of sun, sand and sea.

But there's a far more interesting side to the Balearic islands

Qui vol peix, que es banyi es cul, runs the Menorquín proverb. ("You don't catch fish with dry trousers.") Every country, every region, has its old multi-purpose proverbs; the Balearics are no exception. The particular not-quite-truism above has had its day now as a literal saying, although it is unlikely that the islanders were ever in the habit of chucking themselves, fully clothed, at passing mackerel. They would never do anything in such a hurry.

Fishing on the islands has waned, but tourism has waxed to an awe-inspiring degree; nowadays, fishing boats make a better living as tourist boats, and their owners get their trousers wet only when a holidaymaker spills warm beer. There are more tourist beds in the bay of Palma de Mallorca than there are in the whole of the Eastern Mediterranean, and the number is still growing. Palma is the grand-daddy of mass tourism, and its children continue to produce grand-children on the coasts of all four islands.

Certainly, everyone accepts that the Balearic economy is inextri-cably linked to tourism. But the question today is how to make it sustainable and last all year round. While for decades the islands have been marketed as a cheap and cheerful kiss-me-quick location where the beer goes down a treat and the girls go topless on the beaches, a great deal of effort is now being expended on taking the tourist industry upmarket.

The most striking development of the 1990s has been the appear-ance of dozens of luxury country hotels in carefully-restored mansions – most of them well away from the coast. The idea is to appeal to a subtler, more discreet type of tourist, following in the tradition of such appreciative visitors as Robert Graves, Joan Miró, Agatha Christie, Winston Churchill, the British and Spanish Royal Families and many more, in whose shadow are a whole host of the cultured and the artistically-inclined.

They know, and a lot of quieter tourists know, that there is more to the Balearics than meets the brochure, and this book is also party to that knowledge. These pages dig behind the hackneyed image of Mallorca, Menorca, Ibiza and Formentera, combining the elements of an illustrated lecture, a magazine, an academic text, a collection of anecdotes and a gazetteer of everything of interest, animating a group of islands which is in danger of looking like a tired hostess in a rather cheap establishment.

But, like the fishermen who don't get to catch their fish unless they wet their trousers, you don't get to fully understand the Balearics unless you go out and take a closer look. ❏

PRECEDING PAGES: Ibizan farm-workers; the Menorcan village of Binibeca Vell; splashes of colour in Santa Gertrudis; intricate details grace a Mallorcan façade.
LEFT: Ibizan folk-dancer.

Decisive Dates

5000 BC: Food-gatherers and fishermen arrive from eastern Spain, settling in strategically-situated caves and constructing large cave-complexes.

2000 BC: The race known as the Beaker People arrives on the islands. They build stone houses, develop pottery technology and work metals not indigenous to the Balearics. Evidence of foreign trade and communication.

1300–1000 BC: Height of the Talayotic culture on Mallorca and Menorca. Warring tribes engage in primitive trade around the eastern Mediterranean.

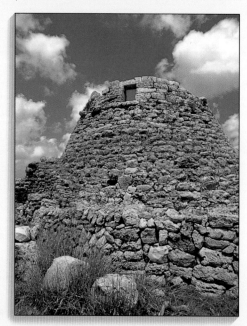

COLONIZATION AND CONTROL

700–146 BC: The Balearics are colonized first by the Phoenicians, then the Carthaginians. The countryside is exploited for agriculture; oil and wine are the principal products. In 146 BC, Carthage finally falls to Rome after losing the Punic Wars. The Romans annex the Balearics.

123 BC: Mallorca and Menorca are occupied by the Romans under the leadership of consul Quintus Metellus. Ibiza avoids military conquest by Rome despite backing Carthage, and remains distinctly Carthaginian.

AD 74: Roman settlers arrive on Ibiza, which becomes a municipality in the province of Tarraconensis (Tarragona).

AD 200: The islands are converted to Christianity.

426: Vandals devastate the islands, and persecute Christians. Trade decreases. The Dark Ages begin for the Balearics.

534: The Christian religion is restored by the Byzantines, who defeat the Vandals. By 700, North Africans are raiding the islands.

902: The Balearics are incorporated into the Caliphate of Córdoba.

MOORISH RULE

1015: After the collapse of the Caliphate of Córdoba, the Balearics are annexed to another small Muslim kingdom, the *taifa* of Denia.

1087–1114: The islands become an independent kingdom, known as the *taifa* of Mallorca.

1114: A group of Pisa-Catalans manage to conquer Ibiza and Mallorca. The siege of Palma lasts eight months. After the city is defeated and sacked, the invaders go home.

1115–1203: The Almorávides, a Muslim tribe from North Africa, arrive to help the Mallorcan Muslims during the siege of Palma and stay on to occupy the island. The Balearics experience a period of prosperity. The Almorávides' dominion extends beyond the islands to Tunisia and Tripolitania.

1203–29: The Balearics fall into the hands of Almohadian tribes from Algeria and Denia. Political instability allows the reconquest of Mallorca by the Catalans.

THE KINGDOM OF MALLORCA

1229: Catalan King Jaume I of Aragón occupies and conquers Mallorca on 31 December after three months of fierce fighting.

1235: Ibiza is conquered by a group of noblemen on Jaume I's behalf.

1276: On Jaume's death, the independent Kingdom of Mallorca (including Mallorca, Ibiza and enclaves such as Montpellier on the French mainland) is created, ruled by Jaume's son, Jaume II.

1285: First attempt by the Catalans to conquer the Kingdom of Mallorca by force. A later expedition is forced to turn back by order of the Pope. Two years later, the kingdom is finally subsumed into the Kingdom of Aragón by King Alfonso III.

1287: The Moors on Menorca are brutally driven out by Alfonso III

1291: Alfonso's successor, Jaume II of Aragón, returns the Kingdom of Mallorca (now including Menorca) to his exiled uncle, Jaume II of Mallorca.

1312–24: The reign of King Sanç, son of Jaume II of Mallorca.

1324–44: The reign of King Jaume III of Mallorca brings economic prosperity. Palma is by now one of the richest cities in the Mediterranean.

1344: Troops of Pedro IV of Aragón invade and reincorporate the Balearics once again into the Kingdom of Aragón.

1349: Jaume III tries to recover the Kingdom of Mallorca but dies in the Battle of Llucmajor.

UNIFICATION WITH SPAIN

1479: The Kingdom of Spain is formed by uniting the Kingdom of Castile with the Kingdom of Aragón, which includes the Balearics.

1700: Felipe de Bourbón ascends to the throne. Beginning of the War of Succession. Menorca is seized by the British in 1705, who occupy the island, on and off, until 1802.

1713–84: Life and times of Junípero Serra, Mallorcan-born founder of the Californian missions.

1715: Troops loyal to Felipe V arrive on Mallorca. The island's Grand and General Council is replaced by an "Audience" supervised by the Captain General of the king's troops, while the use of Castilian is made obligatory for all official transactions.

1785: Treaty of Algiers signed, establishing the Mallorcan "corsairs" who are given permission by the king to defend their homeland against pirates. The most famous of these is Captain Antoni Barceló, who later becomes Lieutenant General of the Spanish Armada.

THE AGE OF ENLIGHTENMENT

1803–13: The War of Independence against the invading troops of Napoleon. Refugees arrive on the islands, provoking social and political unrest.

1837: Establishment of the first regular steamship service between Mallorca and the mainland.

1879–98: Period of social and commercial success for the islands, thanks largely to a booming trade in wine and almonds. This comes to an abrupt end with the arrival of the *phylloxera* virus, which destroys the wine industry. Economic decline results in widespread emigration to the mainland and to the United States.

THE CIVIL WAR AND BEYOND

1936: General Francisco Franco leads a popular uprising against Spain's newly elected Republican government on 16 July, which soon spreads around

the entire country. Mallorca and Ibiza support Franco's Nationalists, while Menorca backs the Republicans – yet the islands themselves see little actual combat.

1939: The Civil War ends with a Fascist vistory on 1 April. Franco becomes head of state; reprisals against the Republicans are widespread.

1939–75: Franco establishes a one-party state. By keeping Spain neutral during World War II, he survives the fall of Hitler and Mussolini. Mallorca's airport is built in 1960; tourism begins to replace agriculture and fishing as the Balearics' main source of income.

1975: Franco's nominated successor, Prince Juan

Carlos, ascends the throne, and restores parliamentary democracy.

1978: Spain receives a new – and democratic – constitution.

1982: Spain becomes a member of NATO.

1983: The Balearic Islands become an autonomous region; the first elections are held shortly afterwards.

1986: Spain joins the European Community.

1989–99: The economy prospers; by the early 1990s the Balearics enjoy the highest per capita income in Spain. There is a continuing Balearic renaissance in literature, the arts and cuisine. Steps are taken to limit the damage done by mass tourism and to take the industry upmarket. ❏

PRECEDING PAGES: Junípero Serra, island missionary.
LEFT: Menorca's Talaiot de Torre Llonet Vell.
RIGHT: Spain received a new constitution in 1978.

WAREHOUSES OF PREHISTORY

The Balearics are home to a treasure-trove of well-preserved

prehistoric – and particularly Bronze Age – remains

Like islands anywhere, the Balearics are precious warehouses of prehistoric data. More than 180 million years ago, micro-marine organisms accumulated as fossil sediments beneath the primordial seas. Petrified by great pressures, these once-living organisms became the limestone bedrock on which the islands are built today.

Over the next 100 million years or so, continental drift between Africa and Europe forced these ancient limestone sea-floors upward in a buckling movement, creating a finger-like peninsula which jutted out into the water off the present-day coast of Valencia. Gradually, thanks to further land movement and rising sea levels, this spiny land-mass broke up into the separate islands which we know today as the Balearic and Pityussae island group: Mallorca, Menorca, Ibiza and little Formentera.

However, the islands still looked very different from the way they do today. The Mediterranean is a sea in a shallow land-locked basin, emptied and refilled over millions of years thanks to climatic changes. It was particularly affected by the great glaciers that covered northern and western Europe in prehistoric times. As these immense ice-masses slowly melted, emptying themselves into the Mediterranean basin (a process which in itself took eons), so sea levels were raised, shaping the mainland and island coastlines which we know today. The melting of the glaciers also helped give rise to Europe's great lakes and river systems, including the Rhône, the Rhine and the Danube Valleys.

Migrant life

Driven southward by great weather changes in Eurasia, the earliest types of fauna to inhabit the Balearics probably arrived some six to eight million years ago. Making their way over land bridges formed by fallen sea levels, with a good deal of the sea's waters frozen around the en-

croaching glaciers, these migrants would have experienced a much colder Mediterranean climate than we do today.

As microcosms, islands are governed by quite separate environmental laws from the mainland. Because of their limited size, islands can support only a certain number of mammal-

ian and other life forms, and practically none can play host, for very long, to carnivores or meat eaters. As carnivorous animals have a continual need for fresh prey, an island would have to be able to provide plenty of food in the form of vegetation – enough to maintain large herds of animals – in order to maintain an ecological balance. Otherwise the carnivores would end up consuming all existing prey and facing mass starvation and extinction. Few islands are large enough to provide this.

Hence, as a result of the lack of predators, the limited geographic boundaries and other ecological factors, the more docile herbivorous species that arrived and evolved on islands

LEFT: a Menorcan *taule*, evidence of early man.
RIGHT: Ses Païsses prehistoric village on Menorca.

often became very specialised, with adaptations strangely different from mainland species. In some cases, these plant-eating creatures had to develop special mechanisms and feeding habits to cope with the plant life that was available.

Species size, too, becomes an important survival factor on the islands, thanks mainly to the limited flora that is available. Under such conditions, smaller individuals are better equipped to cope, principally because they need less food. This is why, for example, both Cyprus and Crete saw the evolution of dwarf elephants and hippopotami; both species had to regress in order to survive.

was to serve as both food and economy for the early human settlers of the Balearics.

As a result of living without predators, *Myotragus* developed frontally-placed eyes, more suitable for seeking food in the inhospitable rock crevices of mountainous slopes. Fossil remains show that in the later stages of its evolution, *Myotragus* also lost two of the three sets of incisors normal to this species. The remaining set developed into a single ever-growing, chisel-like pair of teeth, an adaptation useful for scraping bark, eating tough vegetation or even turning over stones to get at roots and lichens. Its limbs also changed, growing

An early survivor

An important mammalian Super Family, the cloven-hoofed cattle family or *Bovidae*, evolved in Eurasia some 20 million years ago. Many species of this Super Family migrated southward some eight to ten million years ago, driven probably by changing weather patterns, some making their way to the African continent. Others headed on to Southern Asia and Western Europe. From fossil evidence we know that one species, the *Myotragus* or Balearic antelope, arrived in the region of the Balearic Islands some six to eight million years ago. It was this animal, an oddly-shaped, curiously adapted member of the antelope family, that

short and broad, while the flexible components of the lower limbs fused. All this meant the beast was fairly slow-moving but sure-footed as it searched for food on the craggy and inhospitable slopes of the islands' high mountains.

Enter Neolithic Man

Thanks to the discovery of a large rock-shelter at Son Matge, located in a narrow pass in the mountains near the Mallorcan village of Valldemossa, we can set the earliest date for the arrival of man in the Balearics at around 5000 BC.

Other evidence that these neolithic pastoralists first sought shelter in natural caves and then began to construct large cave complexes, dug out of the soft limestone walls, has been found on Menorca. The best example is at Cales Coves, near Cala d'En Porter.

It is thought that *Myotragus* was finally hunted to extinction some 800 years after the introduction of domesticated goats, sheep, pigs and cattle in about 3000 BC. Pottery technology has also been demonstrated to have occurred around this time. By 2000 BC, metallurgical techniques were being practised, as later levels in the Son Matge rock-shelter show, thanks to the arrival of an obscure race of settlers known as the Beaker People.

Named after their custom of burying their dead with pottery beakers, and widely dispersed across Western Europe, this culture is synonymous with the Copper Age or Chaleolithic Period (around 2500 to 1400 BC) which precedes and includes the Bronze Age. This is believed to be when Europe's first socially structured societies began and humans began to accumulate wealth and surplus through developing trade and technology.

Early lifestyle

The arrival of the Beaker Culture in the Balearics saw the construction of the first open-air settlements in sites such as the Old Settlement (at Mallorca's Prehistoric Settlement Complex of Ferrandell-Oleza-Mas), as well as the first sanctuaries, such as the one at Son Matge. Both discovered by the author in 1978, these sites occupy the soil-rich alluvial plain known as El Pla del Rei (Plain of the King), near the village of Valldemossa. Radiocarbon dating shows that the site of the Old Settlement was occupied some 700 years ago from around 2100 to 1300 BC and was abandoned only when the soils eroded so severely that farming the immediate area was no longer viable.

As a result of Old Settlement findings at the Ferrandell-Oleza-Mas Prehistoric Complex, we can reconstruct the everyday occupation and life-style of these early Copper Age and Initial Bronze Age settlers. We see reflected a prosperous group who delineated their property with high, stoutly-constructed walls, behind which they could shelter their goats, sheep, pigs

and cattle. They also collected wood, milked and slaughtered their animals.

They managed water with a hydraulic water system of some sophistication, bringing it in via a stone slab- and clay-lined water channel into the rear of well-built stone naviformed (boat shaped) houses. They farmed the adjacent fields, growing grain and harvesting it with beautifully worked serrated, tabular flint blades. They made the lovely incised, geometrically decorated pottery known all over Europe as International Beaker Ware.

Further to the south, close to the rich soils of the alluvial Plain of the King. lie the Late

MICROCOSMIC TREASURE-TROVES

Often seen merely as backwaters, islands are perfectly capable of giving us key details of the past – of uniquely-developed animal species, for example – which are more complete than those present elsewhere. This is because data may better survive the ravages of time in the microcosmic environment of an island than on the more active mainland. Collecting on their shores most of what occurs around them on a wider scale – either in terms of people or in architecture – islands are important places in which the interested visitor can follow the trails of evidence left by evolution and history. You just have to know where to look.

LEFT: caves in Menorca with evidence of modern troglodytes.
RIGHT: prehistoric doorway, Capocorp Vell, Menorca.

Bronze Age and Iron Age settlement areas of the Ferrandell-Oleza-Mas Prehistoric Settlement Complex, which date from around 1000 BC to the Roman colonisation of the islands in 123 BC. They are good examples of Talayotic settlements of the period, the megalithic remains of which are scattered all over Mallorca and Menorca – although, curiously enough, there are none on Ibiza.

> ### ROCK BANDS
>
> The skills of the Balearic slingers were legendary. Hannibal took 5,000 of them across the Alps to fight the Romans in the Second Punic War; their services were rewarded with women and wine.

Living and working in their stone radial buildings connected in beehive fashion to

talaiots (cone-shaped towers built without mortar or cement – the word comes from *atalaya*, Arabic for "watchtower") – the Talayotic settlers practised a successful combination of agriculture and basic animal husbandry.

Evidence of their burial practices comes once again from the Son Matge rock shelter, which was used as a burial-ground from around 1400 BC until Roman colonisation. Here, over 6,000 individuals were cremated (during the Bronze Age), inhumed in quicklime (Iron Age) or laid to rest in elongated stone burial-chambers known as *navetas*, along with grave-goods of pottery, tools, arms and jewellery *(see also Prehistoric Menorca, page 226).*

Culture clash

Situated as they are on the great trading routes that crisscross the Mediterranean, it was inevitable that the Balearics would come into contact during the first millennium BC with the Phoenicians, the Carthaginians and the Greeks. The Phoenicians and the Greeks seem merely to have used the islands as a staging-post, for hardly any remains have survived.

More enduring has been the Greeks' name for the islands – the Balearics – which comes from the word *ballein*, meaning "to throw from a sling". Always on their guard against attack from the sea, the islanders became highly skilled at this brand of warfare.

By the 3rd century BC, the islands had fallen under Carthaginian control, completing a westward series of settlements extending from Carthage (modern Tunis) to Gades (modern Cádiz) that were to remain influential in Mediterranean politics and trade right up until the 2nd century BC. Then, as their influence in the Mediterranean was gradually eclipsed by the Romans, the Carthaginian empire began to crumble. Mallorca and Menorca were both annexed by the Romans after Carthage lost the Second Punic War in 202 BC. Ibiza, the chief Balearic settlement of the Carthaginians, followed suit in 146 BC, after the city of Carthage itself finally fell to Rome.

Although the Romans occupied Mallorca and Menorca in 123 BC, they left it until AD 74 to settle on Ibiza, which in the meantime remained defiantly Carthaginian in character. Yet the islands flourished under Roman rule, which saw the introduction of olive cultivation, viniculture and salt-mining, as well as the founding of such towns as Pollentia ("the powerful") and Palmaris ("the symbol of victory") on Mallorca. The islands were Christianised in the 2nd century AD.

But by AD 414 Barbarian tribes had conquered Spain; in 426 Mallorca was attacked for the first time by the Vandal leader Gunderico, and by 465 the Balearics had been completely subdued and incorporated into the Vandal Empire. The Dark Ages had begun. ❑

LEFT: Roman remains at Alcúdia, Mallorca.
RIGHT: islands off Mallorca: precious storehouses.

FROM MOORS TO CHRISTIANS

After three centuries of Moorish rule, the Balearics' Christian reconquest
was ruthless, bloody and quick – and motivated by greed for land

The Moors were latecomers to the Balearic Islands, and they left relatively early, too. The total period of Islamic domination in Mallorca and Ibiza lasted just over 300 years: little more than in Sicily and less than half the corresponding period in the history of Granada, in mainland Spain.

Recent studies of Mediterranean sea-lanes in the middle ages help to explain why this was. The patterns of currents and prevailing winds ensured that in the age of galleys and cogs the islands would tend to be dominated from the north or west; though the Balearics were bound to send traffic towards Africa, the sailing season from the south was short and could be very hard work.

Yet whatever the religion of the ruling élite, the islands were attractive to oriental settlers; in Mallorca, especially, Moors and Jews were enduring and influential elements in the population who helped to shape some of the most distinctive features of the archipelago's history.

The post-Roman period of Balearic history is a genuine "dark age". Although Christianity had taken root here during the Roman occupation, the Vandals persecuted orthodox islanders and destroyed their churches (very few Roman remains survived, either). It was only when the islands were conquered by the Byzantines in AD 534 that Christianity was restored, along with some semblance of peace and prosperity.

Justinian ruled the Balearic islands as part of the province of Sardinia. However, they were too remote as far as Constantinople was concerned to be of much use to the empire, and when Byzantium began to be threatened from the east at the end of the 7th century, they were all but abandoned.

Initially, though, they managed to hold out against the Moorish conquerors of the Iberian peninsula. An appeal to Charlemagne in 798 against Moorish pirates shows that, locally, Christian rule prevailed.

LEFT: the Arab Baths in Palma.
RIGHT: an Arab tombstone dated AD 968.

Cordoban claims

In 848 the Emir of Córdoba, Abderrahman II, sent a fleet, reputedly of 300 ships, to suppress the Balearic islanders' reprisals against Moorish shipping and to place Mallorca and Menorca under tribute. But while Andalucian control remained limited, Córdoban pretensions

to sovereignty were either defied or ignored. Instead, close relationships of dependence seem to have bound the Balearics to Catalonia, from where religious jurisdiction was exercised over the Church on the islands.

However, towards the end of the 9th century, the Moorish ruler al-Khaulani is said to have spent time in Mallorca on his way to Mecca. Seduced by its beauty and convinced of its exploitability, he returned in force in 902 and turned the Balearics into a nominal fief of the Emirate of Córdoba, with himself at its head.

For 100 years or so after his death in 912, little is known of the history of the islands beyond the names of the *walis*, or governors, who exercised effective authority, until 1014, when the empire of Córdoba disintegrated and the islands became part of one of the numerous petty successor-states, known as *taifa* kingdoms, with its capital at Denia, on the Spanish mainland near Valencia.

Rule from the mainland

Mujahid, the first ruler of this sea-straddling and diverse kingdom, established at Denia a sybaritic, cosmopolitan court. He was a self-designated literary critic who liked to have works dedicated to him but not, it seems, to pay for them. His relatively long reign of some 30

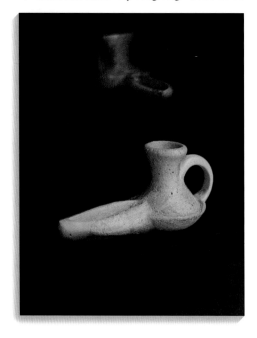

years defined features of Balearic history that would characterise most of the rest of the middle ages: fragile rule from the mainland and a tendency to seek overseas conquests.

In 1015, he launched an ill-fated expedition against Sardinia from Mallorca; it failed, apparently because of storms. The attempt seems to have had little effect on the security of his home bases. In about 1036, he appointed a governor, al-Aghlab, to rule the Balearics; the relationship was cemented by exceptional loyalty, for al-Aghlab served until his master's death, then departed on a pilgrimage for Mecca.

His successor introduced to Mallorca the brilliant court life of Denia without usurping the sovereign authority of the new mainland king, Ali ibn Mujahid. The latter, son of a Christian concubine and for a long time a captive of Sardinia, was exceptionally indulgent towards Christians. He gave the Bishop of Barcelona surveillance of their rights and enjoined their prayers for himself. His reign was an era of peace until he fell victim in 1076 to the ambitions of al-Muqtadir, king of Zaragoza (the warrior-aesthete who was later to employ El Cid).

Commerce and corsairs

The Balearics then enjoyed a brief period of independence: the incumbent governor at the time of Ali's death, al-Mu'tada, issued coins in his own name between 1077 and 1093. Thereafter, the islands were an unruly outpost of the north African empire of the Almoravids – a sect of Berber nomads who would today be classed as Islamic fundamentalists. The islands were equally convenient for commerce and corsairs. According to al-Maqqari they "supplied much of Africa with wood and salt". Naturally the effect of such trade was to excite the greed of would-be conquerors or raiders.

The first well-documented Christian attack of the period was made by Sigurd of Norway in 1108 on his way to Jerusalem. Sigurd made a conspicuous sideline of combining pillage with pilgrimage, and he was said to have burned the defenders of Formentera to death in the cave known as Cova des Fum, towards the eastern end of the island.

Sigurd was a vulture of passage but the next invaders appear to have intended to stay. In 1114, a powerful Catalo-Pisan alliance was formed to attack the islands and drive out the Moors. For the merchants of Pisa the attractions of the Balearics were obvious: Mallorca was an ideal staging-post for growing trade with Spain and North Africa; it was a piratical base from which they would be able to harass their Genoese rivals; and Ibiza was a major salt-producer in her own right.

The interests which moved Count Ramón Berenguer III of Barcelona to join the alliance as its leader are less clear: Catalan commercial interest in the Balearics was still at a rudimentary stage, though the Christians of Mallorca probably looked to their parent-see in Catalonia, Barcelona, for protection.

An army of 70,000 troops was duly landed on Ibiza. At first the campaign went badly, and although the count was soon anxious to return to his own lands, the Pisans preferred to struggle on in the hope of recouping their investment. Exasperation inspired a policy of scorched earth and wanton massacre, and Ibiza was virtually destroyed. Mallorca proved a more difficult proposition, but by March 1115, Moorish resistance had been reduced to Palma's citadel, the last *wali* escaping by swimming away "like a dolphin". Yet almost at the moment of final victory, the Christians were

AN EPIC ACHIEVEMENT

Count Berenguer's Moorish exploits were commemorated by an epic poem in Latin, the *Liber Maiolichinus*, which inspired periodic attempts to emulate him over the next 100 years.

Ganiya (1115–85); he rebuilt ruins unrestored since the Catalo-Pisan invasion, and revived prosperity based on African trade. By the end of the 12th century, Mallorca was acting as protectorate over a number of coastal trading stations of mainland Africa, and a Ganiyid "empire" appeared to be taking shape.

However, in 1202 a rebellion in Mallorca itself, stimulated by Islamic extremists, halted that empire's development. A Maghribi army invaded, the last of the Ganiyids was beheaded

forced to flee with their booty before an Almoravid relief expedition, which put the Berber sect back in power.

A Mallorcan empire stillborn

Pisan and Genoese commercial involvement in the Balearic islands continued to increase during the 12th century, but politically the islands remained an offshore outpost of the Arab Maghribi world. For most of the time they were ruled in effective independence by governors or "kings", the greatest of whom was Ishaq ibn

or fled, and the Balearics passed under the nominal suzerainty of the Almohad dynasty, which had enjoyed supremacy in North Africa and al-Andalus for about two generations. They forcibly converted the islands' Christian population to Islam and began sporadic raids on the mainland.

The Ganiyids left Mallorca both rich and vulnerable. Medina Mayurka – "the city of Mallorca" as Palma was then called – was by this time one of the ornaments of the western Mediterranean, with its busy quays, its 50 bakeries, its watermills and its elegant bathouses. But it had run out of the physical means of self-defence and of friends to fight for it.

LEFT: an early Arab oil-lamp.
ABOVE: the Almudaina as it looked in the 13th century.

Jaume's rule

A new alliance capable of exploiting the Balearics' vulnerability was soon to form under King Jaume I of Aragón and Catalonia (in power 1213–76). When King Jaume described in his *Book of Deeds* his conquest of Mallorca, the arguments which moved him to undertake it and the experience of crossing the sea to carry it out, he described a vision of maritime war as a chivalric adventure *par excellence*, something he obviously found exhilarating. There was more honour in conquering a kingdom "in the midst of the sea, where God has been pleased to put it" than three on dry land, he said.

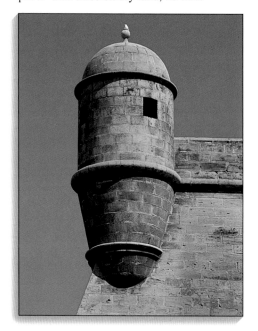

When the king wrote "The best thing man has done for a hundred years past, God willed that I should do when I took Mallorca," he probably meant that it was the best by the standards of chivalry, the deed of most daring and renown. It was to be an achievement of great importance for his dynasty, which began henceforth to create a network of island dominions in the Mediterranean. By the end of the 13th century, the chronicler Desclot could claim, with pardonable exaggeration, that no fish could go swimming without the King of Aragón's leave.

At first, however, Jaume's nobles were unenthusiastic about the projected conquest. They would have preferred to tackle Valencia – a lush Islamic kingdom approachable across a land frontier, without all the complications of boats. Mallorca proved an acceptable alternative partly because the king was lavish with promises of reward. When one of the greatest lords, Nuño Sanz, promised to aid the conquest with horse, foot soldiers and ships, including a hundred of his household knights, he was explicit in his demands for land and wealth by return. Jaume's response was embodied in a charter addressed to all the nobility: "We shall give just portions to you and yours, according to the numbers of knights and men-at-arms whom you take with you".

Rich pickings

As well as the work of contingents from this feudal world of give-and-take, the conquest was the work of militias, mercenaries and ships from the commercial world of the cities. Jaume describes a great banquet on the mainland in November or December, 1228, when a leading citizen and shipowner, Pedro Martel, explained to the magnates the whereabouts of the Balearics, perhaps with an early map spread before him, and commended the islands as the richest pickings then available in the world. Jaume liked to discuss business after dinner: it was a typical social ritual of the Catalonia of his day. The account books of the city of Mallorca after its conquest show that banquets to honour great events or stimulate appetites for civic transactions were a major source of expense, like the business lunch today.

It was characteristic, too, that a nautical technician like Martel could act as host to the king and sit down with great nobles without embarrassment due to lack of social status: this feature of the Catalan social world was also transplanted to the post-conquest Balearics.

But Barcelona, alone or even in combination with the other great Catalan port of Tarrogona, could not launch enough ships to conquer Mallorca. The shipping for Jaume's expedition was in a sense a joint effort of the Catalan and Provençal worlds, suggesting that the commercial rewards promised must indeed have been considerable.

Jaume may have denounced the Balearics as nests of pirates, but while being a rather rough-and-ready form of exchange, piracy should probably not be too sharply distinguished from trade in this period. Most seafarers and most ships slipped in and out of both vocations without specialisation. It is reasonable to suppose that the merchants who backed the king aimed not only to suppress the pirates but also to supplant them in their more legitimate lines of business. Although many new products would be introduced by the conquerors, the islands' role in western Mediterranean trade was well established. The wealth of the Balearics, the entrenched positions of the Moorish traders, and of their privileged partners from Genoa and Pisa, more than adequately explain the jealous anxiety of the Catalans and Provençals to break into the cartel, by force if necessary.

The king's expedition of 150 ships, 16,000 men and 1,500 horses finally set sail for Mallorca in September 1229. After three months the island was conquered, and annexed to Aragón. Jaume was hailed as "El Conqueridor".

Thus the Christian reconquest of Mallorca was determined by greed for commerce and land. It was bloody, ruthless and quick, and evidence of it is scant. Today's visitor can compare King Jaume's beach-head of September, 1229, at Platja Camp de Mar (now smothered by hotels) with the gaunt ruins of the castle of Santueri, near Felanitx, the only Moorish stronghold to resist for any length of time. ❏

The role of faith

Crusading rhetoric justified the expedition and papal indulgences helped to launch it. Can religious motives be distinguished in the background? Pious avowals, beyond conventional assurances of godliness of purpose, are rare in Jaume's *Book of Deeds*. The emphasis here was on making the conquest seem legitimate rather than trying to turn it into a crusade. Above all else, Jaume justified his war as a war justly waged for the recovery of usurped lands.

LEFT: remnant of Palma's mighty city walls.
ABOVE: jousting Moors and Christians, a ceiling panel from the Almudaina.

COMPLETING THE JOB

Mindful of the huge cost of launching an island invasion, King Jaume subcontracted out Ibiza's capture in 1231. Troops led by the Crown Prince of Portugal and the Count of Roussillon conquered the island in 1235, although suzerainty passed to Jaume. The cash-strapped king then turned his attention to Menorca, devising a cunning plan. He returned to Mallorca in 1232 with just three galleys carrying envoys, who were dispatched to Menorca to open negotiations. Jaume, meanwhile, camped out in the Capdepera mountains, lighting bonfires to create the illusion of a huge army. It fooled the Moors, who promptly surrendered.

GREATNESS AND DECLINE

*Despite a spell as Christendom's most dynamic society, the discovery of
the Americas left the islands little more than a far-flung backwater*

The late medieval era was an age of greatness for the Balearics, and Mallorca in particular: a greatness never since experienced. For a brief period in the 14th century they were the *mise-en-scène* of the most dynamic and economically successful society in Christendom and led the medieval "space-race" – the quest for new colonies and trade.

The *conquistadores* who set about erasing the influence of the Moors initially envisaged a Mallorca created from scratch, and thickly planted with new settlers and their crops. Thus the division of the towns proceeded house by house, and of the soil plot by plot, thanks to one of the most efficient and pernickety royal bureaucracies in Christendom.

After discounting what was passed on to the Templars, the towns and the nobles, King Jaume was left with direct control of more than twice the land granted to the biggest magnate proprietor. It was a huge bonanza for the impoverished crown.

The king's half of Palma went in rewards to the soldiers of his urban militias, the sailors of his fleet and the merchants who backed his invasion: 307 houses to Tarragona, 298 to Marseilles, 226 each to Barcelona and Lérida, 100 to Montpellier, and corresponding proportions to small island communities.

The division of the island suggests a programme of intensive colonisation at every social level. The same intention is revealed by the exhortations which Pope Gregory IX distributed around the western Mediterranean basin. He made a gift to all potential settlers (with the exception of Cathar heretics) of indulgences equivalent to those given to pilgrims to the Holy Land.

Enough colonists responded to make the island Catalan-speaking, with marked influence from the dialects of Ampurias and Roussillon, and to saturate the place-names of lowland areas with Catalan. But the extent to which this colonial population displaced the Moors is a much-debated topic of Mallorcan history.

Moorish remains

The myth that the Moors were all enslaved or expelled initially arose from a misreading of

the chronicles, fortified by a false analogy with what happened later on Menorca. Evidence of Moorish survival is overwhelming. First, there were Moors whose autonomy in the mountains was not ended by the conquest: the largest contingent, which surrendered conditionally in June 1232, was reckoned by the king at 16,000 strong. Then there is considerable evidence that in the interests of keeping the island well-populated, the king and other proprietors came to look favourably on their Moorish tenants, ignoring their initial hostility.

The Templars brought "Saracens" from the mainland; the king encouraged Moors from Menorca. A number of surviving documents of

LEFT: a stained-glass window in Palma Cathedral – the *conquistadores* marking their territory.
RIGHT: King Jaume I.

the late 13th and 14th centuries indicate the continued presence of Moors on a considerable scale, especially as artisans in the towns – smiths, metal workers, leather and textile workers, shopkeepers and even a painter.

Many of these documents are records of slavery, but it was evidently common for Moors to slip in and out of slavery for debt with little or no change in their way of life. Contracts in which slaves, who were given land to work for the purchase of their freedom, stayed on as serfs and tenants,

of foreign residents and a lively trade in slaves of diverse nationalities.

One of the most important foreign communities was the Genoese, which was tolerated or encouraged even in times of war between Genoa and the Crown of Aragón. In 1233, the king granted them a trading precinct in Palma, in the street that led up to the Templars' castle. They were a valuable property, more profitable to persecute fiscally than by embargo or expulsion. Between 1320 and 1344, for instance, they paid an

allow us a glimpse of the means by which many lords must have exploited their land-grants.

Finally, the evidence of place-names is probably as good a guide as any: the poorer uplands and central mountains remained Arabic. So while the thoroughly Catalan appearance of Mallorca in the late Middle Ages was a result of Catalan predominance in the main population centres, this did not exclude other influences outside those areas.

Early expatriates

The Catalans may have dominated, but in its commercial zone Mallorca retained a cosmopolitan atmosphere, thanks to growing numbers

import tax 10 times as high as that charged to the Pisans: the high level was justified on the grounds that it provided indemnities for Mallorcan goods against Genoese piracy.

The Jews were even more numerous and at least as important to the economic life of the island. At the time of the conquest, a prosperous Jewish community seems to have acted as a magnet for poor co-religionists from all over the western Mediterranean.

Jewish wealth

Until the end of the 14th century, the Jews were highly regarded as a "treasure house… from whom the trades and traders of this kingdom in peacetime derive great abundance". Most Jewish wealth was accumulated in crafts or professions. Jews were active as silversmiths, silk merchants, veterinarians, peddlers, freelance postmen, armourers, cobblers, tailors, dyers, kosher butchers, carpenters, physicians, illuminators, bookbinders, soap-makers, map-makers, wet-nurses, wine merchants and millers.

You can get a flavour of the ambience in their ghetto from the Carrer de Argenteria, Palma's Jewish quarter's best surviving street, where the silversmiths worked. They were disadvantaged in long-range trade by fiscal victimisation and exclusion from some ports. The only routes on which they played a major role were those to Barbary, where they were much too deeply entrenched for their grip to be forcibly relaxed.

The Jews had a peculiar relationship with the crown, which, as in much of the rest of Christendom, generally worked to their advantage. They were the "king's coffers of money", generously endowed with privileges, of which the most valuable was that no Jew could be convicted by Christian or Moorish testimony. Under King Sanç (in power 1311–24), fiscal exploitation of Jews grew more abrasive; but almost throughout the 1300s, Jews maintained a favoured status. Despite occasional prohibitions from 1285 onwards, they continued to hold public offices up to the level of members of the royal council.

Ghettoes of privilege

Growing popular resentment was their undoing. Their characteristic "crimes" were false coining and "dwelling in Saracen lands". The first reflects Jewish prominence in the handling of precious metals, the second their leading position in the Barbary trade. What seems most to have vexed their Christian neighbours were, first, their discharge of detested functions as moneylenders and tax-farmers and, secondly, the conspicuous distinctions which set their society apart from others.

They lived in their own ghettos where they were numerous enough to do so, as at Inca and Palma. With few exceptions granted – as in the case of the royal cartographer, Abraham Cresques, for exceptional service – they wore a prescribed form of dress. They could re-marry on divorce, by royal leave, and (as is shown by a plea of 1258, made on grounds of childlessness) were allowed lawfully to contract bigamous marriages. Jews also "flouted" the Christian Sabbath and aroused the resentment of other market vendors by their pre-emptive habit of early rising.

However, since their legal privileges were greater than those of Christians, so were their punishments more severe. A Jew guilty of a hanging offence was suspended upside-down – "mouth downwards" – to protract the death and aggravate the agony.

This xenophobic resentment of a community apart was exacerbated by accusations of usury. As the Jews' taxes fell due at Easter, Holy Week yielded an annual crop of outrages and hard times, while febrile preachers could stir popular hatred with astonishing ease. In 1374, the king had to quell demands for the Jews' expulsion at a time of famine by recalling that they had paid for relief ships. In 1370, the preaching licence of the rabid, footloose mendicant, Fray Bonanto, was withdrawn because of his anti-semitic excesses. The pogroms and forcible conversions of future generations were being prepared. In the riots of 1391, perhaps as many as 300 Jews were slaughtered in Palma.

LEFT: Moorish pot, found in a cave used by the retreating Arabs.

RIGHT: alley in Palma's El Call Jewish ghetto.

Crossroads of trade

The majority of other foreigners were slaves, reflecting the Balearic islands' role as an *entrepôt*. Mallorca was a centre of re-export for the whole of the Aragó-Catalan world. The iron of Bayonee and Castile, figs from Murcia and Alcudia, Ibizan salt, Sevillian oil and Greek or Calabrian wine, with slaves from Greece and Sardinia, were the most common market commodities. They were traded to the Aragónese dominions and North Africa: about half the sailing licences surviving from the 14th century are for Catalonia, the rest divided between Valencia and Barbary.

Mallorca was dependent on this re-export trade but also fostered new industries. Commerce bred shipbuilding, especially after Sanç I turned one of the Jewish cemeteries into a shipyard. Mallorcan cogs were the best ships in the sea in the 1300s, leading the way in Atlantic exploration. A thriving arms industry around the 1380s shipped thousands of crossbows to Flanders and England. But the greatest industrial success was textiles, the most important product of the medieval industrial revolution.

This range of new commercial and industrial activity, the prodigious economic growth of the century after the Christian conquest, made the Balearics as a whole a land of medieval *Wirtschaftswunder*, as Germany was after World War II. Jaume I expressed the kingdom's potential eloquently: it was the finest land, with the most beautiful city in the world.

After Jaume I's death in 1276, however, the islands were separated from Aragón. Jaume's kingdom was divided up between his two sons, with Pedro receiving Catalonia, Aragón and Valencia, and the newly-created Kingdom of Mallorca being entrusted to Jaume II.

A top-heavy system

The government of this era presented problems which Aragonese kings found hard to resolve and historians hard to classify. Devolution of power in the regions to municipal communities and lords was combined with a bureaucratic layer of royal or seigneurial representatives called *batles* and two central representative institutions: the *jurats* (nominated by the king) to advise on policy and administer justice, and the *Consell* (elected partly by the *jurats* and partly by syndics in the localities) as a representative assembly.

Because so much of the great nobility was based in mainland Spain, and represented in the islands by administration trained in the law, both institutions had a deceptively bourgeois air. The potentially conflictive division was between the representatives of the *part forana*, from outside the city, and the élite of Palma: the numbers of the former grew from three after the conquest to 10 under Sanç, and to a total of 63 by the end of the 14th century.

Unreliable kings

The Kingdom of Mallorca was made up of a group of enclaves and islands – including Roussillon, Perpignan and Montpellier, on the mainland of what is now France – on the very fringes of the Aragó-Catalan world. It was typical of the Aragonese medieval dominions in that its place in the monarchy was defined only vaguely and haphazardly. Indeed, like most other areas of Aragó-Catalan expansion, it was often hived off to local rulers whose loyalty, secured only by oath, was generally unreliable.

At times, its kings could break their oaths and defy the senior line, but Mallorca was never really viable as a wholly independent state. Its manpower was made up of Catalans, who retained a loyalty to the historic dynasty; it was largely dependent on peninsular trade; its magnates were peninsula-based. Yet despite these strong ties with the mainland, there were numerous attempts by Aragonese leaders to conquer the kingdom.

The first of these was Jaume II's brother Pedro. He had designs on Mallorca as it straddled the trade route between Barcelona and Sicily, where his wife was queen. Although Jaume was powerless to resist Pedro's demand for homage in 1279 or to oppose the Aragonese invasion of 1285, led by Pedro's son, Alfonso III, his even-

> **PATRON TO A SAINT**
>
> Jaume II was a staunch patron of Mallorca's greatest missionary and scholar, Ramon Llull, granting him the finance to build a monastic school of Oriental languages near Valldemossa.

by his nephew, Jaume III, in 1324. Jaume III's two-decade-long reign was a period of great economic prosperity for Mallorca, bringing about the flowering of the island's agriculture, industry and navigation.

More new towns were founded, Bellver Castle was built, the Almudiana was transformed into a splendid Gothic palace, and work began on the construction of the Convent of Sant Francesc. Palma was, by now, one of the richest cities anywhere in the Mediterranean.

tual restoration in 1299 was made in the interests of the dynasty as a whole by the next King of Aragón: Alfonso's brother, Jaume.

Once restored to the crown, Jaume II devoted himself to improving the economic policies of the Balearics, establishing a weekly market in Palma and reissuing the currency in gold and silver to stimulate trade. He also founded 11 towns, including Manacor and Llucmajor.

On his death in 1311, Jaume was succeeded by his son, Sanç, who was in turn succeeded

---

LEFT: splendid stone carvings adorn Palma's Basílica de Sant Francesc.
ABOVE: another Palma showpiece: the Almudiana.

Yet when the ambiguities of the relationship between island and mainland were finally swept away by the definitive Aragonese conquest of 1344, led by Pedro IV, the operation took only a week. The invaders were welcomed almost everywhere and there was little or no support for the vengeful schemes of the pretender Jaume III, who died in a hapless invasion attempt in 1349.

Beyond Mallorca

Ibiza and Formentera were also conquered by "crusaders" but, unlike Mallorca, by crusaders working on their own initiative. The crown played no part, except perhaps as a source of legitimation. Don Pedro of Portugal and Nuño Sanz, on their Mallorcan expedition, were granted a right of conquest to Ibiza which they failed to take up.

It was therefore re-allocated, with their agreement, between December 1234 and April 1235, to Guillermo de Montgrí, a sacristan of Gerona cathedral. He was acting on behalf of the Archbishopric of Tarragona, which had got little out of the conquest of Mallorca. For a while, however, he was to rule Ibiza unchallenged. Don Pedro and Nuño were to hold their portions of Ibiza town in fee from him and to perform homage.

Despite the exalted language in which the Pope had exhorted the conquerors "to snatch the island (of Ibiza) from impious hands", the conquerors' bargain was quite explicit: as in Mallorca, their investment would be recouped from the spoils of conquest.

When Ibiza castle and town were taken by storm in August 1235, it seemed at first as if the partners would have a free hand. Montgrí, who had provided the biggest contingent, appointed himself governor of the principal castle and took half the land. Pedro and Nuño divided the rest equally. Gradually, however, the crown's right to possession of strongholds was enforced. Pedro's fief passed to the crown;

Nuño sold out to the see of Tarragona. After about a generation, the island thus became governed by a royal-ecclesiastical coalition.

The society of post-conquest Ibiza resembled Mallorca in miniature, save that sub-letting of territory was rare. The big exception was little Formentera, granted away by Montgrí in fee perpetual, with exemption only of Don Pedro's share and a few sites intended for a hospice and hermitages. The lord was to receive a quarter of the profits of justice and a tenth of wheat and meat "according to the custom of Ibiza", in addition to the dues owed to the church. In colonised areas, the seigneurial economy evidently relied on ecclesiastical dues.

Settlers, sin and salt

Throughout Ibiza, settlers were at first difficult to attract, to such an extent that in 1237, the Pope authorised the Bishop of Tarragona to re-admit to Communion those who had committed arson, profaners of sacred persons and suppliers of illicit arms to the Saracens – on condition that they settled in Ibiza in person or by proxy. Like Mallorca, Ibiza relied on the survival or reintroduction of Moors, many of them brought in by Pedro of Portugal.

Nothing better illustrated the difficulty of attracting settlers and the narrow economic base of the island than the failure of the lords to increase revenue from salt. Their efforts lasted for eight years before they yielded to the necessity of exercising liberality in allowing settlers user-rights. Apart from slave-trading and piracy salt was the only available economic activity of promise, and the only "perk" that would attract colonists.

Despite the early preponderance of Moors, the fragile economy and the hesitant colonisation, Ibiza was remarkably successful. By the late 14th century, there was an island council of 250 members, a large élite for a small island. The scale of these institutions seem to belong to a solidly established society, with deeply rooted settlements. Yet at the same time the insecurity of life on small islands in pirate-infested seas was starkly illustrated by Formentera's abandonment. By 1403, the island was deserted.

Menorca

The second island of the Balearics suffered the most ruthless form of Aragonese imperialism. At first, it was left undisturbed, save for token tribute, as a Moorish vassal-state: this was a common solution in the Iberian peninsula for Moorish states which could not be practically or profitably absorbed by Christian kingdoms.

In the 1280s, however, Menorca assumed a new importance en route to further conquests in Sardinia and Sicily. It was both a tempting prospect for its potential commercial rivals, both Pisan and Genoese, and something of an embarrassment to the Aragonese kings' crusading propaganda.

> ### A BLOODY TAKEOVER
>
> Alfonso's brutal takeover of Menorca in 1287 was thorough. Those Muslims unable to buy their freedom were enslaved, while the old, the sick and the very young were simply massacred.

Culturally, it remained fairly rough-and-ready. In 1358, an island governor was killed by a blow from a candlestick in a brawl at the high altar of the island's main church. Such was the tenor of life in this showpiece-conquest of Aragonese imperialism.

Decline and fall

As part of the kingdom of Aragón, the Balearics were absorbed into the new Spanish superstate of Ferdinand and Isabella in 1479, This proved a disaster for the islands. From

Thus it was that Menorca offered an opportunity for the young Alfonso III to demonstrate his mettle. His conquest of the island in 1287 was the most brutal in the history of the Aragónese monarchy. Departing from the practice evolved in Mallorca and Ibiza, Alfonso aimed at a radical extirpation of the native population. A century after the conquest, the wreckage remained. Food shortages were still chronic: corn-bearing ships that called at the island were compelled to offer their cargo for sale.

LEFT: exterior detail, Portal de ses Taules, Eivissa (Ibiza Town), taken by storm in 1235.
ABOVE: 15th-century depiction of the port of Palma.

central government's point of view, they were little more than a far-flung, provincial backwater – a trend compounded by Spain's discovery of the Americas in 1492. As attention turned from the Mediterranean to the Atlantic, the Balearics were left starved of foreign currency; the formerly renowned Mallorcan shipping fleets almost disappeared, and the islands' dwindling trade fell into the hands of foreign carriers. The unreliability of grain supplies (which had condemned the islands to chronic shortages) and high tax demands from the mainland did nothing to ease the situation. To make matters worse, the unprotected islands were easy prey for the depredations of North

African pirates, who alternatively sacked the towns and established their own bases there for raiding parties.

The inhabitants did little to help themselves. Exacerbated by economic failure, the divisions between port and hinterland became increasingly violent, especially in Mallorca, where a virtual civil war raged from 1450 to 1453.

The introduction of the Inquisition in 1484 was a grisly bloodletting of local tensions: a cheap tribunal in which one could denounce one's neighbour on irrational grounds. It began with a burst of fire and bloodshed in which 85 penitents were burned between 1484 and 1512.

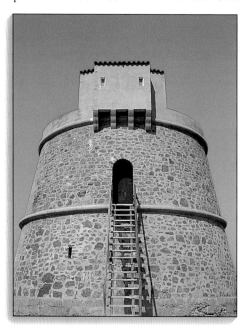

Carnival riot

The social unrest of which these figures are a symptom abated with equal suddenness; after 1517, the Inquisition was virtually inert for over a century and a half. This is an indication, perhaps, that conditions were already beginning to improve when the bloodiest conflict in Mallorca's history erupted in 1521. On Carnival Day, traditional excess overspilled into riots when seven leading guildsmen were jailed.

These circumstances, which launched a bloody revolt known as that of the *Germanía,* or "brotherhood" of rebels, bound together by common oaths, seems to have been a protest to do with the economy: the guildsmen's main

demand was for the alleviation of taxes. It was also animated in part by anti-clericalism and in part by desperation at grain shortages.

On 16 April 1521 the governor was forced to flee to Ibiza. The guildsmen, still professing loyalty to the crown, took the Castle of Bellver by storm and massacred the garrison. As has so often happened in the history of such revolts, an exploitative demagogue rose to the fore and only in the spring of 1523 was the bloody dictatorship of Joanot Colom brought to an end by the combined efforts of crown and aristocracy.

The revolt gave the aristocrats a means to explain the moral decline by which they felt increasingly surrounded. In 1539, the conservative *jurats* complained "how much respect for God and His Majesty the common people have lost since the *Germanía* and how much our difficulty in confronting crimes has increased."

Coastal raiders

Insecurity and insufficiency remained the keynotes of island life, with pirates, bandits and famine the three chief enemies. The effort Charles V and, subsequently, Philip II invested in the protection of their subjects can be seen in the surviving fortifications of Eivissa (Ibiza Town), initiated by the Italian engineer Calvi in 1554. Maó's Fort San Felipe dates from the same period, built after the town had been destroyed in two major Turkish raids. The stone watchtowers that still stand on promontories and high hilltops in parts of Ibiza, Mallorca and Formentera are another legacy of this era.

The chronic shortage of grain arose not only from threats to transport but from problems of supply which afflicted the entire western Mediterranean. A particularly bad famine in 1674 coincided with renewed persecution of Mallorca's Jewish population by the Holy Office of the Inquisition.

The growing number of religious communities in the 17th century was, however, one indication of returning affluence; in addition, the fortunes of some great dynasties were laid by a recovery of trade in the last third of the century. The general renewal of prosperity, however, had to await recovery from a new trauma: the War of the Spanish Succession. ❑

LEFT: Ibiza's Torre Campanitx, built as a watchtower in the days when pirates were a constant threat.
RIGHT: Palma's Puerto Pintado, or "painted gate".

TIDES OF CHANGE

Having endured war, foreign occupation, plagues and pirate attacks over the past two centuries, the Balearics today enjoy Spain's highest per capita income

The Balearics sided firmly with the losing side in the War of the Spanish Succession. Here, as in the rest of the kingdom of Aragón, most of the élite wanted a traditional, even a contractual monarchy, which would devolve power into local hands – an aspiration which seemed best represented by the cause of the Habsburg pretender, Charles III, rather that the French-style absolutism threatened by the Bourbon Felipe V.

Mallorca thus welcomed Charles's representative, the Conde de Zavellá, with enthusiasm, sabotaging the Bourbon governor's guns. Mallorcans were instrumental in beating the Bourbon blockade of Barcelona. And in July, 1715, when the entire mainland had fallen, Mallorca was the last outpost to surrender to Felipe V.

Menorca never did so. Seized in 1705 by Charles III's British paymasters with the collusion of most of the population it was retained under British sovereignty at the end of the war and became the key point in the new Mediterranean naval strategy which Britain was to sustain throughout the following century.

Occupational hazards

Thus both main islands of the archipelago ended the war under armies of occupation, yet for both the long-term effects of occupation were favourable. Menorca smarted under redcoat rule. Welcomed as liberators, the English were resented as rulers. The local clergy encouraged contempt for the Protestant heretics and terrorist outrages against British personnel were commonplace.

In Mallorca and Ibiza, Bourbon rule also had the semblance of foreign occupation. The traditional status and privileges of the kingdom were abolished; the functions of the *jurats* or local magistrates, who by now had become a hereditary oligarchy, were transferred to a court

---

LEFT: symbol of the Enlightenment: the library in Palma's gracious 18th-century Can Vivot mansion.
RIGHT: Maó's British-built Hotel del Almirante is still decorated in its original 18th-century ochre shades.

of royal nominees. Both regimes, however, tempered severity with conciliatory acts.

Menorca was particularly favoured by the changes of fortune that befell the occupiers. In 1756 the English were driven out for the duration of the Seven Years War by a French task force, in an encounter that supposedly gave the

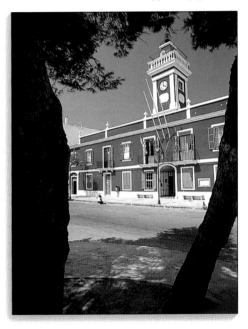

world *mayonnaise* (which is said to have been invented by the French commander's chef) and led to the execution for negligence of Admiral Byng – *pour encourager les autres*, as Voltaire famously and wryly remarked. In consequence, the island, which already had the benefit of the model British garrison town of Georgetown (now known as Villacarlos), acquired a French successor at San Luis. The improvements made by the British to the roads were continued by the French, putting in place the good local infrastructure that still benefits the island today.

The most enlightened British governor, Richard Kane, had already embellished Maó, which owes its status as the island's chief town to the occupiers' choice: the well-preserved Catalan charm of the displaced capital, Ciutadella, is a by-product of that decision. In Maó, the sash windows of Hanover Street are a memento of Georgian supremacy.

Mallorca, too, benefited from the policies of its new rulers. The island was able to thrive as a garrison and naval base thanks to the renewed activity of the Bourbons in the Mediterranean. Though politically repressive, the new regime was economically successful and a mood of *enrichissez-vous* gripped the island élite. There was more new enterprise and more new building than at any time since the 14th century. The

embellishments of the parish church of Santa Cruz in Palma betray the wealth of its early 18th-century parishioners.

The elliptical cloister of San Antonio Abad is only the most startling of the ornaments of Baroque Mallorca. The painter Mesquida, who was active in his native island at this time, was one of the most accomplished in Spain.

Inner debates

Island society remained introspective. Between 1749 and 1777, for instance, the entire community was divided by a dispute over the status of the cult of the Blessed Ramon Llull, the great mystic, missionary and poet who was one of the island's greatest sons, and who, before his supposed martyrdom in Barbary in 1314, established himself as a leading influence in late mediaeval intellectual tradition.

At one level, it was a conflict between Llull's own order, the Franciscans, and the Dominicans. At another, it was a vow between supporters and enemies of the Enlightenment, the former anxious to degrade a candidate for sanctity (Llull) whose works reeked of irrationalism, the latter equally keen to vindicate a traditional cause. But it spread and mobilised hostile factions, waging war by street violence and pulpit-thumping iconoclasm. In the end the cult survived and the only long-term casualty was the advanced-thinking Bishop Díaz de Guerra, who was driven out of the diocese.

The Enlightenment was, however, probably as thoroughly received in Mallorca as in any part of Spain. The libraries of the palaces of Campofranco and Vivot bear witness to the aristocratic patronage of new ideas and the accessibility on the island of texts which had previously been banned.

Famous sons

The second half of the eighteenth century saw Mallorca plagued once more by pirate attacks from North Africa. In response, several generations of notable Mallorcan sailors were given permission by the king in 1785 to "defend" their homeland. Needless to say, the licence – the *patente de corso* – proved enormously beneficial. The most famous of the corsairs (named after this licence) was Captain Antoni Barceló, who eventually achieved the rank of Lieutenant General of the Spanish Armada by such acts as renting ships to the navy whenever it was short of sea power.

Another local celebrity of the same era was the Mallorcan missionary, Fray Junípero Serra. Born in the tiny island village of Petra, Serra travelled considerably further than Barceló. He was the founder of the very first missions in California, including San Francisco (*see also Junípero Serra, page 186*).

The Napoleonic wars at the beginning of the 19th century saw the arrival of a stream of Catalan refugees on Mallorca, causing both social and economic unrest among the islanders. But the same century was also to see the birth of a powerful island bourgeoisie, and an impulse for social change.

Liberal zeal

By the mid-1830s moderate liberals predominated in the island, but they remained wary of the abiding strength of the rebellious reactionaries. The majority of islanders stood aloof from the constitutional conflicts of the following 40 years, concentrating instead on self-enrichment. They voted for the ruling party in the minority of Isabel II; responded so enthusiastically to the government's anti-clerical policies that the arch of the Almudaina

> ### DIFFICULT TIMES
>
> The first decades of the 19th century brought great hardship to the still desperately poor Balearics, including famine and epidemics of cholera, bubonic plague and yellow fever.

Slowly, economic activity grew apace. 1834 was an *annus mirabilis*, which saw new roads, a new theatre in Manacor, a new newspaper, the first steamship sailing to the Iberian mainland and the foundation of a company to exploit trade with the Indies.

A new era

Perhaps as a result of this consequent increase of wealth, the islands' reputation for being politically progressive waned. Under the First Republic, two-thirds of the adult population

was almost knocked down along with redundant monasteries in an excess of liberal zeal; and swamped the polls with votes in favour of the Liberal Union when its leader, O'Donnell, was in power.

They also celebrated the proclamation of a "democratic monarchy" in 1868 by burning the house of a famous reactionary hero of the 1822 rising; and made a virtue of necessity when the First Republic was declared by hoping for increased Mallorcan autonomy.

subscribed to the petitions of the right-wing Unión Católica, which was led in the islands by J.M. Quadrado, the Balearics' most distinguished historian. The restoration of the monarchy on the mainland in 1875 was received enthusiastically on the islands.

Meanwhile, however, republican policies had promoted important material effects, such as laying a railway system and enlarging the harbours. With the restoration of the monarchy, the paddy-like Albufera marshland was drained for pig-farming. A timid regionalism emerged with the renewed use of the Catalan language.

But the end of the century saw another falling of local economic fortunes. The dreaded

LEFT: painting of a 17th-century Mallorcan knight, from a collection in Palma's *Ajuntament*, or Town Hall.
ABOVE: Palma's waterfront in the mid-17th century.

phylloxera virus did away with the Balearics' booming wine business, while Spain's loss of Cuba, Puerto Rico and the Philippines as colonies put an abrupt halt to local shipbuilding. Many islanders saw the writing on the wall and promptly emigrated to the peninsula and the United States.

The 20th century

Nonetheless, the year 1902 saw great changes on Mallorca. The city walls of Palma were destroyed in an extraordinary orgy of destructive progressivism as building began on an electricity station and a "Grand Hotel". Palma

ALL IN THE NAME OF PROGRESS

Between 1900 and 1902, Palma's immensely strong, thousand-year-old city walls were systematically pulled down in an attempt to "modernise" the capital. Yet there was one section of the Roman walls which everyone believed the City Fathers would not dare to touch: the Puerta de Santa Margarita. This was the gate by which King Jaume, the Catalan Conqueror of Mallorca, had entered the city to receive its surrender from the Moors in 1229, and it was almost as sacred as a church. Sadly, though, by 1910 the desire for progress had become too great for the gate, and at midnight on a moonless night, down it came.

also unveiled an opera house with a capacity for 3,000, and the island got its first soccer team! Tourism was beginning to grow with improved communications, and in 1905 a society was established to promote it.

Industrialisation was also taking off. There was a locomotive factory by 1901, a car factory by 1922; and for most of the First World War Mallorcan and Menorcan manufacturers supplied the French army with soldiers' boots. A spate of food and fuel riots occurred in 1918–19, as the economically-favourable war-time conditions came to an end, but did not last, thanks in part to the paternalistic influence of the self-styled "capitalist worker", Joan March. March's was the archetypal "rags-to-riches" story; born in a Mallorcan village during an era of strong class prejudices on the part of the ruling elite, he became not only the richest man in Spain, but was considered the third richest man in the world (after John Paul Getty and Howard Hughes). His grand summer residence in the northeast of the island is now open to visitors.

Mallorca also produced one of the leading politicians of the day, Antoni Maura. As leader of the Spanish conservative party, Maura spent all of his political life in Madrid but never lost the support of his loyal fellow-islanders.

Islands at war

And so the Balearics continued into the third decade of this century much as they had left the 1800s – provincial, extremely religious and politically conservative. There was a large potential left-wing vote waiting to emerge with the fall of the Primo de Rivera dictatorship in 1930, but monarchists easily predominated in the general elections of 1931.

On the national front, however, a Republican government was voted into power, while anti-monarchist parties won the municipal elections later in the year. In response, the king promptly abdicated.

The new Republican government was committed to a programme of radical reform, but protest action by a whole range of splinter groups – anarchists, Marxists and Fascists, as well as separatists from Catalonia, Galicia and the Basque country – stirred industrial and political discontent. Governmental authority was steadily undermined until, by 1936, the country had polarised to the political left and right, and was in a dangerously volatile state.

On 13 July, the right-wing leader Calvo Sotelo was assassinated. General Francisco Franco seized the opportunity to lead a right-wing military uprising against the Republicans which soon spread country-wide. The country was plunged into bloody civil war.

On the islands, Menorca remained strongly Republican, while the ruling classes in Mallorca and Ibiza supported Franco,

Mallorca became an important base for the fascists under General Goded, but despite a build-up of air superiority which turned the island into a sort of permanently-anchored aircraft-carrier for the duration of the war, it

Franco's rule – and beyond

The Franco era (1939–75) saw repression throughout Spain; Catalan and other regional languages were banned, and all expressions of non-Castilian culture ruthlessly suppressed. The Balearics themselves were used as a testing-ground for mass tourism, with little thought given to the impact on the islanders themselves.

Tourism had brought perhaps 40,000 visitors a year just before the civil war, chiefly to Mallorca, but the new airborne invasion boosted numbers from 100,000 in 1950 to nearly 8 million by the 1990s. Certainly, this meant an influx of valuable foreign exchange into the

saw very little action. A Republican invasion of Mallorca's Porto Cristo from Menorca in August 1938 was aborted when the expected rising in its favour failed to materialise.

Menorca nonetheless stuck it out as the last Republican stronghold, surrendering only in February 1939 after Barcelona had fallen to the Nationalists. The British intervened to broker a peace deal aboard HMS *Devonshire*, and Franco's troops finally occupied the island in April 1939.

LEFT: Palma's Grand Hotel, elegant precursor of the tourist boom.
ABOVE: the beach at busy Port d'Alcúdia, Mallorca.

country, together with work and often wealth to small village communities and fishing-ports. Yet in the rush to take advantage of this cornucopia of cash, serious mistakes were made which have only recently been recognised (*see also Surviving Tourism, page 123*).

Franco's chosen successor, King Juan Carlos, surprised many by his early restoration of parliamentary democracy. A period of social liberalisation followed, as Spain threw off the shackles imposed by a puritan alliance of church and state to embrace the changes which had already occurred elsewhere in Europe. Contraception, divorce and homosexuality were legalised. An exciting new arts scene began to blossom – film-maker Pedro Almodóvar is perhaps its best-known exponent – while the cities were suddenly full of late-night clubs and bars.

Just as significant, the new parliament decided to return power to the regions. The 1978 constitution allowed for a measure of devolution, and by 1983 the country had been divided into 17 semi-autonomous regions, with wide-ranging powers over everything from education to tourism. The Govern Balear (Balearic government) was established in Palma, with representatives from all four islands, and Catalan was given equal status to Castilian Spanish across the region.

A HAVEN FOR NON-CONFORMISTS

Whatever the official political affiliations of Mallorca and Ibiza were during the Civil War, they always maintained an independent streak. Later on, during General Franco's rule, the islands gave shelter to many anti-Franquist artists, intellectuals and the like, including the famous painter Joan Miró (see pages 154–5), and Barcelona's radical cartoonist-turned-architect, Javier Mariscal, who spent some years on Ibiza. Today, this tradition continues. There are more than 20 galleries dealing in local artists' work in Palma alone, and there are more artists – both Spanish and otherwise – living on the islands than in any other part of Spain.

A cultural Renaissance

The revival of the local language is the most visible sign of the Balearic's cultural renaissance. Road signs have gradually been replaced in Catalan; it is the language of education and of government. Catalan – along with its Balearic dialects, Mallorquín, Menorquín and Eivissenc – is once again heard on the streets. Yet not everyone is happy with the situation. Older people, for example, educated during the Franco era, were not taught to read and write in Catalan. It is notable, too, that all major newspapers are still published in Spanish.

During the 1980s, under the Socialist government of Felipe González, Spain entered the European mainstream, joining NATO in 1982 and the European Community (now European Union) in 1986. The economy grew rapidly and the Balearics enjoyed their share of this success; by the 1990s, the region had the highest per capita income in Spain. Where once the people of Mallorca had emigrated to Cuba and Argentina to make a living, now the island was importing a huge seasonal workforce from other regions of Spain.

The 1990s also saw a continuing Balearic renaissance in literature, the arts and cuisine. Bookshops were full of novels in Catalan, and the smartest restaurants were those featuring "new Balearic" cuisine. Palma, with its chic cafés, all-night clubbing and vibrant street life, began more and more to resemble a mini-Barcelona.

In 1996, after 14 years of Socialist rule, Spain elected a conservative government led by José María Aznar. Aznar's colleagues, the Partit Popular, have controlled the Balearic parliament ever since it was established. His government is dependent on the support of Catalan nationalists, so – in theory, at least – the Balearics now have powerful allies in Madrid.

But things are never as simple as that. The more extreme Catalan radicals like to talk of a "Greater Catalonia", encompassing the Balearics, Valencia, and parts of the French Pyrenees. It was Catalan invaders who first "liberated" the islands from the Moors. Now people are starting to ask: do we have more to fear from Catalonia than from Spain?   ❑

LEFT: keeping up with the news, Valldemossa.
RIGHT: Ibiza's peaceful rural interior is largely untouched by mass tourism.

THE ISLANDER

Three very different types of people represent three very different sides to the Balearics – but their Catalan roots unite them all

A *Ciutadella, es cul no els hi quep dins sa barcella.* ("In Ciutadella, their bottoms don't fit on a tray.") *A Maó, mostren sa panxa per un boto.* ("In Maó, they show their bellies for a button.")

Islands and islanders always have plenty of individual peculiarities and quirky customs. Think of the British, the Japanese, the Tongans, the Fijians... the list goes on and on. Yet at least all these groups have a collective name. The people of the Balearics do not even have that; they are either Mallorcans, Ibicencos, Menorcans or Formenterans, and they don't always see eye to eye with each other, not even on the same island – as the Menorcan proverbs quoted above demonstrate.

Of course, the islanders have always shared many characteristics with their fellow Mediterraneans. A certain reserved hospitality and a marked respect for tradition are typical of all those seaside populations which have in common a primarily agricultural economy, along with a dependence on seaborne trade.

Curiously, however – rather like their fellow-islanders, the Corsicans and the Sardinians – the inhabitants of the Balearics never became overly dependent on sea commerce. Indeed, a large part of the population always preferred to live in complete ignorance of the sea – even to the extent of never leaving the island's interior so far as to venture into the capital (which was invariably the major port).

At the same time, the *marineros* and fishermen who inhabited the islands' coast seldom ventured into the interior. As a result, the relationship between the traders and the farmers tended to be strictly commercial in nature. The two groups remained culturally quite distinct.

Over the past 50 years, with tourism having almost totally displaced the islands' reliance on maritime commerce and agriculture, all that has

---

PRECEDING PAGES: reflections on a rural life, Ibiza; ploughing land near Sant Miquel, Ibiza.
LEFT AND RIGHT: Ibizan farmer's wife; traditional costume is always at its best on special occasions.

changed. The new generation growing up in the Balearics today has outgrown the individual traits that once distinguished the *campesino* from the coast dweller. Island by island, the populations are far more unified than they once were. Yet throughout the archipelago, some important distinctions remain.

The Mallorcans

It's hard to characterise the inhabitants of the Balearics' largest island, mainly because they lack many extreme behaviour traits. The Mallorcan doesn't like exaggeration or haste and moves with a calm that can enervate others.

The soubriquet *Isla de la Calma,* given to Mallorca by the Catalan painter Santiago Rusinol, was so apt that it has now become a cliché. Today, with its seething coasts in the summer, its excess of cars and its overcrowded airport, the island has lost a great deal of its traditional calm, but the islanders haven't changed the quiet way in which they march through life, disliking the unexpected and the improvised.

Xuetes and Judaism

Xuete (also spelt "*Chuete*") is the name given to descendants of the *Conversos* – Mallorcan Jews forcibly converted to Catholicism during the Inquisition – who as late as the 1970s still constituted a distinctive group on the island.

Some say that the word derives from the old Mallorcan word for Jew, *Xuhita*, which translates literally as "Jewette"; others suggest it is from the word for pork-chop, Xua, and refers to the fact that converts would eat

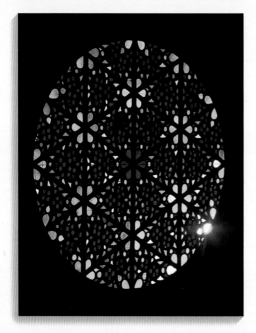

pork-chops on the street to demonstrate that they really were Catholic, and did not follow Jewish dietary laws.

When the officers of the Inquisition arrived in Mallorca in the 16th century, their main focus of attention was the island's large and prosperous Jewish community, most of whom were confined within El Call ghetto in Palma. Given the harsh choice of converting to Catholicism, being burned at the stake or leaving the island, many took the path of least resistance and converted, but hundreds of others were burnt to death.

Despite supposedly having converted, a good many Jews stuck to their old customs,

as you might expect. Publicly, they practised Catholicism but privately they held their own Jewish services. Indeed, it wasn't until the end of the 17th century that the "*Xuete*" label could really be said to hold true.

Yet even those Jews who did convert still suffered discrimination: they were not allowed to leave their ghettos in order to hold office, for instance, or to marry outside their community. Only in the 18th century were *Xuete* priests granted permission to hold Mass in Palma's Catholic cathedral, La Seu.

Up until the 1970s, the *Xuetes* still operated as a small but distinct community in Palma, many working as gold- and silversmiths on the Calle de Plateria ("street of the silversmiths") where their Jewish ancestors had first set up shop nearly a thousand years before. They retained a few Jewish traits, notably a deep respect for family elders, who were always cared for at home.

Today, however, changing economic and cultural factors have worn down community bonds. There are too few *Xuetes* to really constitute a distinct social grouping. Yet in such surnames as Aguiló, Bonnín, Cortés, Fuster, Forteza, Martí, Picó, Pomar, Segura, Tarongí, Valentí, Valleriola and Valls, the *Xuete* legacy lives on.

Judaism experienced a modest rebirth on Mallorca in the 1960s, with the arrival of a pioneering group of settlers from Britain and the United States. In 1987, the community converted an ex-Christian Scientist church into a synagogue – the first on the island since the Inquisition, when almost all Jewish monuments were systematically and ruthlessly destroyed.

Perhaps the most obvious relic of Jewish history left is in Palma Cathedral, where one of the rose windows is shaped like the Star of David. In addition, in some parts of the island crespell cookies are still made in the form of a six-pointed star, and you can still buy the braided bread eaten by Jews on the Sabbath.

But despite the fact that there is once again a Jewish community on Mallorca it has no *Xuete* members, and it probably never will have: the *Xuetes* are, by now, far too far away from their origins. ❑

LEFT: this stained-glass window in Palma Cathedral is based on the shape of the Star of David.

They see an ally in time itself; to put an idea into practice or to take a decision is often a matter of considerable length. The answer to the question "when?" is normally "next week" or "next month" or even "next year". Not that this means Mallorcans are allergic to hard work – in fact, they are very industrious – but they are definitely sceptical of new projects and novelties that threaten to alter their daily routine.Not for nothing is the saying *Hay més díes que llonganisses* ("There are more days than sausages") still a popular one.

Foreigners passing through the island may, with some justification, conclude that the

to benefit from their devotion towards their guests. The Mallorcan warms to those who are capable of understanding this.

The Menorcans

The Mallorcans and the Menorcans share a common bond in their affability and their quietness. But in spite of this obvious brotherhood, the two groups could never be confused.

The Menorcans may *seem* to have an easy smile and a happy-go-lucky temperament, but their setting out here on this island has made them vastly different in character from, say, those extroverted Spaniards living down in the

Mallorcans are very closed, idiosyncratic and are full of complexes. This judgement is the result of a frustration at not being able to introduce themselves easily into island society. They are quite right in their diagnosis, but it is one that applies to any small community which has had a long history of being forced to live by itself – as is the case with all four of the Balearic islands.

Besides, tourists' impressions will always be superficial. A bit of patience and respect is enough to penetrate into Mallorcan society and

ABOVE: Mallorcans making *sobrasada*, the speciality pork sausage tinted red with *pimentón* peppers.

REVIVAL OF AN ANCIENT ART

The S'Hort del Rei gardens in Palma are home to a famous statue of the Balearic Slinger, for in antiquity the islanders' accuracy with the sling was legendary. In modern times (or at least until the 1960s), Mallorcans were taught the art in early youth as a pastime – but today, thanks to a resurgence of interest in Balearic culture, it has been revived. Several slingshot clubs have been formed, their members (most of them under 20) meeting up in large open spaces to practise. Public contests are regularly organised; experienced spectators keep a respectable distance from beginners, however, as shot number one often backfires.

south of the Spanish mainland. Nonetheless, their nature is to be optimistic. The fatalistic scepticism of the Mallorcan is converted into clever well-meant irony in the Menorcan.

Island society, ever relaxed, doesn't invite uproars, irritations or envies. The Menorcan desire for harmony also inspires their dislike of disorder and dirtiness. Their neighbours in Mallorca certainly admire this love for order, putting it down to the influence of utilitarian values and a general appreciation of good taste cultivated during British rule – a period of Menorcan history looked upon most affectionately by the locals.

BALEARIC SPOKEN HERE

Most inhabitants of the Balearic islands are bilingual, speaking both Castilian Spanish and – thanks to Jaume the Conqueror – a local version of Catalan Spanish much influenced by the dialect of the Ampurdán region on the north coast of Catalonia (which is where many of Jaime's soldiers came from). Officially called Balearic, this language is known on Mallorca as *Mallorquín*, by the Menorcans as *Menorquín* and by the Ibizans as *Eivissenc*. During the Franco regime, even speaking the dialect on the street could incur a prison sentence; however, both "pure" Catalan and the Balearic dialect are officially recognised nowadays.

Yet an old quarrel between the two "capitals" of Menorca, located at either end of the island – Maó, proud of its port and dominating the traffic with the continent, and Ciutadella, bastion of the island's tradition and aristocracy – blemishes, ever so slightly, the perfect balance of Menorcan society. It is said that this rivalry has to do with Maó's failure to come to Ciutadella's aid during a punishing seige by the Turkish pirate Red Beard in 1558.

The Ibicencos

If the Mallorcans and Menorcans are rather like brothers in character, the Ibicencos are hardly even distant cousins. The island has suffered from the effects of isolation throughout its history. Indeed, some would say this island, the only one without a Roman name, has been bypassed by time itself. Despite Ibiza's location between two large and influential cities – Alicante on the mainland and Palma in Mallorca – and the fact that it occupies less treacherous waters than those which surround Menorca, the Ibicencos developed a surprisingly introverted traditional life and culture.

Rather stand-offish they may be, but the Mallorcans and Menorcans try hard to open and adapt themselves to their visitors. The Ibicencos, on the other hand, are not nearly so flexible. To bend their thought, will or behaviour is impossible. To insist is useless. Their lives march on parallel tracks to that of the tourists who visit the island each year, with little interconnection. And thus the Ibicencos have maintained a pure and singular character in the midst of the extraordinarily colourful stream of foreigners – both long-stay and short-stay visitors – who enliven the island today. Indeed, it's a good bet that no other islanders would have managed to tolerate such unusual expatriates.

Of course, this refers to the "traditional" Ibicenco – he of the countryside. Society on the island has always been primarily rural, with a complexity of austere virtues, honour codes and silences all more seemingly appropriate to a character of mythology than to a flesh-and-blood human being. The Ibicencos look as if they have escaped from an unwritten book, and the only thing easily identifiable about them is the fact that they are Mediterranean. ❑

LEFT: a musical interlude, Eivissa's Cathedral Square.
RIGHT: a moment of quiet in Palma.

ISLAND PIETY MIXED WITH PLEASURE

Most Balearic festivals are religious in origin. Every town and village celebrates its saint's day with music, dancing, fireworks and fancy dress

The processions that take place at Easter are perhaps the most striking spectacle to be seen in the Balearics. During Semana Santa (Holy Week) hooded penitents representing various religious fraternities *(left)* process solemnly through the islands' city streets, carrying huge crosses and sculpted Passion scenes on floats. The biggest procession takes place in Palma on Maundy Thursday, involving up to 5,000 people. Marchers play drums and trumpets, and hand out sugared almonds to the crowds.

Holy Week begins on Palm Sunday, with the blessing of palms and olive branches at village churches, and ends a week later on Easter Day. The tradition on Easter morning is for two processions to depart from different churches, one carrying a figure of Mary and one of the risen Christ, and then to be reunited with dramatic gestures.

One of the most moving processions takes place on Good Friday in Pollença, when a figure of Christ crucified is carried down the Calvary steps in silence by torchlight. The *Devallement*, as it is known, has its origins in a medieval Passion play. A similar ceremony takes place on the church steps in Felanitx.

▷ **HEROES AND VILLAINS**
Devils taunt the crowd with firecrackers at Sa Pobla's Festa de Sant Bartomeu – but in this battle, fortunately, the good guys always win.

△ **LA VERGE DEL CARME**
Sailors carry effigies of the Virgin through the fishing ports of the islands on 16 July in honour of the protector of seafarers and fishermen.

▽ **LOS CORSAIRES**
Fireworks over Eivissa harbour mark the end of a week of August festivities, marking the anniversary of Ibiza's Christian reconquest in 1235.

▽ **DEVIL OF A TIME**
Costumed devils, once banned by the church authorities, are a feature of several Mallorcan fiestas.

MOORS AND CHRISTIANS

Mallorca's own version of a popular Spanish festival recalls the island's history of piracy, with mock battles enacted between local "heroes" and infidel Moors. Sóller's festivities (*above*) each May commemorate a famous battle of 1561, in which valiant local women helped to defeat a band of Algerian pirates. A mock landing takes place on the beach, a villager calls on the locals to defend their port, and a very noisy battle ensues. There is no need to tell you who wins.

A similar event takes place at Pollença in August. Large crowds turn out to watch as hundreds of youths in Moorish costume attack the town, only to be repelled by bands of "Christians" wearing shirts and white shorts. The battle – which is fuelled by large amounts of alcohol and the firing of antique rifles into the air – is usually extremely colourful.

◁ **BLESSING THE BOATS**
Formentera's big festival takes place in July, when the island's fleet of fishing boats – gaily decorated for the occasion – sails out to sea to be blessed in Sa Savina harbour.

▷ **HORSE PLAY**
Menorcan *caixers*, riders representing the medieval social classes, enliven the island's biggest party, the Festa de Sant Joan.

MALLORCA AS IT WAS

A personal recollection by Neville Waters,
a long-time resident of Mallorca

I will never forget the day that I first arrived on the island of Mallorca. It was late in the month of November 1958. I had motored from Copenhagen in a little Morris Minor, down across a freezing Europe almost entirely covered in snow.

I came to Barcelona to catch the midnight ferry, and I do not recall that I saw the sun throughout the whole journey. The wind was strong in Barcelona, and icy cold. My car was hauled up and lashed to the deck of the boat.

The next morning at dawn, after a rough night, I could see the island of Mallorca across a calming sea, bathed in the rays of the rising sun. I watched with interest as all the many white and stone-coloured houses, the church towers and spires of the city of Palma came more and more clearly into view. The great Gothic cathedral at the end of the harbour looked like an immense old galleon come to rest with all its sails furled.

The hotel where I spent my first night was comfortable and clean, with a private bathroom to each bedroom. The room, with three meals and wine and coffee, cost a pound.

The following morning I visited a Spanish lawyer whose name I had got from the British Consulate before leaving Scandinavia. I told him I intended to buy a house and hoped that he would act for me, although I expected to take six months before deciding where to live. He commended my common sense.

"Many people," he said, "come here on holiday, think that they would like to live here, and buy a house at the end of their summer holidays. They have no idea what it will be like in winter, and are rarely satisfied as a result."

Later that day I noticed a cluster of white houses up on a mountainside, and by the afternoon I was back at the lawyer's office to confess that I had bought a house! And for the past 30 years I have lived in that very same village.

PRECEDING PAGES: letting time pass, Mallorca.
LEFT: Neville Waters, committing memories to canvas.
RIGHT: the older generation clings on to old customs.

Customs in the *casa*

The first morning that I opened the front door of my new home it was to discover plates of green figs on my doorstep. A welcome from my neighbours.

In those days it was the custom to leave one's front door key on the outside of the door if you

were leaving the house as an indication to any caller that you were not at home. Collectors came round with bills for gas, electricity, house and car insurance, etc. You did not keep such people waiting on your doorstep, but invited them in and offered them a glass of brandy with the words *mi casa es su casa*, my house is your house. This practice meant that you had at all times to keep a sizeable sum of ready cash about the house. In those days it was quite safe to do so; house-breaking and burglary were virtually unknown.

My much-esteemed friend was Jaume the postman. If you needed your garden walls or your cellar whitewashed, he would dump the bag of undelivered letters in the entrance hall, take off his coat and start work. If the work took longer than he anticipated he would, on leaving say, "Ah well, they can have this lot tomorrow." Postal deliveries are still slow and unreliable, but not because the postman is whitewashing my cellar.

Language, food and church

I did not speak any Spanish when I first arrived and my Italian proved of no use at all. Often, words in Spanish that sound familiar are more of a trap than a help. I remember one dignified Spanish *señora* informing me that she was very

constipada. The lozenges I gave her can have been of no help, for today I know that she was informing me that she had a cold.

When I arrived on Mallorca it was not possible to buy tea, and butter was available in only one shop on the island, where it was heavily salted and kept in a tub. The shop was nick-named Fortnum and Masons by expatriates, for though it was only a small grocer's shop one could buy things unavailable anywhere else, particularly at Christmas time.

In those days if you were Church of England, you attended services in a converted soda-water factory, in a slight atmosphere of persecution. Services could not be advertised, and armed

Civil Guards frequently came into the church to stand, arms akimbo, usually during the sermon. It was enough to make one fidgety.

The law of Religious Liberty was passed during the last years of Franco's dictatorship, and today, through the efforts of the English and American residents, we have a church and chaplaincy house.

Evening habits

In my early years in Mallorca the pavements of the towns and villages were lined with women fanning charcoal in the early evenings of winter. All types of basins and dishes were used to hold the charcoal, basins of enamel, copper, brass, or whatever they had. The breeze and a newspaper fan having well ignited the contents, the bowls were carried indoors and put beneath a special table, known as a *camilla*. It was circular and draped with a cloth that came down to touch the floor all the way around. If going to read, write, play a game, eat, or just sit, you picked up the cloth, inserted your legs beneath, dropped the cloth and allowed the comforting warmth to rise to where it was most needed. Sadly *camillas* are no longer in use.

The *serenos* have also gone. They were a sort of vigilante who roamed the streets of the towns at night calling out the hour and that all was well. As burglary was almost unknown their duty was mainly directed to seeing drunks home, helping them up the steps and getting the key in the keyhole.

City dressing

Palma is a provincial capital city with a magnificent Gothic cathedral, two palaces, many streets of noble mansions, elegant shopping thoroughfares, avenues of trees and fountains. Thirty years ago people dressed as you would expect them to be dressed in so beautiful a city. Almost all heads were covered, all taxi-drivers wore caps, and on a Sunday, after mass, Spanish *señoritas*, holding their missals, would slowly parade up and down the main avenue, the Passeig des Born, with their *dueñas* beside them, and the sibilant sound of *piropos* filled the air. It was gracious and lovely.

A *piropo* is a compliment paid by a young man to a passing girl or girls. Though quite clearly heard by the young woman for whom it was intended, she was supposed never to acknowledge it in any way. Not even by the slightest inclination of the head, or the flick of an eye. These *piropos*, now alas gone, were always in good taste, and any woman up to late middle-age who had not received one as she walked about Palma, would see to it that almost every item of her wardrobe was immediately renewed.

Nowadays, English youths on holiday walk through the streets of Palma dressed in the briefest possible shorts, while girls in the smallest bikinis try to gain entrance

MALLORCA AS IT IS

Unlike in 1950s Palma, there's a relatively high risk of theft in the city today. In crowds, watch out for pickpockets, and never leave anything valuable in your car.

Talking of water, it was only in the 1980s that my village (which is less than three miles from the centre of Palma) was given piped city water and a piped sewage system. Prior to these modernisations, every single drop of rain that fell was caught upon the roofs and terraces of our houses, and drained down into enormous cisterns which had been built below. Despite the modern pipes, most of us still prefer to go on pumping up the water from these old cisterns. That way, there's no chlorine, and no salt.

to the cathedral. Theirs is a display which should be confined to the beaches.

A place of windmills

Mass tourism has necessitated a vast increase in the use of island water, but as the water-table sank so the water became salty, and therefore useless for irrigation. Accordingly, the hundreds of windmills – variously coloured, merrily twirling – which thirty years ago enlivened the journey in from Palma airport have ceased turning, and have fallen into decay.

LEFT: Ibizan *campesinos* stacking hay.
ABOVE: shepherd and his dog.

Transports of dismay

Another major change is the traffic. Almost none when I came – but the lanes have now been turned into four-lane motorways, and all roads are at all times heavy with traffic. Thanks be my village street is too narrow, and those coaches that have tried to use it get stuck, loaded with tourists, like a cork in a bottle.

It certainly seems a long time since I came, a homeless bachelor in my late forties, to live on an island I have grown to love. Now I have a loving wife, two English step-daughters, two Spanish sons-in-law, six Anglo-Spanish grandchildren, and four step-great-grandchildren! What Zorba called "the full catastrophe". ❑

BAR TALK

Jobs, drugs, politics, inflation... Mallorca may look like a wealthy island of perpetual sunshine, but the locals have their worries like everyone else

For the vast majority of the millions of tourists who visit the Balearics every year, the things that matter are sun, sand, sex and sangria. Perhaps this is as it should be: the whole purpose of a holiday is to get away from it all; having left your own problems behind you don't particularly want to become embroiled with anyone else's.

In any case, it is hard to believe that – in a land of almost perpetual sunshine and evident prosperity – the locals have much to worry about. But beneath the glossy surface, the residents are at times troubled, preoccupied and entertained by issues of local importance, few of which ever get into the pages of the island's English-language newspapers. The closest the visitor who does not read Spanish is going to get to the local news is via a particularly garrulous hotel receptionist or a local whose tongue has been loosened by the profits of his car-hire business in a local bar – and he will usually be speaking Mallorquín.

Issues in the news

Spanish bars are not the easiest places for conversation. It is always necessary to compete with at least one television set (on full blast), the rattle of slot machines and the whistle and grind of coffee makers, plus the happy bellow of the other customers. Bars are not the forum for intellectual exchanges.

In any case, it is said that Mallorcan men are only interested in three things: women, football and gambling. Football certainly provides plenty to talk about; *Real Mallorca*, the island's leading side, has led a yo-yo existence of relegation and promotion between the Spanish Divisions One and Two for more than three decades. There are more than 200 football clubs in the Balearics and there is strong support for the local sides at all levels and foreigners who can play are always welcome to participate;

many Mallorcans are devoted fans of Everton, Chelsea or Manchester United.

Bull-fighting, once a Spanish passion, is holding its own but no more than that, and expatriate attitudes are gradually rubbing off on younger, local opinion. The Coliseo Balear in Palma was once numbered with the great

bull-rings of mainland Spain but it has declined in the past fifty years. Some say it is bad management, and "cowardly bulls and cowardly *toreros*" has been a Press judgement for many years, but whatever the reason, the great *toreros* rarely come to Palma. Others blame the depopulation of the countryside, where support for bull-fighting was strongest.

Gambling is a pervasive presence: from the remote, but entrancing, possibilities of winning *El Gordo* ("The Fat One") – the huge main prize in the National Lottery – to the daily drawings of the ONCE (Society for the Blind) numbers, and to the face-to-face immediacy of the bar card game.

PRECEDING PAGES: salt workers, Formentera.
LEFT: gathering material for conversations with friends.
RIGHT: did you hear the news ...?

Drugs, jobs and more

So, when the unholy trinity of women, football and gambling has been disposed of, what more is there to talk about over a *cerveza* or laced coffee? Inflation, of course. In Palma's hyper-markets one sometimes has the impression that the prices are moving up while the goods sit on the shelves. Cars, of course, and where to park them; the Balearics have the highest ratio of cars per head of population in Spain and parking in Palma is hellish. Drugs, of course; perhaps perceived as a plague brought by for-eigners but now reluctantly recognised as a problem that is creeping down to the young of

suppliers on the estate is remarkable and all of them are busy, with a large number of "sun-rise" industries in computing services and design being especially prominent.

Nonetheless, Mallorca's more traditional forms of employment are in decline. Shoe man-ufacturing, once a thriving industry, is in a depression from which it may not recover. One of the centres of the craft, Inca, a small town 25 km (15 miles) from Palma, had 30 factories in the 1980s but now has only three. Higher wages, heavy social security contributions and what many employers regard as inflexible employee-biased contract conditions have all

every village. Crime, of course; the loss of what was virtually total personal security during Franco's time is still regretted – without there being any significant wish for the return of those times.

Jobs, of course. Employment in Mallorca is related to tourism, but this is still largely sea-sonal and the problem goes wider. Agriculture is important but Mallorca has no heavy indus-try and most industrial and commercial activ-ity is in construction, infrastructure, and expanding the tourist services. A visit to the *Poligono de son Castello*, a new industrial estate on the outskirts of Palma, can be highly instructive. The range of service industries and

combined to price Mallorcan shoes out of their once extensive and profitable export markets – and those who visit the factory outlets no longer find the products cheap.

Agriculture, traditionally based on almonds and olives, also has its problems. Neither of these crops is now profitable in international markets; Mallorca's 7 million almond trees and countless ancient olive groves do not produce high-quality fruit and are labour-intensive to harvest. Early potatoes, capers, wines and milk products achieve some small export success but, by and large, those parts of Mallorca's agri-culture which are most successful are those which use modern methods – and therefore fewer workers. These supply fruit and vegetables to the hotels and the local markets, where they are snapped up by tourists living in villas and self-catering apartments. With village industry declining, the drift from the small towns and villages to Palma and the tourist centres – and increasingly, to Barcelona and the Peninsula – accelerates. The farmhouses and cottages thus vacated are bought by well-to-do Palma residents as their second homes – or else by foreigners.

Scandalmongering

Are there, then, no scandals, no corruption, no political favouritism, for the locals to talk about? Well, of course there are. Considering the exponential growth of the Balearic economy over the past fifty years – a period which also included the giant leap from dictatorship to democracy – it would be surprising if some cracks at least had not shown on the surface of local society.

These 40 years have turned many centuries-old values upside down. Traditionally, for example, the youngest son of a family of landowners always received the agriculturally poor land near the coast as his inheritance. Suddenly, this land is worth immeasurably more for hotels and apartments than his older brothers' rural holdings. Shocks of this kind are difficult for a society to absorb without damage to its indigenous structures.

Mallorcans are no less interested in making money than any one else; expatriates claim rather more so. Tourism has changed Mallorca, culturally and visibly. Once it was a land of windmills; today it is a land of cranes. There have been times during the past forty years when the pouring of concrete has seemed like the flow of lava from a constantly erupting volcano of greed and opportunism.

If it were possible to tune in at one time to conversations in the thousands of bars in the Balearics, the dominant topic – after women, football and gambling, naturally – would almost certainly be construction. Who is getting away with what, and how; who is getting his private road surfaced at public expense; how that permission for a new *urbanizacion* was obtained; why developers were allowed

into an area designated as being of special natural beauty… and so on.

Faced with a mass of restrictions and permissions to be obtained before building, many Mallorcans simply go ahead regardless and worry about the consequences (and permits) later. Quite often there aren't any, as an overworked bureaucracy and legal system tries to keep pace with new developments. Sometimes fines are imposed, but not always collected, and – albeit occasionally – illegal buildings are bulldozed without compensation. The job of head of planning in a local authority may not be an easy one, but it must at least be profitable. ❑

LEFT: GOB demonstration in Palma's Plaça d'Espanya.
RIGHT: an overburdened runway at Palma airport.

GOB TALK

A reliably lively topic of discussion in Mallorcan bars is the influential environmental movement, *Grup Balear d'Ornitológia i Defensa de la Naturalesa*, or GOB. Hardly a week goes by when the media are not reporting GOB's views on some proposed new tourist or industrial project, for these Mallorquín "Greens" have had some striking victories. In the 1970s, GOB helped save the uninhabited islet of Dragonera from an insensitive development plan; it is now owned by the *Consell Insular*. GOB has also successfully lobbied to save Menorca's S'Albufera reserve from development, and to increase the penalties for hunting protected birds.

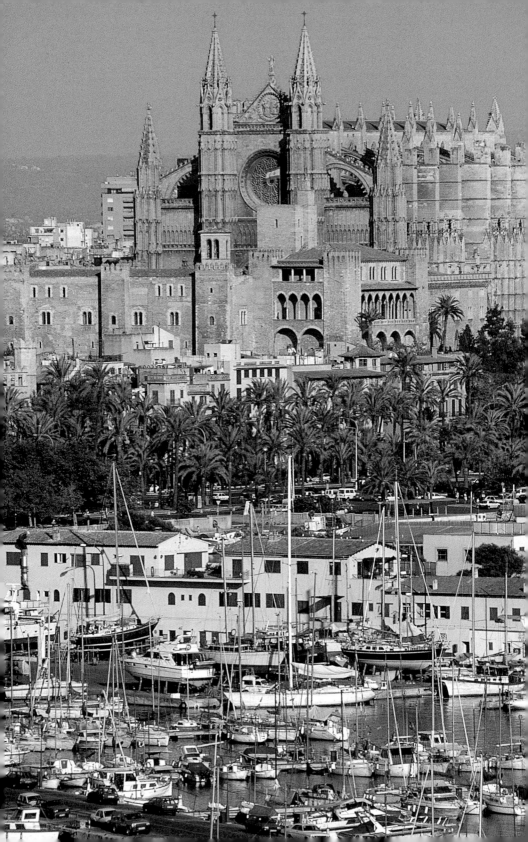

JET-SETTERS, PAST AND PRESENT

Mass tourism might have steamrollered its way around the coasts,
but the Balearics' beauty still attracts plenty of the rich and famous

In the Balearic summer season – a moveable feast which seems to include most of spring and all of autumn as well – barely a week goes by without one or other of the newspapers mentioning the arrival of someone significant at the airport and the departure of someone else.

Sheiks, artists and aristocrats, screen and singing stars who have made money, society figures who have inherited it, and beauties who have married it – the jet-setters who come to the Balearics are no different to those anywhere else in the world, but here, on these small islands, they are noticed.

The tradition of just dropping by for a taste of sun was started by Frédéric Chopin and his common-law wife, George Sand. They came to spend the winter of 1838-39 in Valldemossa, Mallorca, hoping the weather would be good for the composer's health. Unfortunately, the monastery where they stayed is cold and damp in the winter, and Chopin almost died; moreover George Sand disliked the island and its people, who for their part, didn't view her with much favour either.

By contrast, Archduke Luis Salvador of Austria, who arrived on his yacht *Nixe* in 1869 and stayed for 22 years, loved the locals and they loved him. He blazed a trail which many have followed. The estate he bought for his Mallorcan mistress, the peasant girl Catalina Homar, is today owned by the film star Michael Douglas; it was so expensive that locals have since nicknamed him "Archdouglas".

Other "residents" include rock star Annie Lennox, who has a property at Esporlas, and Lynne Franks (the model for the high-flying PR Edina in BBC Television's sitcom *Absolutely Fabulous*) at Deià. Virgin's Richard Branson has a hotel in Mallorca, a house in Menorca, and also owns 4 km (2½ miles) of pristine coastline near Banyalbufar.

PRECEDING PAGES: playground for the rich.
LEFT: Palma's yacht-clogged marina.
RIGHT: taking the helm: King Juan Carlos of Spain in action during a Palma regatta.

Royalty

Perhaps the most significant jet-setters are the members of one of Europe's best-loved Royal Families. King Juan Carlos and Queen Sofía of Spain, and occasionally their three children, spend the month of August in Mallorca's Royal Palace, former home of the famous Greek

painter, Juan Saridakis. The family sail around the island on the Royal Yacht *Fortuna,* and compete in such regattas as the "King's Cup" and the "Princess Sofía Cup" in Palma bay. Princess Elena takes part in show-jumping competitions, including the HRH Princess Elena Horse Jumping Trophy in Bunyola, while the King often plays golf with his father, Don Juan, count of Barcelona.

The main venues

Although sophisticated Palmaian venues like the 17th-century Palacio Ca Sa Galesa attract some *glitterati*, most head out of town to such classy establishments as the Son Vida – set just outside the capital in a restored 18th-century mansion – and Richard Branson's La Residencia. The latter's guest list has included Jack Nicholson, Sting and Princess Diana.

When the Son Vida Hotel was inaugurated in 1961, Prince Rainier and Princess Grace of Monaco were guests of the management, as were many famous names from society and show business, some of whom have returned and purchased property here. Their huge villas, hidden in sumptuous, sub-tropical gardens on the luxurious Son Vida estates (and nearby Bendinat and Portals Nous), count among the most desirable addresses in the Balearics.

At the other end of the island the Hotel Formentor, discreet and colonial, has played host to Winston Churchill, Douglas Fairbanks, Charlie Chaplin, Christopher Plummer, the Prince of Wales, the Prince and Princess of Monaco and countless others.

The Ibizaphiles

Plenty of influential figures have flitted through Ibiza on yachts and been snapped by *paparazzi* in the nightclubs, but it has also attracted artists and showbiz types by the score. In the 1960s, Diana Rigg and Denholm Elliot both bought houses at Santa Eulàlia, while Terry-Thomas retired to a villa at Cala Boix near San Carlos.

Roman Polanski still owns a place in the swish modern *urbanización* of Roca Llisa.

A number of rock stars are confirmed Ibizaphiles: George Michael uses the island as a base for his Spanish concert dates, while Roger Taylor of Queen is another fan of Santa Eulàlia, and has bought a property there. German punk singer, Nina Hagen, lives on the island, too.

Pike's Hotel near Sant Antoni – a rambling converted farmhouse in a pastoral setting – has long been the haunt of assorted music-biz celebrities, including Julio Iglesias. As for little Formentera, plenty of stars have stretched out on its nudist beaches over the years, including Brigitte Nielsen and Grace Jones.

Playgrounds

Where jet-setters go, they must have their places to play. The Royal Family's favourites include the Peppone Italian restaurant in Palma, as well as the Shangri-La Chinese and the Mediterraneo 1930 restaurants.

The yachting fraternity have colonised Wellies in the Puerto Portals yacht club; swish Latino, with its impressive cocktail list, and Tristans, with its Michelin star and punitive prices to match, are also popular. Head for Club Mosquito in Palma and you could find yourself dancing side by side with the Crown Prince of Spain or one of his sisters. Michael Douglas, however, prefers nearby Pachá.

New image

Over the past 15 years, the Balearics have increasingly come to be recognised as a prime site for property investment by some of the most gilt-edged speculators in the world. Palma's identity as a chic, prosperous, cosmopolitan city was confirmed in the 1990s when it was nominated by the newspaper *El Pais* as the best place to live in Spain.

The number of expensive restaurants and famous-label boutiques continues to increase, while events such as Valldemossa's Chopin Festival give the islands the stamp of cultural credibility. Never mind the boom in mass tourism on its coasts; in general, the Balearics' image is emphatically an upmarket one. ❑

LEFT: Claudia Schiffer, one of Mallorca's many celebrity residents.
RIGHT: Finça s'Estaca in Mallorca, owned by film star Michael Douglas.

THE EXPATRIATE EXISTENCE

The Balearics attract a wide variety of foreign residents, but they all share the same dream: to find a life in the sun and a sanctuary from stress

Everyone has an image of life in the sun: sitting on a shady terrace, looking out beyond the orange trees to that distant glint of warm, blue sea, living far from the cold, dreary, northern winters in a place where the money goes further than it might do at home, and the company largely consists of like-minded friends. We may not want to work there, and we will certainly miss the children; it may even be a little dull, but as somewhere to retire to, to finally put one's feet up and enjoy life, free from stress, it sounds ideal.

The Balearic islands measure up to this picture reasonably well. In the past 60 years or so, they have attracted a great quantity of expatriates, all of whom live on the islands for at least part of the year and regard the islands as their principal place of residence – if not actually as *Home*. The attractions are broadly those outlined above, but the expatriates themselves vary widely.

There is no one type of expatriate, no dominant nation. They come from all countries and all classes and have tastes that vary from the extravagant to the spartan. Even the common image of the "expat" as retired is no longer entirely accurate; at the turn of the 21st century, not all expatriates are elderly or pensioners. An increasing number have come to the islands to work, and, since Spain's entry into the EU, this number has grown – a process accelerated by the ease of global communications. Thanks to computers, fax machines and especially e-mail, many international businessmen and women now find it easy to conduct business from an office in their villa in the sun.

New breed

In the main, the new type of working expatriate is involved in the tourist trade (the islands' principal industry) or serves the needs of the expatriate community itself. Expatriates run the local offices for holiday companies, act as guides or resident representatives, manage hotels or bars or restaurants, run beach concessions like sailing or windsurfing, or work in such places as full-time staff where their language skills and willingness to work long hours are their principal assets.

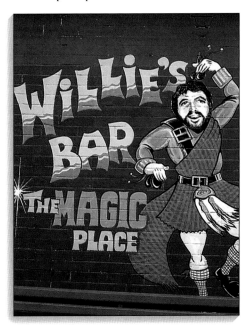

Increasingly, however, this new breed run their own service industries, looking after flats, houses or gardens while the expatriate owner is abroad, handling lettings, liaising with local builders for construction work or repairs, or running estate agency offices. Then there are those who, having made their pile elsewhere, offer professional services in banking, finance, architecture and computing, both to the expats and to the islanders, as a way of avoiding boredom and keeping in touch.

Clearly, "a knowledge of island ways" and "the ability to get on with the locals" are essential qualifications for these sorts of jobs, and it is these skills that distinguishes the new breed

---

PRECEDING PAGES: the lifestyle has its appeal.
LEFT: fine for two weeks, but for a lifetime?
RIGHT: try a dash of sun with your highland fling.

most sharply from the old – many of whom still find it difficult to accept that life on the islands is very different from the way it is back home.

For these younger expatriates, the Balearics are their home and quite possibly their future. Some are married to islanders, speak Spanish – or even Mallorquín – and, having decided to make their homes on the island, have come to terms with the fact that the pace of life there is not actually that much slower than in other European countries, and is speeding up all the time. Their children tend to be educated at local nursery schools to begin with, where they get a good basic education and become fluent in

perceptible increase in the number of Chinese restaurants – a boon, given the islands' not always varied cuisine.

The majority, however, are relics of World War II or the decline of empire in the post-war period: Britons from Malaya and India, French *pied-noirs* from Algeria, and Dutch from the Far East.

Flat or *finca*

Where to live on Mallorca will depend on personal preferences, but the basic choice usually boils down to either a flat or a small country house, or *finca*. Flats can vary from a small

Mallorquín, but will then be sent to a bilingual (Mallorquín-Spanish) establishment in Palma before a secondary school in America, England or Continental Europe.

Races apart

The second, and larger part of the expatriate community, fits into a more traditional mould, though here again, not all of them are necessarily old or retired. Some are refugees, political or economic, fleeing to these islands from war and insecurity at home. Thus the South African community has grown in recent years, and when Hong Kong began to wind down before re-integration with China, there was a

pied-à-terre in a side-street of Palma to a luxurious coastal apartment with a boat dock at the marina. Similarly, "*finca*" can mean anything from a modern villa in a new development to an old farmhouse set among the olive trees.

The choice here usually depends on the amount of use envisaged for the property. Those who spend long summers on the islands go for flats or apartments, while those who live there all year round tend to favour houses with some sort of garden. Flats have the advantage that owners can close the door and walk away, with the disadvantage that the other flats in the block may be let out throughout the summer to holiday companies and filled with tourists and their noisy children. *Finques* have gardens which must be maintained; many lack water during the dry summer months and are beyond the reach of electricity and telephone lines – though this problem is declining. In either case the property intended for year-round use must be insulated against the winter chill and made secure against burglars. Mallorca is still a safe island, but not as safe as it used to be.

Nor is it easy to pick up a bargain. Property prices have remained stable largely because the

> **WEATHER ALERT**
>
> Would-be expats take note: the Mallorcan weather is not always benign. From late August onwards heavy rain and violent storms are common, while central heating is essential from November to March.

and all the other problems that expatriates inevitably encounter, most residents seem happy. Medical services and hospitals are surprisingly good, and the expatriate social life generally agreeable. Plenty of expatriates claim it is even better in wintertime, when the summer visitors have gone and they can socialise among their island friends in peace. Many have boats, or enjoy their gardens, and take advantage of the good communications with "the Peninsula" (mainland Spain) and the rest of the world.

stock of property is continually increasing; however, the heady days when a beautiful old farmhouse could be picked up for a few thousand pesetas are now long gone, and those who decide to go ahead and build must learn to cope with local builders, who are a race apart. Indeed, one expert suggests that the best way to get what you want from local builders is to sit by the works with a chequebook in one hand and a whip in the other.

Even so, despite rising prices (many goods cost more here than they do on the mainland)

Although everyone has friends among the islanders, the Mallorcans are clannish; few expatriates of any age are fully integrated with island life. Here, the main difficulties arise because not many expatriates speak more than shopping Spanish, and fewer still Mallorquín. The island people, for the most part, keep their socialising within the wide boundaries of their own families, or to the confines of the numerous *fiestas*.

Even so, few Mallorcan birthday parties, or children's *santos* – saint days – are without a handful of expatriate friends, who have learned to bring presents and enjoy a colourful glimpse of local culture. ❑

LEFT: expats enjoy open-air eating as much as tourists.
ABOVE: Pollença in Mallorca, popular with expats.

ISLAND CUISINE

A continuing renaissance in Balearic culture has seen the revival of traditional island cooking, as well as the emergence of a "new Catalan" cuisine

Until the 1990s the Balearics were something of a blank on the Spanish gastronomic map, known for little more than tourist barbecues with paella, chips and plonk, Two closely-connected trends have now challenged that view. One is the revival of traditional island cooking, with restaurants offering *cuina mallorquína, menorquína* and *ibizenca* based on fresh local ingredients. The other, at the upmarket end of the scale, is the appearance of a Balearic version of nouvelle cuisine (sometimes referred to as "new Balearic" or "new Catalan"), featuring exotic ingredients like snails and pigs' trotters but not afraid to mix them with influences from elsewhere.

The traditional cooking of the islands reflects their landscape and history. Olives arrived with the Romans, almonds and oranges with the Moors. Peppers, tomatoes and potatoes were brought back from Spain's New World colonies. The British introduced a dairy industry to Menorca, while the French are said to have invented mayonnaise – now blended with garlic to make *allioli*, a sauce for meat and fish.

Key ingredients

Many of Mallorca's most appealing dishes are based on pork and vegetables, They include *frit mallorquí*, a fry-up of offal and potatoes which is traditionally made following the annual *matança*, or pig-slaughtering; *sopas mallorquínas*, a steaming bowl of broth poured over vegetables and thin slices of bread; *tumbet*, a robust summer dish of fried peppers, tomatoes, potatoes and aubergines; and *arroz brut*, the Mallorcan equivalent of paella, with meat and game instead of seafood.

Poultry is traditionally reserved for special occasions. At Christmas, most families will roast a turkey or prepare *capó al Rei en Jaume*: capon, King James' style, stuffed with apples, raisins and breadcrumbs.

PRECEDING PAGES: Palma greengrocer.
LEFT: paella-style *arròs brut* for the farmworkers.
RIGHT: succulent mountain hams in a country bar.

Menorca is known for its spiny lobsters, made into wonderful casseroles and fish soups, and for the abundance of seafood around its coasts. Mullet, prawns and sea-bass are all fished here, along with more unusual offerings like scorpion fish and the mussels known as sea-dates. Aubergines feature in a good many

Menorcan dishes, frequently stuffed either with meat or prawns, while another Menorcan favourite, roast meat with *grevi* (gravy), is a legacy of the British occupation. The most interesting specialities of Ibizan and Formenteran cuisine – dried salted skate, for example – are getting harder to find, but there are good fish stews, and herby roast lamb.

Islands' pride

The most famous local product is the *sobrasada*, a sausage of finely-minced raw pork tinted red with *pimentón* peppers. Traditionally made from lean cuts of black pigs fattened on beans, barley, acorns and prickly pears, it comes mild or spicy, soft or hard, according to taste. Other specialities include *botifarró*, a herby blood sausage, and *cuixot*, a type of brawn. It was probably these that George Sand encountered when she wrote: "I am sure that more than two thousand dishes are prepared from the pig in Mallorca, and at least two hundred kinds of black pudding, so liberally seasoned with garlic, black and red pepper ... that you hazard your life with every bite." Whatever Sand may have thought, the pork products of the Balearics are treated with a reverence not usually accorded to mere foodstuffs; during the annual Balear craft fair in Palma,

sobrasada-makers take their place alongside carpenters, leatherworkers and potters in the rollcall of Balearic master artisans.

The other main object of culinary pride is the *ensaimada*, a puffy spiral of sugar-dusted bread which can be as small as a croisssant or as large as a lifebelt, packaged into an elegant hatbox. The secret of its feathery richness, enviously but unsuccessfully imitated all over mainland Spain, rests in the use of pure pork fat in the cooking. *Ensaimadas* can be dunked into coffee or chocolate for breakfast, filled like a cream bun with confectioner's custard or pumpkin jam, or even, believe it or not, topped with slices of *sobrasada*. To an outsider, the fatty

blandness of the dough is an acquired taste, but some people love it and fly home clutching a stack of *ensaimada* boxes bought at the airport.

Specials on the side

The best take-away food is available in bakeries and markets. Sweetmeats like *flaó*, an Ibizan cheese pastry, *coca de patatas*, an airy potato-based bun from Valldemossa, and *galletas*, olive oil biscuits from Alaior, all have their origins in *fiesta* treats. Arab and Jewish influences are especially obvious in the *empanadas, cocas* and *cocarrois*: flatbreads and pies with a huge variety of toppings and fillings. *Cocas* might be a blazing red sheet of roasted peppers, or a bed of sugar-sprinkled *sobrasada*; spinach pies and pasties come studded with pine kernels and sultanas.

The markets also sell local cheeses, often made from sheep's or goat's milk, as well as the ubiquitous *queso de Mahón* (*see also page 220*). Slices of cheese and cured ham, plus fruity tomatoes and olive oil from Sóller, are all you need to make that favourite Balearic snack, *pa amb oli*, an open sandwich of rough country bread rubbed with tomato and drizzled with olive oil.

Almonds, sultanas, fig cake and oranges always make good buys, along with strawberries and new potatoes in late spring and early summer. Olives are everywhere, in a bewildering range of varieties. "The olive tree has been to the Mallorcans what the seal is to the Eskimos: a cherished source of materials put to infinite use with nothing wasted," writes Toby Molenaar in *Discovering the Art of Mallorcan Cookery*. And he's not wrong: the oil provides soap and polish as well as cooking fat; it is an important ingredient in a number of traditional remedies; the branches are used as fuel, and the wood is carved into salad bowls to be sold to tourists. The early green olives, harvested in autumn while still slightly bitter, are delicious marinated with wild fennel.

Where to go

Palma is the gastronomic capital of the islands and the most likely venue for a special meal out, with restaurants specialising in Galician, Basque, Castilian and Catalan cuisine, not to mention French, Italian and Japanese. Pollença has a reputation for its excellent French-style restaurants; Algaida and Orient for their hearty *cuina mallorquína*. And Es Mercadal is the place to find traditional Menorcan cuisine.

Some of the best local cooking is to be found in *cellers* (converted wine-cellars), especially those out on the Mallorcan plain in towns such as Sineu, Inca and Binissalem. The emphasis here is usually on rustic meat dishes such as roast suckling pig, roast kid and *llom amb col* (pork wrapped in cabbage leaves with pine nuts and raisins). In winter, this might be made with *tords* (thrushes) instead of pork.

As for seafood, it should be good anywhere on the coast, particularly at Fornells and Ciutadella in Menorca. Unfortunately, however, as the Mediterranean fish stocks are gradually depleted, so much of the fish has to be imported and frozen – a depressing trend indeed.

The best of the modern Balearic style of cooking is generally found in the restaurants of the smarter hotels, as well as in the more upmarket resorts. Here, *nouvelle cuisine* takes on Balearic touches, with local ingredients assuming unexpected disguises – *sobrasada* with steak, perhaps, or even duck stuffed with *torró* (nougat).

A recovering industry

Mallorca's wine production is only just starting to recover from the devastation caused by the *phylloxera* plague of the 1890s. As the wine industry develops, an interesting debate is taking shape between those who want to experiment with new varieties (Cabernet, Merlot, Syrah, Pinot Noir) and those who believe that this will endanger the distinctiveness of Mallorcan wines.

The traditional red wines, from Binissalem, are based on the indigenous grape, Manto Negro, though Jaume Mesquida in Porreres is turning out an excellent Cabernet Sauvignon and experimenting with white wine varieties from Gewurztraminer to Sauternes.

Elsewhere, a vineyard in Algaida has produced an organic Chardonnay, and some of the more innovative wine-makers are working on a Mallorcan version of *cava*, the Catalan sparkling wine. There is even talk of reviving the production of sweet Malvasia wine in Banyulbufar.

LEFT: squash for sale at Inca's Thursday market.
RIGHT: Palma's Mercat Olivar is a great place to find fresh fish and seafood.

Menorcan gin, another legacy of the British occupation, is at its best mixed with lemonade to make *pomada*. The only remaining producer left on the island, Xoriguer, also makes a number of gin-based herbal liqueurs, one of which, *calent* – made with aniseed, cinnamon and saffron – is traditionally served warm in winter. Aromatic liqueurs such as *palo* (made from carob seeds) and *herbes* (packed with herbs) are also produced at distilleries in Ibiza and Mallorca. These are enough to leave happy memories of any meal, although you are more likely to see the locals with a Spanish brandy – or even a glass of Scotch. ❏

SPINACH A LA CATALANA

☛ Heat 1 tablespoon of olive oil in a small saucepan, add 40g (1½ oz) pine nuts and fry until golden. Using a slotted spoon, transfer to kitchen paper to drain.
☛ Heat another 2 tablespoons of oil in a large saucepan. Wash, but do not dry 750g (1½ lb) fresh spinach, and remove the stalks.
☛ Add to the pan with 2 chopped cloves of garlic and cook over a high heat for 5 minutes, stirring with a wooden spoon, until the spinach is wilted.
☛ Stir in the toasted pine nuts and 40g (1½ oz) raisins and season to taste. Cook through for a minute or two.
☛ Serve with grilled meat; this makes enough for four.

NIGHTLIFE

Famous worldwide for their no-holds-barred hedonism, Ibiza's
extraordinary clubs set the standard for nightlife on all the islands

Nightlife on Ibiza is famous for two things: a unique brand of unbridled hedonism that sets it apart from all other Spanish resorts, and its luridly fashionable clubs.

However, visitors should not expect to find this kind of thing all over the Balearics. Formentera is so small that it can only support two nightclubs, both in the mini-resort of Es Pujols. And while Menorca's main cities, Maó and Ciutadella, have a range of bars and clubs, they are nothing special; even the giant disco-chain Pachá could not be persuaded to open an outlet near Maó until 1988, finally providing the island with a place which stayed open until early morning (the most unusual night-spot on the island is **Cova d'En Xoroi** at Cala d'En Porter, set in a series of natural caves overlooking the sea). And even Mallorca's lively, sophisticated nightlife is largely inspired by trends set on the third-largest island.

Ibiza

In the island's two main towns, the evening begins in bars and cafés around the port. The waterfront bars have always been popular gathering spots before a long night; in Sant Antoni people sit on the terraces of the **Café del Mar**, **Mambo** or **Savanna**, sip drinks and watch the sunset, while in Eivissa (Ibiza Town) a series of bars fronting converted fishermen's houses draw the crowds at dusk.

Here, bars **Vogue**, **Tango** and **Zoo** make up the legendary "Ibiza Triangle", where the most beautiful and bizarre exhibitionists strut their stuff. It's a psychedelic world of gold-sprayed stilt-walkers, be-sequinned drag queens and fiery devils, either promoting a nightclub or simply dressed that way because – well, this is Ibiza. A stroll through the Marina quarter leads to Carrer Virgen and **Bar Zuka**, the hippest place to be seen before the clubs open.

Gays have always been drawn to tolerant

PRECEDING PAGES: going wild, Sant Antoni disco, Ibiza.
LEFT: Ibiza's club Privilege can hold 10,000 dancers.
RIGHT: getting in the drinks, Palma.

Ibiza. A number of gay bars with accompanying terraces are concentrated just inside the walls of Dalt Vila, overlooked by an enormous rampart. **Anfora** is the main exclusively gay club, while **Manumission** at Privilege attracts a mixed crowd, gay and straight – as does the fetish **Club Submission** at **El Divino**.

At the foot of Dalt Vila is Ibiza's original disco, **Lola's**, built into the ground floor of an old house and still going strong as a pre-club venue. There's a different scene around the Botafoch Marina on the opposite side of the port, favoured by well-heeled Eurotrash summering on their yachts.

Nothing much gets going in clubland until around one in the morning. In Eivissa, everybody drifts towards **Pachá** and **Angel** on the Botafoch Marina: both operate a door policy on popular nights, and only the "suitably dressed" are admitted. Pachá is one of the oldest establishments on the island, part of a chain of some 20 clubs located all over Spain. The

Ibiza venue is expensive, hip and happening, hosting London's famous **Ministry of Sound** DJs throughout the summer in assorted dance rooms, with drinks served from 15 bars. There's a huge chill-out terrace on the roof, from which you can watch the sun rise over the harbour.

Angel's began as Charly Max in the late 1970s, and for a time made Pachá tremble for its disco primacy. However, it lost the struggle for the elite crowd, closed for a year, and opened again with its present name. It's not as exclusive as Pachá, but it has a well-regarded sound-and-light show, and regular theme parties. Also on the marina is the stylish El

Over the road is Brazilian-owned Privilege (formerly KU), a barn-like venue that holds a staggering 10,000 dancers. Privilege is like a small town, complete with shops, bars, restaurants and a swimming-pool, over which the dance-floor is suspended. The DJ travels up and down in a glass lift; at dawn, the roof opens to reveal the orange-streaked sky. Needless to say, chilling out in the pool is all part of the fun.

Privilege hosts some of Ibiza's wildest theme evenings, including a Brazilian spectacular, as well as the outrageous Manumission club, which features fire-eaters, drag artistes and a live sex show.

Divino, famous for its fetish parties as well as its theme evenings.

No self-respecting partygoer can visit Ibiza without making a pilgrimage to the two mega-clubs, **Amnesia** and **Privilege**, located outside the tiny hamlet of Sant Rafel on the road to Sant Antoni. Amnesia is built around an old *finca* and thrives on its Spanish setting, with whitewashed buildings and lush gardens. Here, the chill-out room is a vast greenhouse, complete with palms and cascading bougainvillaea. Hottest tickets are for the nights hosted by the Liverpool club, **Cream**, and for the famous foam parties, when 1.8 metres (5 ft) of foam is pumped onto the packed dance-floor just before dawn.

THE PRICE OF EXCESS

A word about drugs. These are illegal on Ibiza, as they are on mainland Spain, and the penalties for possession are severe. Nonetheless, Red Bull and vodka alone do not fuel 12 hours' hard dancing, and drugs – especially Ecstasy – play a large part in the local club scene. Ibiza's Ecstasy culture is the latest chapter in a 40-year history of turning on, tuning in and dropping out, for since the early 1960s Ibiza has been a Beat and then a hippie haven, a place to live out a counter-cultural dream in which drugs are simply part of the package. Needless to say, though, clubbing under the influence is dangerous as well as illegal.

Sant Antoni has its share of spectacular clubs, too. **Extasis** and **Es Paradis** are the biggest, the latter located under a huge glass pyramid on the bay. It's famous for water parties, during which the dance floor is – literally – flooded.

When the clubs close at first light, die-hard clubbers head for Platja d'En Bossa and **Space**, another cavernous venue which opens at breakfast-time and goes on pumping out ferocious techno-house beats until midday.

Of course, clubbing isn't the only nightlife available on the island. In Eivissa, the café-music bar **Pereira**, a former theatre, stays open all night; its restaurant is open 20 hours

old part of town. A speciality of the house continues to be barbecued spare-ribs, and it must be the only place on the island that offers Mexican food. Phyllis has brought some of her gypsy friends across the port, and on Saturday nights they dance and sing flamenco.

Mallorca

Over the years, the hub of Palma's nightlife has shifted away from the El Terreno district towards the Passeig Marítim; the Plaça Gomila, once the only place to be, has become a seedy, run-down area of sex shops and topless bars. All that is left of Gomila's former lustre is

a day. Dutch owner Eric-Jan Harmsen's jazz performances on the piano are part of the nightly entertainment, and thanks to his extensive contacts in the music world, he is able to book well-known jazz artists. Live music is a regular feature of **Mirage** on Santa Eulàlia marina, too, a friendly place with funky décor and a good line in cocktails.

Another place that breaks the mould in Eivissa is called **Phyllis** after its American owner, who for 13 years had a restaurant in the

LEFT: full moon party on Ibiza's Benirràs beach.
ABOVE: a foam party in action at Amnesia, with young revellers dancing in several feet of foam.

Tito's, for many years the district's centrepiece. Starting out in 1923 as a swish nightclub, it featured such entertainers as Marlene Dietrich and Charles Aznavour; it is now run as a futuristic mega-disco, reached by a panoramic glass elevator from the waterfront.

A young crowd gathers at **Pachá**, on the Passeig Marítim, and at **Ib's**, a nightclub beneath the promenade. However, much the smartest place to pose is outside one of the late-night terrace bars. The **Cappucino**, **Café de Paris**, **Dàrsena** and **El Pesquero** all opened on the Passeig Marítim in the late 1990s, along with **Varadero** overlooking the sea at the end of the old quay. The younger Spanish royals visit

Mosquito, beside the Club de Mar, or hang out at the chic waterfront cafés in Portals Nous.

Not far from La Llotja in Carrer Sant Joan is the best place in Palma for a pre-dinner drink. Abaco is set in a 17th-century mansion, strewn with antiques and embellished with courtyards, fountains and caged birds. Baskets of fruit tumble to the floor where they lie piled up in heaps; you sip cocktails by candlelight to the sound of opera in the background. Exotic drinks are sold at extremely high prices, but then what is being sold is the atmosphere. And if the atmosphere here appeals, you may also like Abaco's big brother, Abacanto, a nightclub set in

largest disco in Europe, with laser shows, theme fiestas and dance floors on two separate levels. While the upper level is packed to the hilt with lager-swilling British teenagers, the lower is reserved for those whom the upstairs crowd call *carozas* (carts) – that is, anyone over the age of 30.

For entertainment a little less loud and louche, head out to Port Andratx to see and be seen at ultra-trendy Tim's or Idó, or to dinner at the waterfront Miramar or the Club Naútico. For those who fail to make it home before dawn breaks, the café and bakery Consignia is open from 7am for breakfast.

another extravagantly revamped country mansion, a short way out of the city in the *barrio* of S'Indioteria. It's best to take a taxi – Abacanto isn't easy to find.

Outside Palma, there are as many centres of nightlife as there are beach resorts, with the biggest concentration occurring on both sides of Palma bay. The clubs here are hardly hip – anyone with aspirations to that sort of thing heads for Ibiza – but they offer a chance to dance to familiar hits from home, rather than cutting-edge DJ mixes, and the drinks are cheap. The disco at RIU-Palace, in Platja de Palma, has room for 2,000 people, but this is dwarfed by BCM in Magalluf. BCM claims to be the

The tour groups make for Son Amar, a *finça* on the outskirts of Palma with a star-studded cabaret show, or the Pirate's Adventure Show in Magalluf. More skin and fewer frills are on display at the Dorado Night City nearby, entertainment of a less wholesome kind. This "theme town" of discos and bars features a Wild West show, karaoke nights and an "erotic district", with audience participation encouraged. One price covers all the food and drink you can consume in a night – although some of the other, seedier attractions on offer bring a whole new meaning to the term "all-inclusive". ❑

ABOVE: elegant outdoor dining in Mallorca's Cala d'Or.

Magic Ibiza

Ibiza's magical nightlife has its roots in something more than just the chemically-induced fantasies of a few spacy hippies. Since Punic times, the island has been a magnet for mystics and followers of the occult; throughout the twentieth century, writers and artists have waxed lyrical about the beauty of the *Pityussai* ("pine islands" – the name Greek traders gave to Ibiza and Formentera), and their powers of regeneration.

Ibiza is ruled by Scorpio, the sign of the occult, of enchantment and extremes. The island's history is peppered with tales of powerful gods and mischievous spirits, UFO sightings and strange magnetic forces. Scorpio also represents rebirth – is there a link here with the ostrich eggs (a symbol of resurrection) found in the Carthaginian necropolis at Puig d'Es Molins outside Eivissa Town?

The Carthaginians, who first began to colonise the Balearics in the 7th century BC, used ibiza as a burial-ground because for them it was holy, a place without poisonous plants and snakes and where even the clay was thought to have curative properties. They believed it was protected by the sacred power of their gods: fierce Baal, whose terrifying wrath could only be placated by offerings of oil, wine and children; benevolent Bes (always depicted with a giant phallus) who, according to legend, killed off all the island's poisonous animals, and Melkart, the fishermen's god. Most powerful of all the pantheon was Tanit, goddess of love, sexuality and death.

There is still a pagan element to the islanders' traditional dances, which are believed to date back to Carthaginian times: while the men's moves symbolise fire and strength, the women's evoke submission and darkness. Custom dictates that these dances should be performed beside wells, fountains and waterwheels; the Carthaginians did the same in order to summon the life-giving spirit of the revered Tanit.

Gods aside, island culture is also endowed with three bizarre spirits which still feature in everyday folklore: the *barruguet*, the *fameliar*

and the *follet*. The *barruguet* is a lascivious, stunted goblin with a scraggly goatee beard and a roaring voice. He lives in wells and water-wheels, eats bread and cheese and delights in playing practical jokes on housewives. Once tamed, however, a *barraguet* is useful around the house as he likes hard work – so much so that there's a local saying that these goblins built the ramparts of Eivissa.

The *fameliar* is a different story. Trapped in bottles, these spirits eat and work insatiably when released and have to be kept busy with impossible tasks – or recaptured on 24 June, the night of the feast of St John. Anyone

lucky enough to come into possession of a *follet*, meanwhile, is said to acquire great strength and wisdom.

Modern-day Ibiza is awash with tales of curious sightings and encounters worthy of the *X-Files*. Many centre on the islet of Es Vedrà, a barren, pyramid-shaped chunk of rock lying opposite Cala d'Hort cove to the south; it is supposed to radiate strange energies. Some people believe it channels a powerful beam of energy which lures UFOs, and there have been several cases of fishermen reporting inexplicable circles of light glowing in the sea nearby. Whatever the truth, Es Vedrà makes a great photograph at sunset. ❏

RIGHT: the pyramid-shaped islet of Es Vedrà: a communication beacon for UFOs?

BALEARIC BIRD LIFE

Blessed with a variety of habitats in relatively close proximity, the islands attract birds – and birdwatchers – from all over the globe

In recent years, the Balearic Islands and Mallorca in particular have become firmly established as one of Europe's finest birdwatching locations. Not only do the Balearics enjoy a prime position in the Mediterranean where many migrating birds land each spring and autumn, but there is also a great diversity of habitats in relatively close proximity, which attract further varieties. Mallorca is particularly well blessed in this regard: there are marshes and reedbeds, freshwater lagoons and salt-pans, scrubland, fields, orchards and woods, rocky sea cliffs and, most impressive of all, mountains with wild peaks and plunging gorges.

Local residents

One of the Balearic's most striking birds is the hoopoe, unmistakable thanks to its crest which can be raised to resemble a Red Indian chief's head-dress. Yet for such a handsome bird, it can be surprisingly difficult to spot when foraging on bare ground, its sandy-pink plumage blending with the colour of the earth.

Also common throughout the islands is the little Sardinian warbler. The male, a dapper grey and white bird with a distinctive black cap and red eye, delivers his rattling song and scolds passers-by from the tops of bushes and tangled vegetation.

Other common birds are the stonechat, the corn bunting, serin, greenfinch, goldfinch and linnet, all of which frequently choose exposed perches on posts, wires and tree tops to sing and call. The tiny fan-tailed warbler, however, usually delivers its repetitive, single-note song in mid-air, fluttering upwards in a bouncing song-flight before dropping down again into a clump of weeds and grasses. Blackcaps are more difficult to observe, as they tend to skulk inside bushes and thickets.

Wherever you come across pine trees it is worth looking for crossbills and firecrests,

whereas thekla larks and red-legged partridges usually frequent rough, uncultivated farmland, stony fields and dry scrubland. Here, the keen-eyed observer may find rock sparrows, Marmora's warbler and the mysterious, secretive stone curlew. The Dartford warbler also occurs in Menorca, while it is less common in Mallorca; however, the opposite is the case with the cirl bunting.

From boulder-strewn hillsides, rocky coves and cliffs comes the lovely, flute-like song of the blue rock thrush; the midnight-blue cock bird is a most handsome creature. Sharing the same rugged locations, crag martins – action-packed little birds – can be seen zipping around the cliff-faces. Kestrels and ravens are here too, familiar sights in the skies above Menorca and Ibiza as well as in the hillier parts of Mallorca.

From cliff-top vantage-points it is possible to sight Cory's shearwater and the Balearic race of the Manx shearwater passing by off-shore. And there is always a chance of finding

PRECEDING PAGES: Mallorca's coast is rich in bird life.
LEFT: hoopoe, with lunch.
RIGHT: male Sardinian warbler.

Audouin's gull, one of the world's rarest gulls. You may catch a glimpse of one in the harbours of Palma, Maó and Eivissa Town, but you are more likely to spot them on little Cabrera island, just off Mallorca's southern coast.

Spring migrants

Although there are plenty of birds to be seen at all times of the year, the most popular months are April and May, when there is a huge influx of migrants from Africa, some merely passing through, others intending to stay and breed during the summer. The most favoured sites can become quite crowded as binoculars, telescopes

and cameras all jostle for the most exclusive views of the rarest birds.

One such site is Cases Velles, an area of fields, orchards and woods nestling in a wide valley, halfway along Mallorca's deserted Formentor peninsula. A combination of topographical and climatic factors conspire to funnel migrating birds into this sheltered hollow. Wryneck, pied and spotted flycatcher, stonechat, whinchat, wheatear, black-eared wheatear, redstart and black redstart can often be found feeding here among the trees and bushes.

Roller, melodious, subalpine and spectacled warbler, rock thrush, ortolan and golden oriole are also recorded regularly. Many of these pass

through the Boquer Valley near Port de Pollença, another fine location to search for migrants.

Among the springtime arrivals are European bee-eaters. Combining an easy, gliding flight with quick twists and swerves, these rainbow birds indulge in the most dazzling aerobatics, sometimes launching forth from roadside wires or power-lines on the outskirts of towns. Bee-eater nest-colonies are extremely vulnerable to disturbance – the sandy cliffs where they excavate their nest chambers all too easily fall victim to industrial activity, or are destroyed to make way for building development.

Summer visitors

An attractive summer visitor is the woodchat shrike, often seen stationed, sentinel-like, on fences and wires. With its bold brown, black and white markings it is one of the prettiest of the shrikes, or "butcher birds" as they are known because of their habit of impaling their prey on thorns. In summer, turtle doves and spotted flycatchers are common breeding birds; blue-headed wagtails favour damp, grassy patches, while short-toed larks and tawny pipits are normally restricted to the drier, dustier parts of the islands. Nightingales, on the other hand, seem to be everywhere: their song bursts from every copse and thicket.

At night, the Scops owl can be located by its persistent call, reminiscent of a sonar "bleep". Like the resident barn owl, the Scops owl often hunts close to farms and other human habitation, and can be heard beeping occasionally in the gardens of some holiday hotels.

On summer days hordes of swifts, swallows and martins swoop over farmland and town rooftops. Close scrutiny may reveal the uncommon red-rumpled swallow, on its way across the Mediterranean, as well as the pallid swift and its much larger relative, the Alpine swift.

Birds of prey

If there is one thing that distinguishes Mallorca as a birdwatching destination from its smaller neighbours, it is the high sierra that stretches along the north-western coast. For this wild kingdom is the domain of numerous birds of prey, among them some of Europe's rarest.

The Balearic colonies of the Eleanora's falcon – a dashing acrobatic hunter which breeds on the islands's sea-cliffs and off-shore islets – represent an important part of the world population of this endangered species. Among the more accessible colonies are those on the cliffs near the Boquer Valley, around the Formentor lighthouse, on Dragonera island and on the tiny islets just off Cabrera. Soon after their arrival in April, Eleanora's falcons gather to hunt beetles over marshes and, sometimes, over Port Pollença and Alcudia on the coast.

The peregrine falcon also breeds in these parts of Mallorca, although it is frequently seen over the smaller islands as well. This powerful aerial predator can sometimes be watched making breathtaking dives from high above the sea, in pursuit of rock doves nesting in the cliffs.

and tilting its reddish-brown forked tail from side to side like a sensitive rudder.

Raptor viewpoints

The booted eagle, which occurs in Menorca and Ibiza as well as Mallorca, is not uncommon, although like many of the birds of prey its numbers are declining steadily. Not averse to dropping down into farmyards in search of easy pickings, the booted eagle is unpopular with some farmers.

By contrast, Bonelli's eagle is extremely scarce and only infrequently seen by the fortunate observer deep in the mountains.

The Egyptian vulture is an occasional visitor to Mallorca but is comparatively common in Menorca. The red kite, similarly, is more abundant in Menorca than Mallorca. It, too, has suffered needless persecution by hunters and farmers, which has greatly reduced its numbers on the islands – even though it is a harmless scavenger, and not a killer.

It is a supremely elegant bird in flight as it glides effortlessly on long, crooked, drooping wings, delicately fingering the hot air currents

LEFT: a black-winged stilt, searching for food.
ABOVE: the cormorant is just one of many species to be spotted off the coast of Mallorca.

A RARE BREED

The mighty black eagle is one of Europe's most endangered species. Mallorca's population has had to contend not only with persecution by poisoning and shooting, but also a dwindling food supply as improved animal husbandry reduces the amount of carrion available. However, a fragile breeding population (estimated at about 50 birds) clings on in Mallorca's mountains. Good spots for a sighting include the area around Puig de Massanella in the Serra de Tramuntana, and the Boquer Valley near Port de Pollença. Drifting on broad, sail-like wings across the sky (their wingspan is nearly 3 metres/10 ft), they are truly a magnificent sight.

Other raptors (birds of prey) in the mountain passes, usually on spring or autumn passage, include black kite, honey buzzard, Montagu's harrier, hobby and lesser kestrel. The latter also breeds in Menorca; less commonly in Mallorca.

Several birds of prey species can usually be notched up in any part of the mountain range but some places are more likely to reward the keen raptor enthusiast. On the Pollença-Sóller mountain road there are several good observation points in the vicinity of Puig Major, at the reservoir at Cúber (Embalse de Cúber) and in the valley near the Lluc monastery. The Boquer Valley is also a favoured haunt of birds of prey

and the cliff-top ruins of the Castell del Rei at the seaward end of the Ternelles Valley can provide exciting close-up views against a backdrop of dramatic coastal scenery.

Wetland birds

Not all raptors are inhabitants of the high peaks. Ospreys, although sometimes sighted diving for fish in the mountain reservoirs, more regularly fish in the lowland rivers, marshes and lakes of Mallorca and Menorca. On occasions they can be watched plunging into the shallows along the holiday beaches, particularly near Alcúdia and Port de Pollença, or off the craggy coastline opposite Dragonera. Likewise, marsh

harriers, as their name suggests, are more or less confined to a watery habitat and can often be spotted in Mallorca and Menorca, lazily quartering reed beds and marshes.

The main wetland sites are the Albufera Marsh on the north coast of Mallorca (the largest area of marshland in the Mediterranean), the Salines de Llevant in the south of the island and the Albufera Lake in Menorca. Others include the Ses Salines saltpans near the airport in Ibiza and Albufereta just outside Mallorca's Port Pollença on the road to Alcudia.

In the best of these locations, year-round residents include spotted crake, little ringed and Kentish plover, Savi's, Cetti's, Marmora's and moustached warbler. In spring, an extraordinary assortment arrives, some to breed, others to rest and feed on their journey north. Among their number are purple heron, egret, squacco and night heron, little bittern, black-winged stilt, avocet. Temminck's and little stint, collared pratincole and various sandpiper, little gull, gull-billed, black, white-winged black and whiskered tern, reed, great reed and aquatic warbler. In winter, too, these watery areas are important, supporting numerous waders, wildfowl, and small groups of flamingos.

Threat of tourism

The wetland sites are the richest wildlife habitats in the Balearics, yet they are also the most threatened as more and more hotels, apartments and *urbanizaciones* spring up. Happily, the Albufera Marsh, a protected *parc natural* since 1985, seems set to survive as one of Europe's most important wetlands, though the burgeoning tourist developments creep ever closer. Menorca's Albufera Lake has also been given reserve status, while Mallorca's offshore islet of Cabrera is now designated a national park.

However, other valuable sites remain at risk each year. Not all holiday-makers who visit the Balearics do so merely to soak up sunshine and sangria among tasteless modern buildings. There are many who come to enjoy the islands' quiet charm, the natural beauty of their varied landscapes and their rich flora and fauna. The Balearics still have much to offer such visitors, but for how much longer? ❏

LEFT: Mallorca's Albufera marsh has been a protected reserve since 1985.
RIGHT: the brilliantly coloured European bee-eater.

THE ISLANDS' FAUNA AND FLORA

Wild flowers, migrating birds and a wide variety of landscapes make the Balearics one of the richest wildlife areas in the Mediterranean

The Balearics have a remarkable diversity of wildlife. In part, this is due to the enormous variety of habitats – mountains and cliffs, forest and dunes, limestone gorges and agricultural plains. It is also a result of the protection offered by the sea. Predators which managed to eliminate certain species elsewhere never reached the Balearics, allowing the islands' endemic fauna and flora to survive. Even within the Balearic archipelago this holds true. The Balearic lizard, for example, has been exterminated throughout the major islands, but thrives on barren little Cabrera in the absence of weasels and snakes.

Mallorca alone has more than 1,300 flowering plants, of which around 40 are unique to the island, including the Balearic cyclamen and the native St John's wort. Spot a dwarf fan palm, the Balearics' only native palm, and you can be sure that you are never far from other endemic plants. Giant orchids thrive in the woodland glades in February, while the delicate bee orchid and other species can be seen in the pine woods and on the coastal cliffs from March to May. And look out for the asphodel, with its tall spikes and clusters of pink flowers, on over-grazed farmland between April and June.

The best time for birdwatching is during the spring and autumn migrations, from March to May and September to October. Top sites include the S'Albufera marshes, Cap de Formentor, the Bóquer valley near Pollença and anywhere on the coast. Wading birds head for the Salines de Llevant on Mallorca's south coast, and bee-eaters can be seen in summer among Menorca's beaches and dunes.

▷ **DRAGON ARUM**
This rare plant, with healing properties, flowers on Cabrera in early summer. Other plants commonly found on the island include Balearic peonies and giant fennel.

◁ WILD OLIVE TREES

"When walking in their shade at dusk, I have to remind myself that they are only trees", wrote George Sand (*see page 165*).

▽ A RARE BREED

In 1970, there were only 12 black vultures left in the Serra de Tramuntana, but the population has now grown to around 70.

▽ AUDOUIN'S GULL

Many seabirds, including shearwaters, shags and yellow-legged gulls, breed on Mallorca's coastal cliffs in spring. Little Dragonera is also home to a large colony of Audouin's gulls.

△ LILFORD'S LIZARDS

These lizards – endemic to the Balearics – thrive on Menorca's offshore islets and on Cabrera. One spot off Fornells Bay is even known as *Illa Sargantanes*, or "Lizard Island".

◁ CARETTA CARETTA

This endangered Mediterranean sea turtle survives in the clean waters around Dragonera and Cabrera. Feeding mainly on crustaceans (it breaks open their shells with its powerful jaws), it can weigh up to 100 kg.

▷ ROCK ROSES

The grey-leaved cistus, or rock-rose, flowers in the Serra de Tramuntana mountains in spring. Mallorca's maquis landscape is rich in flowering shrubs, including rosemary and broom.

WETLANDS OR WASTELANDS?

The most important wetland area of Mallorca has the misfortune to be situated right behind the island's longest beach. The S'Albufera marshes (*above*) have been around since Roman times – Pliny writes of night herons being exported for the tables of Rome – but the rapid tourist development of the 1960s threatened their very existence. The construction of hotels, the growth in human traffic and the introduction of garden plants all damaged the stability of a precarious ecosystem, causing species to disappear and prompting concern about the future.

The resulting debate had a happy outcome. S'Albufera was declared a nature reserve in 1985, and under the Natural Areas Law of 1991 a total of 76 Balearic sites are now protected.

ISLAND ARCHITECTURE

*From grand Rococo mansions to Catalan modernism and classic
cube-style farmhouses, there's a wealth of styles to be explored*

Some authors divide the "typical" Mallorcan house into three categories: rural, village and city. Although the three may be discussed separately, there is an interdependence and interchange of style and structure which crosses the rural-urban divide to the point that it is almost impossible to talk about one without talking about them all.

Rural houses on the island normally grew from a central structure, the kitchen fireplace. The design was always functional, and the dwelling invariably expanded in such a way that a central patio, or *clastra,* became the pivotal element. In the *fincas,* as the country houses are called, this interior courtyard became the heart of the dwelling. It not only served as a meeting place, but also had the important strategic function of providing some protection for the inhabitants.

If the estate was substantial, it was generally divided into three parts: a section for the owners (*casa de los señores*), one for the farm manager (*casa de los amos*), and then all the usual barns, pens and outhouses of the working farm.

Good manors

The appearance of the country house depended a good deal on such interrelated aspects as geography and the kind of agricultural enterprise being carried out. Visually, the productive mountain *finques* with their stone walls had a richer appearance than their inland counterparts, usually built of sandstone blocks.

In the north, olive-trees formed the agricultural base of the farm. Consequently, mountain estates required large spaces for the oil press (*tafona*), and for the storage and curing of the olives themselves. In the central plain where the local economy was based upon grain, the building was certain to have a mill, or, in the case of wine production, a wine press.

PRECEDING PAGES: distinctive Es Castell bow window, Villacarlos, Menorca.
LEFT: modernist staircase in Sóller's Can Prunera.
RIGHT: Puig d'En Missa church, Santa Eulàlia, Ibiza.

Meanwhile, the houses on the less economically productive coast of the island (where local people relied on hunting, fishing and forestry, and where times were often hard) were usually dependent on a defensive tower. Indeed, in some cases (such as the Son Forteza Vell estate in Manacor) the tower dominated the house.

Family rooms

Traditionally, country houses' living quarters were divided into two independent sections. In large estates, the *casa de los señores* was always located on an upper floor, reached by way of a monumental staircase with a smart salon for receiving guests.

Most also had a chapel or *capilla*, its grandeur indicating the family's social status as much as religious necessity. If the chapel was connected directly to the house, as in the case of the Raixa estate in Bunyola, it invariably had two entrances – one inside for the family, and another for visitors and the farm workers who came daily to take Mass. At times, the *capilla* took on a size and stature quite out of proportion to the house. The *finca* of Sa Torre near Llucmajor, for example, is thus named for its nearby cathedral-like structure, which can be seen for miles around.

The *casa de los amos,* that half of the house inhabited by the farm manager and his family as well as the master's servants, centred on the kitchen. Used as a living-room, meeting-place and cooking area, this was usually the hub of the entire *finca*.

During the 16th century, many country landowners moved to the city, leaving their *amos* to maintain the productivity of the farm.

styles from Europe, and so baroque, rococo and neo-classical embellishment was added to the lines of the Gothic city structure built by the Catalans in the 13th century.

During the 16th and 17th centuries, houses grew through acquisitions to become aristocratic palaces with grand entrance patios and interiors. Elegant Palmanian houses such as Can Vivot, Ca N'Oleza and Can Morell (Palau Sollerich) became the models for future renovations and development throughout the city. Eventually, the new architecture was taken to the countryside, as the wealthiest owners adopted the new styles too.

Some of the *finques* were subsequently turned into summer retreats.

In town

Unlike the expansive "add-on" architecture that typified the country *finca*, city houses were designed and built to fit into the confines of urban life. These residences shared many elements with their rural counterparts, including stone floors, vaulted vestibules, interior cisterns, semi-circular arched doorways and open-beamed ceilings.

However, the city houses' architectural styles were far more complex and "cultured". Architects were hired to build or rebuild in the latest

TRADITIONAL IBIZAN ARCHITECTURE

Le Corbusier is only the most famous of the many architects who have found inspiration in the striking simplicity of Ibiza's traditional farmhouses. A classic dwelling may consist of just one cube; other cubes are added on as circumstance dictates. Thick walls are whitewashed and have either no windows or tiny ones which prevent the sun from penetrating the interior. A *porxet* (porch) provides shade and space to store vegetables and fruit. Beams support a flat roof, while an outdoor *horno* (oven) and *pozo* (well) are usually located close by. Today, such buildings are recognised as cultural treasures – and are priced accordingly.

The shock of the new

It is difficult to pinpoint exactly when "modern" architecture began in Mallorca. Certainly, by the end of the 19th century, many of Spain's largest cities – choking with the smoke of industrialisation – were searching for a response to the inhuman face of progress. By now, "traditional" architecture in all its complexities had fallen by the wayside. The grand Renaissance-style mansions with their loggias, arcades and patios were *passé*; divided up into small apartments, many fell into neglect.

Meanwhile on the mainland, a revival of Catalan culture led by Barcelona's bourgeoisie grate to the far corners of Europe in search of work. When they returned at the beginning of the 20th century, the most prosperous among them contracted leading Catalan architects to bring the latest European designs – including *art nouveau* – to Mallorca. Hence the rise of such buildings as Palma's Gran Hotel, designed in 1902 by Lluis Domènech Montaner, and the start of what some called *la época de mal gusto*, or "the epoch of bad taste".

Gaudí in Palma

At the same time, Palma's Bishop Campíns, having seen Gaudí's cathedral in Barcelona,

saw the emergence of *modernismo* – an ornate, often startling Catalan variant on the theme of *art nouveau*. A new breed of radical architects began to leave their surreal signatures on the city, epitomised by Antoní Gaudí's still-unfinished masterpiece, the Sagrada Familia cathedral. Yet it was to take an agricultural disaster to bring the style to the Balearic islands.

In the 1860s, the mountain village of Sóller was devastated by an orange blight. Economically destitute, the villagers were forced to emi-

LEFT: carefully restored entrance hall in a grand Palma house.
ABOVE: elegant patio at Ca N'Oleza mansion, Palma.

invited the famous Catalan architect to restore the city's magnificent 14th-century cathedral. Gaudí arrived to take charge of the work in 1902, and together with his student Joan Rubió, and local architects Gaspar Bennazar Moner and Francesc Roca Simó, spent the next 10 years on the task. He made some radical changes to the cathedral's interior with the introduction of electric lights, wrought-iron railings and a controversial canopy of cardboard, cork, brocade and nails suspended above the altar, symbolising the Crown of Thorns.

Gaudí's influence can be seen in many of Palma's early 20th-century commercial and residential buildings, including the Pensió

Menorquina and Can Casasayas in Plaça del Mercat. Ironically, however, the most memorable legacy of Mallorcan modernism was not left by an architect. Lluis Forteza Rey was a silversmith, and the prime diversion of his life, Can Forteza Rey (Carrer Bolseria), has become the eye-catching standard bearer of the style in Mallorca.

In the meantime, Rubió was busy in Sóller, creating some of the island's finest examples of *Modernista* architecture – the Banco de Sóller, the parish church and also his very own mansion, Can Prunera, with its striking external stone spiral staircase. He and Gaudí also

worked at Lluc, creating five sculptures representing the Mysteries of the Rosary on the mountain behind the monastery.

Tourist style

Just as there is no clear date for modernism's start in Mallorca, the date marking the end of the movement is equally vague. The architectural new wave probably arrived in the late 1950s with the building of a number of office blocks in Palma, though even some of these were faintly neo-classical. But by far the most pervasive influence came with the rise of tourism on the island, and the building of the giant towerblock hotels of the 1960s.

By and large, these were built as faithful replicas of modern hotels in the United States or England, with perhaps a token archway or two by the entrance foyer to remind visitors where they were. All other evidence of Spain or Spanish architecture was absent – perhaps intentionally, since most early package tourists were not particularly adventurous. Spartan cleanliness and comfort were the prime considerations, and Spanish warmth and architectural ambience was at least a decade away from being appreciated by most foreign visitors to Mallorca.

Parts of the coastline suffered badly from this architectural onslaught, even though it was restricted to a handful of resorts occupying only a few miles. It must have seemed strange to the villagers of that time, still building their own homes in traditional stone, to travel to these areas and view a mini-Miami beach where visitors surrounded by breeze-block and plaster talked of "comfort" and "facilities".

Ironically, these villagers – many of whom would have been travelling by donkey cart or bus, for only the wealthy could afford cars, even in the 1960s – were living in a style that many foreign holidaymakers came to appreciate enormously. By the late 1970s, the trend for renovating old *finques* and village houses as holiday homes and installing new kitchens and bathrooms to provide the necessary comforts and facilities was well underway.

The aim of any true *finca* renovation is to retain as much of the original character as possible, yet those same visitors, 15 years earlier, would have viewed the way the villagers lived with disdain – certainly not imagining that the cycle of architectural fashion would find them trading places in the future.

Period revival

Since building in stone was still such a strong tradition, foreigners seeking a good stonemason to renovate their newly-purchased stone holiday homes did not have to look very far. Indeed, the decades after World War II witnessed a minor revival of the style. Jaume III, Palma's main shopping avenue, is a good example – most visitors would put its age at between 1890 and 1910; in fact, it was built in the 1950s. Stone building continued throughout the 1970s, and was particularly popular in inland villages.

As rustic styling became all the vogue with upmarket foreigners, so resort architecture began to change. The requirements for coastal resort living were simple, just as they were in the villages: a sea view, one or two bedrooms, compact lounge and kitchen areas and with generous terrace areas for catching the sun. Ideal for one or two months' occupancy a year.

Pedro Otzoup was probably the first to answer this demand with his development at Cala Fornells, a rustic Mediterranean-style

BLOWIN' IN THE WIND

On Formentera, locals can point out a picturesque windmill on La Mola, the island's only mountain, where Bob Dylan allegedly lived for a time in the 1960s.

been adopted, although here the accent is more strongly on the Provençal, and there is more mixing of colours. To some, the resulting colour contrasts give a vaguely Caribbean flavour to the place, but in achieving the effect of a four-storey village, open terrace space has been sacrificed. The French architect, François Sperry, who also created Port Grimaud, made no excuses for his single-minded adherence to his original plans, even though his consulting Mallorcan architects suggested a more traditional Spanish design.

complex meandering lazily down a hillside, with the buildings linked by paths, archways, gardens and courtyards. The style is eclectic, blending elements of Mallorca, Andalucia, Ibiza and Provence – with practically no two apartments the same. The style has since been copied, though seldom bettered.

A blend of influences

At The Anchorage, a complete waterfront village in Illetas, a similar blending of styles has

LEFT: *modernismo* standard-bearer: the Can Forteza Rey in Palma.
ABOVE: opulent modern residence.

Local flavour

The same group of architects had more of a say in the design of Puerto Portals, a collection of shops, boutiques and restaurants on the edge of a 650-berth luxury marina. Here, traditional archways and the mixing of ochre and white lend a more traditional Mallorcan flavour – although, strictly speaking, the influence for this particular style came originally from Italy and was only introduced into Mallorcan architecture in the 1700s.

More common were natural stone facings; in general ochre and white were employed only if the stone required rendering. However, apart from natural stonework and an often imposed exterior colour scheme, it is certainly more authentically Mallorcan than white – and a lot easier to maintain.

A new era

In general, even though many choice resorts have been plundered by developers with more taste for money than for style and environment, the situation in Mallorca is no longer deteriorating. Developments tend to be more imaginative now; the maximum height in many areas is now down to four floors; and the new coastal development laws restrict building within 100 metres (330 ft) of the coastline – although many

planning permissions were gained before new legislation was passed.

What has probably most aided modern architecture and development is changing public demand. The fashion for small holiday flats with one or two bedrooms has dwindled; larger apartments and villas are now more popular. Generous terrace space, ideally partly open, is also a prime requirement. This means that developers have to stagger each floor, often using the natural fall of the hillside to do so.

More apartments are incorporating gardens and increasing green space, and local hope is that the magic 100 metres between the coast and the first cement will be treated in the same

manner. This would provide a much more attractive coastal tree line when viewed from the water, and would also break up the harsh lines of concrete.

An emphasis on green

Mallorcan city planning can often appear haphazard, perhaps because of the volume of paperwork involved in gaining planning permissions and the slowness of the Spanish bureaucracy. Certainly, listed buildings are still sometimes destroyed to make way for new structures; bad developments still go ahead. But situations like this are rare, and due more to bureaucratic oversight than policy planning. On the whole, listed buildings are heavily protected and, where possible, faithfully restored. Local council grants are available in many cases to fund the renovation work, and some dazzling examples now grace Palma's city centre as a result. Many of them are used as art galleries or exhibition halls.

The next 10 years look brighter than the last. Public opinion tends to guide events more than it used to do. Unspoilt areas such as Dragonera island and Es Trenc have been saved from development by effective lobbying. City planners have been taking more note of public opinion and pressure groups, smart new marinas, palm-lined beach promenades and golf courses are springing up, with the emphasis on "green" or "sustainable" tourism. Projects are now considered more in terms of how they will suit the island in general than how they will benefit a handful of developers.

Another good sign is that most of the hotels and apartments built during the worst period of Spanish architecture and construction (the 1960s) are now coming close to the end of their life cycle, and are being either renovated or, more often than not, knocked down to make way for new structures. Trends and demands are finally swinging heavily away from highrise block styling.

With luck, the skyline of Spain's more notorious resorts could soon be reduced from eight to 10 storeys to four floors, with the emphasis on traditional Spanish styling and ambience. Pretty much as it was, in fact, before the first tourist invasions of the early 1960s. ❏

LEFT: the Anchorage waterfront village in Illetas blends Balearic, Andalucian and Provençal styles.

Windmills

Few travellers have visited Mallorca without scribbling a note or two in their diaries about its windmills. In 1886, Charles Wood wrote in his *Letters from Majorca*: "The curious windmills of Majorca... have six sails instead of four, which gives them a strange and unfamiliar appearance... a mass of ropes and cordage makes the sails look as complicated and as intricate as the rigging of a ship."

Things have changed since then. The six-sailed windmills have disappeared, and the only four-bladed ones left are either museum pieces or sad skeletons, steadily decaying under the hot summer sun.

Windmills (*molinos*) have formed part of the landscape of the island for centuries, but no one knows when they first appeared. Sanchis Guarner, a modern investigator, reports that they were invented by the Persians in the 7th century and widely dispersed throughout the eastern Mediterranean. Certainly, during the Middle Ages both the Byzantines in the south and the Moors in North Africa used them, but while the Moors brought the invention to Spain in the 7th century BC, there is no evidence that it arrived in Mallorca at the same time. But whatever its origins, the windmill was in use here before the 1500s.

The first *molinos* on the island were used to grind grain. Usually, the miller lived in the tower which supported the wind-driven sails and housed the millstone as well. Over the years, the sails were gradually replaced by more efficient wooden slats, divided into sections separated by radial spokes.

It wasn't until the 19th century, when windmills were used to drain water out of the marshy Sant Jordi plain near Palma, that their potential as a pump and irrigation tool began to be exploited. Farmers used an ancient Moorish device called the *noria*, where a loop of jars were lifted and lowered on a continuous belt into an underground well by a blindfolded mule, The *noria* was primitive but effective – and popular. According to Archduke Ludwig Salvator "in the last quarter of the

19th century, there were between 3,500 and 4,000 *norias* in use in Mallorca..."

Later, the wooden elements of the windmill were replaced by metal ones, which were more efficient and easier to manoeuvre. The newer *molinos de hierro* had the added advantage of not having to be de-sailed in a strong wind.

Largely abandoned by the 1960s, thanks to advances in motor technology, Mallorca's picturesque windmills began to fall into decay. During the energy crisis of the early 1970s, however, many were resuscitated, farmers and market gardeners finding them far more

economical to run than a petrol-driven pump. All over the island, the skeletal remains of once-proud windmills came to life, sporting smart new aerodynamically-designed blades, updated machinery, and new paint. Today their multi-coloured blades – often adorned with Mallorca's bright red-and-yellow striped flag – still whirl in the afternoon wind, waiting to be photographed against the sunset, or sketched in a traveller's notebook.

Sadly, many more windmills have ceased to turn forever. Head eastwards from Palma along the *autopista* to S'Arenal, for example, and you'll pass hundreds of tumbledown structures, now left to decay. ❑

RIGHT: Mallorca used to be known as an island of windmills; nowadays, many are sadly neglected.

SURVIVING TOURISM

First the Balearics were a testing-ground for cheap seaside holiday packages.

Now there's a new tourist strategy afoot, in the countryside. But will it work?

In 1910, the British writer Mary Stuart Boyd spent the winter in the Balearic islands, gathering material for her book, *The Fortunate Isles*. Before she left home, a friend offered her some advice. "There are no tourists," the friend began. "Not a soul understands a word of English, and there's nothing whatever to do. If you take my advice, you won't go."

In fact, tourists have been visiting the Balearics ever since George Sand and Frédéric Chopin spent their famous winter in Valldemossa in 1838–39. Sand's northern European manners and morals infuriated the locals – an early foretaste of what was to come – but in a memorable phrase, translated by Robert Graves, she prophesied the subsequent tourist invasion. "The time will doubtless come," she wrote, "when frail dilettantes, and even lovely women, will be able to visit Palma with no more exhaustion and discomfort than Geneva."

By the 1930s, following the opening of the Hotel Formentor, Mallorca had become a fashionable winter resort; Winston Churchill and Charlie Chaplin were among the early guests at the hotel, and Agatha Christie set a story in nearby Pollença Bay. Christie conjured up a world where wealthy British families would arrive with their servants on the steamer from Barcelona to enjoy cocktails on the terrace and flirtations on the beach. But the Civil War put an end to such frivolity; when it was followed by dictatorship and then war in Europe, almost the only visitors to Mallorca for a generation were honeymooners from mainland Spain.

A time of "Poor Tourism"

At first, Franco was happy to keep foreigners out, but in the late 1950s, he embarked on a bold policy to improve Spain's standard of living. The government needed foreign currency, and mass tourism was seen as the easiest way to

provide it. Tourist offices were set up all over Europe and an aggressive marketing campaign aimed to lure people away from the French and Italian Rivieras. The Balearics – along with the Costa Brava in Catalonia – were used as test cases for a new kind of holiday, offering cheap sun, sea and sand and a dose of Mediterranean colour to visitors from cold northern Europe. Accordingly, fishing villages were transformed into concrete resorts and great swathes of coastline were covered in apartment blocks and soulless hotels. Building regulations were minimal – what the tour operators wanted, the tour operators got – and the local communities were able to exercise little control. The philosophy was ruthlessly simple: pile them high and sell them cheap, and never mind the impact. Cynics would say that was because the impact only struck home in the regions – but the money ended up in Madrid.

This was the era of *turismo pobre* ("poor tourism"), which defaced the landscape with

---

PRECEDING PAGES: Cala Lenya, Ibiza.
LEFT: wall-to-wall roasting at Ibiza's Cala Bassa.
RIGHT: the high-rises of Magalluf in Mallorca epitomise *turismo pobre*.

thoughtless *urbanizaciones* and threatened to swamp traditional culture with foreign kitsch. Parts of Mallorca and Ibiza became mini-Britains or mini-Germanys, where the food and drink came straight from home and the only local culture consisted of watered-down *sangría* and fake flamenco shows.

Fishermen and farmers gave up their work on the land as the islands were radically transformed in just a single generation from an agrarian economy into a service economy.

A DRIVING FORCE

In *Not Part of the Package*, Paul Richardson recounts that, while in the mid-1950s there were only 20 or 30 cars on Ibiza, by the 1990s the island had the highest number of cars per head in Europe.

The hippie culture of Deià and Ibiza in the late 1960s seemed to sum up Franco's failure in his self-appointed role as the guardian of conservative Spanish values. (However, there are those who now argue that this particular result of the tourist boom was a liberating rather than a corrupting influence, and that without the effects of tourism Spain would have been much slower to enter the European mainstream.)

In 1950, when the first charter flight landed in Mallorca, just 100,000 tourists visited the

A shock to the system

Faced with these radical changes to the traditional Balearic way of life, family and social structures struggled to cope; certainly, Spain's ultra-orthodox Catholic values were put under severe strain.

Until the 1950s, for example, when the police enforced "public morals", you could be arrested for wearing a bikini; now tourists went topless but everyone turned a blind eye in the interests of hard cash. William Graves, son of Robert, who ran a small hotel in Deià in the 1960s, describes in his autobiography *Wild Olives* how the presence of foreigners in the village also contributed to a growing drugs scene.

Balearics; by 1965 this had risen tenfold and by 1978 it had reached 3 million. The islands had become one of the richest regions in Spain, but at what cost?

Damage limitation

The death of Franco, followed by democracy and devolution, brought a new regional awareness and a reassessment of the benefits of tourism. At the same time, there were the first stirrings of environmental consciousness as the *Grup Balear d'Ornitologia i Defensa de la Naturalesa* or GOB (*see page 73*), a birdwatching group with wider conservation interests, emerged as a prominent political voice. Their successful campaigns in the 1970s to save S'Albufera reserve in Menorca and Dragonera island in Mallorca from development were perhaps the first serious indications that mass tourism had reached its natural limit.

Not that the authorities in Madrid necessarily agreed. Addressing a conference in Palma in 1977, the representative of the Ministry of Tourism declared: "Thanks to tourism, all of Spain was saved. Before, we could do nothing. There was no money. Tourism is a miracle." To his audience, he seemed to be rejecting the whole of Spanish history and culture and worshipping instead at the false shrine of the tourist dollar. Yet they had to admit that he had a point.

Few people in the Balearics wanted to return to the past; the debate was over how to sustain the level of tourist income while containing tourism's worst excesses. Throughout the 1980s and 1990s, the Balearic government – by now an autonomous region – gradually developed the policy which came to be known as "the second tourism revolution".

A focus on quality

The key planks of the policy were these: mass tourism had reached its limit, both in the number of people that could be accommodated and in the pressures it placed on the natural environment; however, as more and more countries copied the Balearic model, new markets in Turkey, North Africa and the Caribbean were able to offer a similar, more exotic, product at a cheaper price. The only way forward, it was decided, was to focus on quality.

Hotels which failed to meet safety standards were blown up and new establishments strictly controlled; in 1988 there were 228 one-star hotels on the islands, but by 1997 the number had been reduced to 69. The new emphasis was on golf courses, marinas and luxury hotels, on agrotourism, nature reserves and off-season walking and cycling. The tackiest resorts were given a facelift, with new parks, green spaces and seafront promenades.

Tough controls were introduced governing sewage disposal and water treatment. Grants were awarded for restoring traditional architecture. The Balearic University set up a

tourism school, and students from around the world travelled to Mallorca to learn about life after the cheap package holiday. The island that led the way into mass tourism was now leading the way out.

Yet still the numbers kept on growing – 5 million tourists in 1984, 8 million a decade later. Taking the peak summer months as a whole, the number of visitors to the islands is now 10 times the local population; on busy days in August, 800 planeloads of tourists arrive in Palma. And whatever the authorities may want, most of these people are still looking for cheap sun, sea and sex.

The nationality of visitors may have changed – in the 1990s, Germany overtook Britain as the Balearics' largest market – but the demand for cheap holidays has not. For all Mallorca's best efforts, Magalluf and S'Arenal remain as seedy and down-market as ever – and the locals have started to tire of the so-called "lager louts" who only want to get drunk as cheaply as possible and wander around town *descamisado* (without a shirt).

An issue of national pride

The issue of culture resurfaced in the 1990s as the tourist boom showed no signs of abating. Now, after decades of repression, Balearic

---

LEFT: as many Germans as glasses of beer in Palma.
RIGHT: menus in English, like this, must now by law also include Catalan.

culture was finally reasserting itself with a revival of traditional crafts and cuisine. Yet while Catalan may have replaced Spanish on street signs and menus, it was nonetheless giving way to German and English throughout the resorts. People started to ask whether there was any point in gaining devolution from Spain if the Balearics were to be taken over by northern European culture instead.

Closely linked to this was an undercurrent of anti-German xenophobia, as German property owners acquired almost a quarter of the land on Mallorca. Quoted in a 1997 newspaper report, the chief minister of the Balearics,

Jaume Matas, captured the prevailing mood perfectly. "Germans are buying up the island," he said, "and they just won't integrate with local people and adopt our customs." Author Carlos Garrido wrote a science fiction novel, *Mallorca de los Alemanes*, about an island taken over by Germans in the 21st century.

An Association for the Defence of Mallorca was formed to campaign against excessive foreign – in other words, northern European – influences; one of its early successes was a new regulation requiring restaurant and bar owners to print their menus in Catalan or Spanish as well as German and English.

A POWERFUL LOBBY

Germans dominate the top end of the property market in Mallorca. Estate agents estimate that about 80 percent of the island's "manor houses" are now German-owned. Celebrities such as Claudia Schiffer, Boris Becker and Michael Schumacher all have substantial properties there. With about 30,000 Germans residents and another 3.13 million German tourists each year, several attempts have been made to establish a Mallorcan political party on the island and present candidates for local elections, but so far these plans have failed. Many German residents fear that such schemes would brand them as imperialists.

An industry under pressure

Everyone accepts that the Balearic economy is now inextricably linked to tourism; the question is how to make it sustainable and year-round. Menorca's designation in 1993 as a UNESCO Biosphere Reserve – protecting both traditional industries and tourism as well as the natural environment – seems to offer one way forward which acknowledges the need for continued economic growth. But then Menorca has never been as dependent on tourism as the other islands; fewer than half of the population work in tourism and there are strong agricultural and industrial sectors. It is Mallorca and Ibiza that have the most to lose.

The Balearics are being carefully watched. By the late 20th century, tourism had become the ultimate cash crop, one which has transformed the landscapes and economies of numerous countries eager to grab their share of the world's fastest-growing industry. Yet more than almost any other product, tourism is subject to the whims of fashion – and when the tourists move on, what is there to replace them? Fragile cultures and economies have been left in ruins, their resorts turned into ghost towns, when the big tour operators decided it was time to withdraw. Nowhere has yet successfully completed the transition away from mass tourism. The Balearics, where mass tourism was invented, are determined to show the way.

New strategies, new dilemmas

So what is the future of Balearic tourism? The most striking development of the 1990s was the appearance of dozens of country house hotels in expensively-restored mansions, most of them well away from the coast. La Residencia in Deià, which opened in 1984 and is now owned by Richard Branson's Virgin group, started the trend – and where Branson leads, others soon follow. Now it seems that almost every country estate in Mallorca is being bought up by a wealthy foreigner and converted into a luxury hotel.

However, this development is being carefully controlled. All new rural hotels must be based in original, pre-1940 buildings, with at least 50,000 sq. metres (500,000 sq. ft) of land and a maximum of 25 double rooms. Another category of accommodation, known as *agroturismo*, is restricted to 12 rooms at a time on working farms. The last thing Mallorca wants is mass tourism in the countryside.

Typical of these new establishments is Son Net, which opened in 1998 in a restored 17th-century *finça* (farmhouse) above the small village of Puigpunyent in Mallorca. The American owner has filled the hotel with his own private art collection – a Warhol on the landing, a Chagall in the bar. Every detail has been individually designed, from the marble-and-stucco bathrooms to the restaurant built into the old olive press. From the poolside terrace where

you gaze out over the mountains and a village of golden stone houses, it's easy to imagine you are the only tourist in paradise.

This is the model of the new Mallorcan tourism, yet it is not without its dangers. Exclusive rural retreats can never replace 8 million package holidays, and as Mallorca attempts to reposition itself up-market it comes up against the eternal tourist dilemma – if the numbers attracted to the interior grow too sharply, they will destroy the very landscape that they have come to see. In *Wild Olives*, William Graves mourns the loss of his beloved childhood village, lamenting that for him, the Deià of the

1980s had become little more than "an up-market holiday resort". There is only room on Mallorca for so many Deiàs.

For 40 years, Mallorca has pulled off a very effective trick, confining tourists to a few crowded ghettos on the coast while the rest of the island lives undisturbed off the proceeds. No one doubts that it has worked, but everyone knows that it cannot go on for ever. If the second tourism revolution succeeds, the Balearics will still be playing host to tourists well into the 21st century. But one nagging question remains. The islands have survived the invasion of their beaches; can they survive the invasion of their villages as well? ❏

LEFT: send a message home: wish you were here?
RIGHT: an estimated 3.13 million German tourists visit Mallorca every year.

MALLORCA

*A detailed guide to the entire island, with principal sites
clearly cross-referenced by number to the maps*

The family Baleares consists of three big brother islands and two little sister islands. The eldest and biggest of these is Mallorca, (population 530,000) with the loudest voice, the most money, the keenest sense of responsibility and the most diverse landscape. Mallorca is a mini continent, with beaches, mountains, plains and a beautiful historic city, not to mention department stores, boutiques and restaurants with Michelin stars where royalty dine.

Everyone thinks they know Mallorca well, but there is far more to the island than is commonly supposed. Serious claims, on a world level, are made about the turnover and scale of the port and airport; serious art, on a world level, is active in the hills and on the plain; serious money, on a world level, is holidaying or investing here.

The island's landscape is amazingly varied: steep rocky coasts, seemingly endless sandy beaches, large tracts of marshland, high mountain ranges sloping down to fertile plains. Despite its relatively small surface area, Mallorca's contrasts are stunning: the wild Serra de Tramuntana with its winding roads and sleepy mountain villages; the fragrant orange groves of the Sóller Valley; the terraced gardens around Banyalbufar with their gnarled olive trees; the delightful fishing villages of Porto Colom and Cala Figuera; the ancient stone walls separating the fields of apricots; almonds and potatoes in the island's interior. Mallorca's broad plains and gentle valleys are full of vineyards, interspersed with olive and fig trees.

A good way of tackling the island is simply to strike off into the wild blue yonder, either by car or bicycle, far away from the signposted routes. There is always another quiet little part of the island waiting to be discovered – particularly in spring or autumn. Visit the picturesque villages of the interior, and travel up through forests of pine and oak to silent hermitages and down to peaceful coves. Admire impressive country estates and elegant Moorish gardens, and experience the noisy fiestas in honour of the local patron saints as well as the bustle of the colourful weekly markets. Stroll along the narrow streets of the capital, Palma, and around a few of its art galleries before sampling some delicious Mallorcan cuisine in a cool *celler*. Take a boat-trip out to little Cabrera, Mallorca's uninhabited sister-island, a haven for wildlife and now a national park.

Volumes have been written on the evils of mass tourism, but anyone who leaves behind the crowded coast and heads inland will soon discover the original, unspoilt Mallorca, with its hidden bays, magnificent natural landscape and rich, cultural heritage. ❏

PRECEDING PAGES: quiet Ibizan countryside; gathering in the harvest; up into the Serra de Tramuntana; the ancient city of Eivissa (Ibiza).
LEFT: checking out the route.

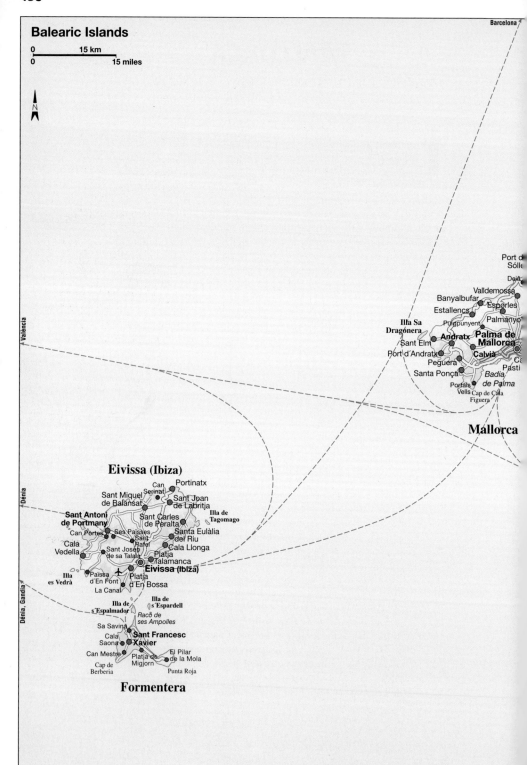

Balearic Islands

0 ——— 15 km
0 ——————— 15 miles

N

Barcelona

València

Dénia

Dénia, Gandia

Port d
Sóller
Deià
Valldemossa
Banyalbufar
Estallencs
Esporles
Palmanyo
Puigpunyent
Palma
Illa Sa
Dragónera
Sant Elm
Andratx
**Palma de
Mallorca**
Port d'Andratx
Calvià
Peguera
Ca
Pasti
Santa Ponça
*Badia
de Palma*
Portals
Vells
Cap de Cala
Figuera

Mallorca

Eivissa (Ibiza)

Portinatx
Can
Serinat
Sant Miquel
de Balansat
Sant Joan
de Labritja
**Sant Antoni
de Portmany**
Sant Carles
de Peralta
**Illa de
Tagomago**
Can Portes
Ses Païsses
Santa Eulàlia
del Riu
Sant
Rafel
Cala
Vedella
Sant Josep
de sa Talaia
Cala Llonga
Platja
Talamanca
Eivissa (Ibiza)
Illa
es Vedrà
Païssa
d'En Font
Platja
d'En Bossa
La Canal

Illa de
s'Espardell
Illa de
s'Espalmador
*Racó de
ses Ampolles*
Sa Savina
Cala
Saona
**Sant Francesc
Xavier**
Can Mestre
El Pilar
de la Mola
Platja de
Migjorn
Cap de
Berberia
Punta Roja

Formentera

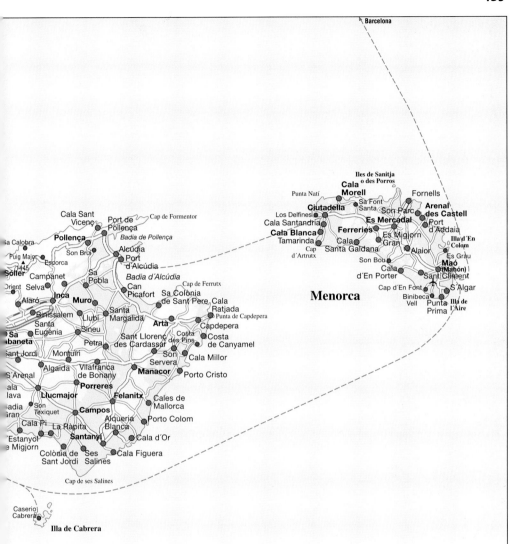

Barcelona

Iles de Sanitja
o des Porros
Cala
Morell
Punta Natí
Fornells
Sa Font
Ciutadella
Santa
Son Parc
Arenal
des Castell
Los Delfines
Es Mercadal
Port
Cala Santandría
Ferreries
Es Migjorn
d'Addaia
Cala Blanca
Cala
Illa d'En
Tamarinda
Gran
Colom
Cap
Santa Galdana
Alaior
Es Grau
d'Artrutx
Son Bou
Maó
Son Bou
Cala
(Mahón)
Cala
Sant Climent
d'En Porter
Menorca
Cap d'En Font
S'Algar
Binibeca
Illa de
Vell
Punta
l'Aire
Prima

Cala Sant
Vicenç
Port de
Cap de Formentor
Pollença
Pollença
Badia de Pollença
a Calobra
Pollença
Son Brull
Alcúdia
Puig Major
Port
1445
Escorca
d'Alcúdia
Sóller
Campanet
Sa
Badia d'Alcúdia
Pobla
Can
Orient
Selva
Picafort
Sa Colònia
Cap de Ferrutx
Alaró
Inca
Muro
de Sant Pere
Cala
Binissalem
Santa
Llubí
Santa
Margalida
Ratjada
Sa
Eugènia
Sineu
Artà
Punta de Capdepera
baneta
Petra
Capdepera
ant Jordi
Montuïri
Sant Llorenç
Costa
Costa
Algaida
Vilafranca
des Cardassar
dés Pins
de Canyamel
S'Arenal
de Bonany
Son
Cala Millor
ala
Manacor
Servera
lava
Porreres
Porto Cristo
adia
Llucmajor
Felanitx
ran
Son
Cales de
Texiquet
Campos
Mallorca
Cala Pi
Alqueria
Porto Colom
La Rapita
Blanca
Estanyol
Santanyí
Cala d'Or
e Migjorn
Colònia de
Ses
Cala Figuera
Sant Jordi
Salines
Cap de ses Salines

Caserio
Cabrera
Illa de Cabrera

M E D I T E R R A N E A N

S E A

PALMA AND SURROUNDINGS

Map on page 144

*It may be the capital of one of Europe's most
popular package holiday islands, but this sophisticated
city has stayed true to its Catalan roots*

There is really only one way to arrive in Palma, and that is by sea. One thousand years of history are etched into the waterfront, where a Gothic cathedral, rising proudly from the city walls, looks down on a royal palace built by Muslim rulers and remodelled by Christian kings. A medieval stock exchange and a 17th-century shipping tribunal stand side by side, reminders of Palma's maritime importance in times past. On its hilltop high above the port, 14th-century Bellver Castle crowns a skyline punctured by the spires of ancient churches. Even the 20th century gets a look-in with the boldly conceived Parc de la Mar, whose artificial lake – on reclaimed land beneath the cathedral – has restored the magnificent effect of golden sandstone reflected in the sea.

The oldest part of the city fans out around the cathedral. **Medina Mayurka**, as Palma was known in the Arab world, was a sophisticated place with street lights and heated baths, stretching between Morey and Miramar streets, Plaça Cort, Passeig des Born and the sea. Centuries later, this was where Palma's wealthy Catalan merchants built their palaces, with their grand patios and graceful arcades. East of here is the old Jewish ghetto, whose cramped alleys belie its 14th-century importance as one of Europe's leading centres of cartography.

But Palma is not only about ancient buildings. This is a city of Renaissance courtyards and *Modernista* (Catalan art nouveau) façades gracing 19th-century boulevards and 20th-century boutiques; a city where ancient dignity blends harmoniously with modern style.

Since 1983 Palma has been given a new lease of life, as the capital of the Balearic region and a focus for the islands' cultural revival. Chic, cosmopolitan, prosperous and energetic, this is a city with a future as well as a past. Art galleries are flourishing; new restaurants open every month – perhaps it is no surprise that Palma has been singled out by the Spanish newspaper *El País* as the city with the best quality of life in Spain.

Gothic majesty

Any tour of Palma has to begin at the cathedral, **La Seu** , begun by Jaume I on the site of the city's main mosque soon after the Catalan conquest of 1229. Almost 400 years in the making, finishing touches were still being added to the building as late as 1914. The great nave was completed in the 14th century, when work began on the magnificent **Portal del Mirador**, on the south front facing the sea.

La Seu was finally finished in 1601 with the completion of the **Portal Major** (Great Door), but an earthquake in 1851 necessitated the rebuilding of this façade. Subsequently, it has been strongly criticised for not blending in with the original building's Gothic

PRECEDING PAGES: *Modernista* shop sign, Carrer Unió, Palma. **LEFT:** view from the Castell de Bellver down to Palma Bay. **BELOW:** La Seu, Palma's cathedral.

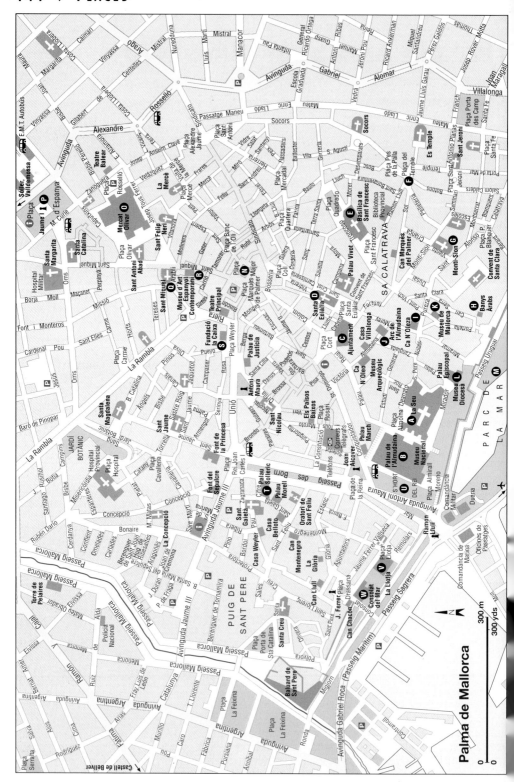

Palma de Mallorca

design (open Mon-Sat; closed Sat pm; entrance fee; free on Sun am for Mass).

There can be few churches in the world with such a spectacular setting. It was clearly designed to be admired from the sea, with pinnacled columns and flying buttresses climbing above the city walls. Inside, sunlight filters in through the stained glass of the cathedral's 35 windows; the **rose window** suspended above the apse is one of the largest in the world with a diameter of 12 metres (40 ft). Seventeen side chapels, lavishly embellished with statues, reredos and gilded altarpieces, render the cathedral a treasury of Gothic, Renaissance and Baroque art. The **Trinity chapel** behind the main altar (the oldest part of the building) contains the tombs of the Mallorcan kings Jaume II and Jaume III.

The Catalan architect Antoni Gaudí was commissioned to redesign the interior at the beginning of the 20th century. It was Gaudí who introduced the electric candelabra which ring the slender columns of the nave – a real novelty for the time – but his most conspicuous innovation was to hang an enormous **baldachin**, or wrought-iron canopy, over the altar. Once its 35 lamps are lit, this bizarre sculpture fashioned from cardboard, cork and brocade becomes a surprisingly powerful symbol of the Eucharistic mystery – and of Palma's ability to take on the spirit of the times while retaining the best of the past.

Ancient quarter

Facing the cathedral across Carrer Palau Reial, the **Palau de l'Almudaina ❸** was built on the site of the Roman citadel, later converted by the Arabs into their *alcàsser* or fortress. The present Gothic palace, designed by Pere Salvà, was constructed at the end of the 13th century, at the command of Jaume II. The salons and hallways are hung with Flemish tapestries, but the main interest is the

Map
on page
144

The main portal of Palma's majestic La Seu cathedral.

BELOW: the cathedral's interior columns are remarkably slender.

Behind Santa Eulàlia church in the Carrer Sanç is the Can Joan de S'Aigo, the chocolate shop where the artist Joan Miró used to indulge in a daily hot chocolate and almond cake.

building itself, with its Moorish-style arches and intricately-carved wooden ceilings. The central courtyard contains two stone lions dating from the Arab era, while one of the four towers is topped by a 14th-century bronze sculpture of the angel Gabriel. The angel acts as a weather-vane; according to Robert Graves, Mallorcans describe an unstable man as being "like the palace angel". Today the palace serves as the Balearics' military headquarters and is also the King's official residence in Palma – though he generally prefers to stay in his summer palace at Marivent (open Mon-Sat; closed Sat pm; also closed Oct-Mar: 2-4pm; entrance fee).

A left turn outside the palace, passing ranks of *galeres* (horse-drawn carriages) offering tours of the old city, leads to Plaça Cort, which is dominated by its **Ajuntament ❻** or Town Hall. Here, a baroque façade is overhung with carved wooden eaves adorned with caryatids and atlantes, the work of a naval carpenter. The English writer Gordon West, visiting Palma in the late 1920s, described this square as "the meeting place of the old men of Palma. All round the front of it they sit, on a long stone ledge in the sun. Their countenances are beautiful with peace. These are the faces of men who have the consciousness of peace well merited after centuries of battling for the freedom of their island." The stone bench, and even the old men, are still there today.

Church of sages

The church of **Santa Eulàlia ❼** in the neighbouring square is one of the oldest in Mallorca, built like La Seu in the years immediately following the Christian conquest. **Bar Moderno**, in the small square facing the church, is a traditional locals' café where lively *tertúlies* (informal debates) are still held.

BELOW: the Palau de l'Almudaina.

A narrow street leads to Plaça Sant Francesc, where the huge sandstone façade of the **Basílica de Sant Francesc ❺** looms up above a statue of Junípero Serra, founder of California's missions, who lived in the convent here. Although much of the church dates from 1281, when Jaume II laid the foundation stone, the original façade was destroyed by a lightning strike in 1580. The present façade is baroque and combines the simplicity of a sheer, stark frontal wall with an exquisitely wrought portal. The cloisters are Gothic, and with their orange and lemon trees make a peaceful retreat in the centre of Palma. Inside the church lies the tomb of Ramon Llull, medieval mystic, missionary and philosopher (open daily; closed 12.30–3.30pm and Sun pm; entrance fee).

The Jewish ghetto

The basilica stands near the entrance to **El Call**, the 14th-century Jewish ghetto, once surrounded by walls. As a group, the Jews earned the island an enormous amount of foreign trade, particularly with Africa; their knowledge of medicine, commerce, map-making and the manufacture of navigational instruments was considerable. El Call was also the setting for one of Palma's darkest days: a violently anti-Semitic crowd stormed the ghetto in 1391, murdering 300 people. Mallorca's Jewish community never fully recovered; before long, most Jews had formally converted to Christianity for their own protection (*see also Xuetes and Judaism, page 56*).

Carrer del Sol, at the heart of the Jewish quarter, contains one of Palma's most impressive mansions, **Can Marquès del Palmer**, built in the 16th century with huge Renaissance windows and a Plateresque façade. The street ends in the **Plaça del Temple ❻**, once the site of a monastery-castle belonging to the

Map on page 144

This stained-glass window adorns the baroque Basílica de Sant Francesc.

BELOW LEFT: the *Modernista* Forn des Teatre bakery on Plaça Weyler.
BELOW RIGHT: a few words on Palma's La Rambla.

Knights Templar. Before their suppression in the early 14th century these military monks provided a service moving money around the Mediterranean – a service vital to Palma's mercantile success. All that is left of the Templars' redoubt now, however, are two Romanesque side-chapels located in an oratory.

There were once two synagogues in the area; one is now the Baroque church of **Monti-Sion** , established by the Jesuits in the 16th century, while the other, the **Seminari Vell**, is a theological college. Just near here, on Carrer Santa Clara, stands the convent of the same name, with its original 13th-century cloister and a baroque 17th-century façade.

Since the 1950s, Palma's main produce market has been the Mercat Olivar, off Carrer Sant Miquel.

Moorish remains

Few traces are left of the Arab's Medina Mayurka, but the **Banys Arabs** (Arab Baths) ❶ on Carrer Can Serra provide a rare glimpse into 10th-century Islamic life. There are two main chambers: a *caldarium*, for hot steam baths, and a *tepidarium*, for lukewarm bathing. The ceiling is sustained by uneven columns with horseshoe arches and round shafts for sunlight; the lack of uniformity among the columns is thought to be a result of their having been salvaged from the ruins of other buildings (open daily; entrance fee).

From here you can plunge into the heart of the old city. Palma's "palace quarter" lies between the churches of Santa Eulàlia and Sant Francesc, and the former city gate of La Portella; here, Gothic and baroque churches grace peaceful squares, while mansions with Renaissance-style façades front huge patios with spacious entrance-halls. Perhaps the most impressive example is **Ca N'Oleza** ❶ on Carrer Morey, remodelled in the 17th century with Ionic columns and a Gothic stairway. While in Carrer Morey, look down Carrer de l'Almudaina to see the **Arc de l'Almudaina** ❶, the only surviving section of Palma's Roman walls.

BELOW: the Arab Baths provide a rare glimpse of Moorish Palma.

The art within

Another 17th-century palace on Carrer Portella – one of the few that have passed into the public domain – houses the rewarding **Museu de Mallorca** ❶. Several thousand exhibits from various epochs make this one of the Balearics' most important collections, including archaeological finds from Tayalotic and Roman times, Moorish ceramics, and a few superb paintings and altar-pieces. Look out for the collection of works by the Gothic school of Mallorcan Primitives, based on the island in the 14th and 15th centuries. One of the most talented exponents of the style, the so-called Master of the Privileges, is well-represented here by his *Santa Quiteria*; in his use of bright colours and precise, cartoon-like detail there are echoes of his Italian contemporaries (open Tues-Sun; closed 2–4pm and Sun pm; entrance fee).

Two streets away, the **Museu Diocesà** (Diocesan Museum) ❶ inside the bishop's palace, has a worthy but dull religious art collection (open daily; closed 1.30–3pm, Sat pm, Sun pm; entrance fee).

From here, Carrer del Mirador runs along the cathedral's south front, past the Portal del Mirador, whose Gothic carvings portray the Last Supper with a supporting cast of angels and prophets. A wide staircase drops down to the **Parc de la Mar **, built in the 1960s on reclaimed land. This is now one of Palma's most popular meeting places, with several terrace cafés and outdoor concerts on a stage beside the lagoon in summer. A giant mural by Joan Miró adorns one of the walls, while the military vaults of the medieval ramparts have been turned into a gallery, **Ses Voltes**, which features 19th- and 20th-century Mallorcan art (open Tues–Sun; closed 1.30–5pm and Sun pm; free).

Markets and Modernista architecture

North of the old city, Palma's main shopping streets spread out around **Plaça Major**, a handsome 19th–century porticoed square which acted as the city's market until the 1950s. Carrer Sant Miquel leads to the present-day market, **Mercat Olivar**, housed on two floors with fresh produce down below and meat and cheese upstairs; from here it is a short walk to **Plaça d'Espanya**, where a statue of Jaume the Conqueror on horseback looks across at the city's two railway stations. Carrer Sant Miquel also contains the church of **Sant Miquel**, where Jaume celebrated the first Mass following the capture of Palma, and the **Museu d'Art Espanyol Contemporani**, with works by 20th-century Spanish artists including Picasso, Miró, Dalí and the Mallorcan Miquel Barceló (open Mon-Sat; closed Sat pm; entrance fee).

South of Plaça Major, an archway leads into Plaça Marquès del Palmer, where a pair of *Modernista* buildings feature multicoloured mosaic façades. The alleys around Carrer Jaume II are home to many of the city's small, specialist shops; Colmado Santo Domingo, with its hundreds of hanging sausages, must be the most photographed shop in Palma. From Plaça Major steps lead down into Plaça Weyler, and the 19th-century neoclassical **Teatre Principal**, an opera

Map on page 144

King Jaume the Conqueror gazes out over Plaça d'Espanya.

BELOW: a section of the Miró mural, Parc de la Mar.

house modelled on the Liceu in Barcelona. Near here is Palma's finest *Modernista* structure, the 1903 **Gran Hotel**, designed by Catalan architect Lluís Domènech i Montaner. This was the first of the great Mallorcan hotels and the building which started the craze for *Modernista* architecture in the city. The hotel closed after the Civil War, but since 1993 it has been given a new lease of life as an art gallery, the **Fundació la Caixa**  (open Tues–Sun; closed Sun pm; free). Across the street, the Forn des Teatre bakery is another fine example of a *Modernista* building.

Look out for island specialities like the ensaimada, a puffy spiral of sugar-dusted bread, in Palma's traditional bakeries.

North of Plaça Weyler is **La Rambla**, a promenade laid out on the site of a diverted river bed in 1613. It may not match its Barcelonan namesake for colour, but still makes a pleasant stroll, with flower stalls set out beneath the plane trees. The statues at the foot of the boulevard, representing Roman emperors, were placed here in 1937 as a Francoist tribute to Italy's Fascist rulers.

On the street

West from Plaça Weyler, Carrer Unió leads into Plaça Rei Joan Carles. Ahead is Avinguda Jaume III, the city's up-market shopping street; while to the left, **Passeig des Born** runs down towards the sea. This tree-lined walkway, built over a narrow creek, derives its name from the jousting tournaments which took place here in the 17th century. During the Fascist era it was renamed after Franco, but everyone continued to call it the Born. The street still plays an important role in city life as a venue for everything from festivals to political demonstrations and the evening *passeig* (the *paseo* in Spanish). The baroque **Palau Solleric** ❼, built on the Born for a family of olive oil merchants, is now a modern art gallery whose ground-floor café and bookshop has become one of the trendiest meeting places in town (open Tues-Sun; closed 2–5pm and Sun pm; free).

BELOW: La Llotja, Palma's Gothic stock exchange.

At the foot of the Born, Plaça de la Reina leads to **S'Hort del Rei** ❽, the former royal gardens beneath the Almudaina palace. For most of the 20th century a hotel and theatre stood on this site, and the gardens were only reclaimed for public use in the 1960s. There is a sculpture by Miró, *Monument* (popularly known as The Egg), and another depicting a Balearic slinger by Llorenç Rosselló. Above a small pond, the **Arc de la Drassana** is a Moorish arch, once the gateway to the royal docks, discovered during restoration work in 1961. On the seafront a few metres away is a memorial to Ramon Llull, with dedications in Catalan, Arabic and Latin.

Along the waterfront

You'll find **La Llotja** ❾, the 15th-century maritime exchange, down on the seafront. Designed by Guillem Sagrera (the architect of the cathedral's Portal del Mirador), embellished with gargoyles and geometrical motifs, it is the supreme example of Palma's civic Gothic architecture. Seen from the sea, its crenellated towers give it the appearance of a castle; inside, the fluted columns and vaulted roof are more suggestive of a church. The building served as the stock exchange for Palma's prosperous merchants; today, like so many of the city's old buildings, it houses an upmarket art

gallery (open Tues–Sun during exhibitions; closed 2–5pm and Sun pm; free). Separated from La Llotja by a small garden is the **Consolat del Mar** , now the seat of the Balearic government. Established as a shipping tribunal by Jaume III in 1326; the present building dates from around 1600. The seaward-facing gallery, with five basket-handle arches supported by a balustrade, is the most visible architectural feature. It's across the road from the fishing port, a colourful fish auction takes place beside the harbour at around 6am each day. West of here, in a small garden, is the oratory of **Sant Elm**, designed as a navigator's chapel, later used as an inn, and moved here stone by stone from its original home in Carrer de la Mar in 1947.

The wide boulevard known as **Passeig Marítim**, constructed in the 1950s, follows the curve of the waterfront from the fishing port to the commercial harbour. This has become the most fashionable area of Palma, with an ever-growing number of designer bars. The promenade comes to an end at Porto Pi, Palma's medieval port, whose 13th-century lighthouse is one of the oldest in the world. An 18th-century defence fortress, **Castell de Sant Carles**, houses Mallorca's military museum, with displays covering everything from the Christian conquest of Palma to the Spanish role in Cuba (open daily; closed 1–4pm; free).

Beyond the centre

Palma's ❶ outstanding military structure is the circular **Castell de Bellver** ❷, designed by Pere Salvà, the same master builder who remodelled the Almudaina palace. It was Jaume II, learning from his father's conquest of the city, who had the castle built high above the harbour to prevent a repetition at the hands of a foreign invader. Originally a summer palace and later a military prison, it

Maps:
City 144
Area 162

TIP

It takes at least an hour to walk the whole way along Palma's waterfront, pausing to look back at the cathedral seen across the bay through a forest of masts. You can return on a No. 1 bus.

BELOW: the elegant Castell de Bellver.

now houses Palma's municipal **history museum** (closed Sun). The rooftop view, looking down over the pine woods to Palma bay, is one of the finest in the city; indeed, the name of the castle means "lovely view" (open daily; entrance fee; free on Sun; museum closed Sun).

During the annual Bellver Festival in July, the Castell de Bellver – the only round castle in all of Spain – is the venue for a series of floodlit evening concerts.

Down below in Palma's western outskirts, the **Poble Espanyol** (Spanish Village) is a purpose-built tourist attraction containing faithful reproductions of famous Spanish buildings such as the Alhambra of Granada and El Greco's house in Toledo, as well as vernacular architecture from the Spanish regions. As an introduction to the history of Spanish architecture, showing its Roman and Islamic influences, it is interesting enough; but the self-conscious displays of handicrafts, together with the numerous coach parties, have the effect of making this "village" seem more theme park than museum. There are just as many interesting buildings in the back streets of the old city (*see box below*), and you don't have to pay to see them (open daily; entrance fee; bus 5).

The Bay of Palma

Palma sits at the centre of a broad, deep bay, which has become the biggest tourist resort in Europe. The 30 km (19 miles) of coastline between S'Arenal and Magalluf has over 70,000 hotel beds; a third of all visitors to Mallorca stay here. Until the 1950s, much of this shore was deserted; now it is a concrete jungle of motorways, beach promenades and high-rise hotels. The cathedral and castle which once dominated their surroundings have become mere specks in the landscape, while quiet fishing villages have been turned into major tourist towns.

BELOW: the Poble Espanyol, modelled on Granada's Alhambra Palace and other famous Spanish buildings.

Mass tourism reaches its nadir at **Platja de Palma**, a 5-km (3-mile) stretch of sand on the eastern side of the bay. Its proximity to the airport means that vis-

PALMA'S MANSIONS

One of Palma's finest features is the wealth of aristocratic mansions which grace the old town. Most date from the late 17th and early 18th centuries, part of an extended urban renewal programme after swathes of the medieval city were destroyed by fire. Architects were hired to follow the latest fashions from Europe, concealing Renaissance-style arcades, loggias and courtyards behind a dignified façade of plain stone. The spacious courtyards around which these houses were arranged came to play an important role in Palmaian social life: births, deaths and marriages became city-wide events as the noble families threw open their doors and invited the community in to mark the occasion. In the 20th century, however, as the aristocracy moved out, many of the mansions were divided into flats and offices; the courtyards went into decline. The 1990s saw an ambitious scheme for their revival as the city council awarded grants for restoration, putting in wrought-iron gates on condition that the massive wooden courtyard doors would be left open.

Don't miss the chance to peep in on Ca N'Oleza *(see page 148)*, Can Vivot (Carrer Can Savellà), opulent Palau Solleric *(see page 150)* and Ca N'Aiamans, which now houses the Museu de Mallorca and can therefore be entered.

itors converge here from all over Europe; **S'Arenal** ❸ and **Can Pastilla** ❹ – the villages at either end of the beach – have gradually merged over the years to become a single mega-resort. The long beach promenade, which provides views of Palma across the bay, is delightful, but behind this much of the resort has become a seedy hotchpotch of discos, strip joints and English and German bars. One of the more notorious bars, Balneario 6 – named after one of the bathing stations which divide the beach into districts – was the inspiration behind the German cult film *Ballerman 6*, about a pair of "lager louts" on a Mediterranean holiday.

Not far from here, a group of Franciscan friars maintain their meditative lifestyle in the seminary of Porci Úncula. Their **museum** features prehistoric artefacts from the area as well as sacred art and a display of Mallorcan coins (open Mon-Sat; closed 1-3pm; entrance fee).

West of Palma, and just beyond the port, **Cala Major** ❺ was one of the earliest resorts on Mallorca. The artist Joan Miró (*see also pages 154–55*) had a house here, now the **Fundació Pilar i Joan Miró** (open Tues–Sun; closed Sun pm; entrance fee), and the king still spends his holidays in Mallorca at his summer palace, Marivent, overlooking the bay.

From glitz to tourist tack

The C719 coast road continues to **Ses Illetes**, a laid-back beach resort named after the rocky islets which guard its harbour entrance. The smart, family-run hotels here have the air of old-fashioned guesthouses, while the beaches are a popular weekend outing for Palma locals. Nearby **Portals Nous** ❻ is home to probably the most glamorous summer address in Palma, the Puerto Portals

Map on pages 162–3

This wooden wheel adorns Miró's Mallorcan home, now the Fundació Pilar i Joan Miró.

BELOW: busy Palma Nova resort.

Map on pages 162–3

marina – just the place to spot celebrities and Spanish royals mooring their yachts before stepping carefully ashore to dine on *nouvelle cuisine* at a waterfront restaurant.

The dolphin shows, shark tanks and crocodile ponds at **Marineland** (open daily; closed mid-Nov to Christmas; entrance fee) signal the onset of another mass tourist agglomeration where Palma Nova merges into Magalluf: the area is now known simply as "Maganova". **Palma Nova ❼**, with three sandy beaches, is still an attractive family resort; but **Magalluf ❽** has become a byword for the tacky excesses of mass tourism. If your idea of a great Mediterranean holiday is 5-litre cocktails, wet T-shirt contests, pubs with names like the *Benny Hill's* and hours spent whirling round your handbag in a Bacardi blur, then this may well be the place for you.

The municipality of **Calvià** which controls Palma Nova and Magalluf has been at the forefront of efforts to change the area's downmarket image. The worst of the hotels have been destroyed to make way for a new seafront promenade. Guided walks have been introduced, along with winter activities like *tai chi* on the beach. Amphibious wheelchairs have been provided for disabled visitors, enabling them to swim in the sea.

Yet still the "lager louts" flood in, and there is not a great deal that Calvià can do about it. Calvià itself, 6 km (4 miles) north of Palma Nova, remains a rather ordinary, if prosperous, country town, living off the proceeds of tourism without allowing it to disrupt everyday life. A tiled mural beside the fountain recounts the history of the town. Founded in 1249 with just 80 inhabitants, Calvià had a population of 3,000 in 1960, which had increased to 11,560 by 1980 – all because of tourism.

BELOW: taking it easy at S'Arenal.
RIGHT: these days, tourism offers an alternative to making a living from fishing.

To the lighthouse

From Magalluf, the C719 heads west to Andratx, passing the ever-popular **Aquapark** with its swimmingpools, rides and giant water castle on the way out of town (open daily, June–Sept 10am–6pm; May–October 10am–5pm; entrance fee).

South from Magalluf, a narrow country road winds through the pine woods on its way round Palma bay and along a little peninsula that has – so far – escaped much development. Eventually the track reaches **Portals Vells ❾**, where a handful of villas look down on an unspoilt sheltered cove. There are two small sandy beaches here, including **Platja El Mago**, Mallorca's official nudist beach, offering sunbeds, showers and a small beach bar.

A short walk along the cliffs leads to the **Cova de la Mare de Déu**, a rock chapel said to have been built by Genoese fishermen to give thanks for a safe landing. The statue of the Virgin which they placed inside the cave is now in the seafront church at Portals Nous.

Two km (1¼ miles) from Portals Vells, the road runs out at a barbed-wire fence, the start of a military zone. As long as the road is not closed and guarded, you may continue your stroll down the peninsula to reach **Cap de Cala Figuera**, with its lonely lighthouse. From here, you can gaze back across the entire bay of Palma, and wonder at the pace of change. ❏

JOAN MIRÓ AND THE LIGHT OF MALLORCA

Drawn by the "light of Mallorca", the Catalan artist Joan Miró spent the last 27 years of his life in a farmhouse on the outskirts of Palma

Joan Miró (1893–1983) was born in Barcelona; his father was a Catalan goldsmith, his mother the daughter of a Mallorcan cabinet-maker. The family had regular holidays in Mallorca, and even as a child Miró was drawn to the island's landscapes, inspired by the clarity of its light and the deep blue of the sea and sky. He was also fascinated by Mallorcan peasant traditions and loved to collect *siurells*, the clay whistles with their bright, simple designs which have been produced on Mallorca since Arab times.

After early experiments with realism, Miró forged links with the Surrealist movement before moving on to develop his own distinctive avant-garde style. Noted for his love of primary colours, his most common subjects were stars, birds and the female form: look out for his ceramic murals at Barcelona airport, and at the UNESCO building in Paris.

In 1956, Miró moved to Mallorca with his Mallorcan wife, Pilar Juncosa. They settled in Son Boter, a 17th-century farmhouse in Cala Major, to which his friend, the architect Josep Lluís Sert, added a purpose-built studio. The star-shaped gallery of the Miró Foundation (above), designed by Rafael Moneo, was added after his death to hold a collection of his Mallorcan works.

▽ **SURREALIST PERIOD**
One of Joan Miró's earliest Surrealist works, painted in 1925. In that same year, his work was included in the Surrealists' first exhibition in Paris.

▷ **ARTIST AT WORK**
"When I pick up a rock, it's a rock; when Miró picks it up, it's a Miró." So said Joan Prats, a Barcelonian shopkeeper who was also Miró's friend and patron.

◁ **GETTING IN SHAPE**
Few visitors to the S'Hort del Rei gardens in Palma seem able to resist having their picture taken framed by Miró's famous *Egg* sculpture.

▽ **A GIFT TO THE PUBLIC**
When Palma's Parc de la Mar was created in the 1960s, reflecting the cathedral in a dazzling ornamental lake, Miró presented this mural as a gift to his adopted city.

MIRO'S ARTISTIC LEGACY

Palma today is a vibrant centre of contemporary art, with more than 50 private galleries and a growing number of exhibition centres. It is often said that painting has taken the place of rock music in Spanish teenagers' hearts, and, while this is certainly an exaggeration, there is no doubt that a revival of the arts has gone hand in hand with the post-Franco Balearic renaissance. The best-known local artist is Miquel Barceló, born in Felanitx in 1956 and now the leading avant-garde painter of his generation. However, only one of his works is on display in Palma, at the Museu d'Art Espanyol Contemporani. The oil *Fum de Cucina* (*above*) is typical of his style.

◁ SIURELLS
Traditional clay figures, a popular children's toy in Mallorca, are credited with influencing Miró's love of bright primary colours.

▷ I MAY BE SOME TIME
Miró's studio, Son Abrines, has been left virtually untouched since his death, with paint-tins still open as if he'd just popped out to the shops.

THE MALLORCAN SIERRA

One of the island's classic drives, the route north above the coast gives a glimpse of the best Mallorca has to offer, both in terms of scenery and sights

Map
on pages
162–3

The Serra de Tramuntana (Mountains of the North Wind) run for more than 80 km (50 miles) along Mallorca's north coast, from the rocky outcrop of Dragonera in the west to the finger-like promontory of Formentor in the east. These are real mountains, torn with gulleys, carpeted with thorn bushes and sculpted by the elements into outlandish shapes. Forests of holm oak and wild olives support large numbers of feral goats, while the higher slopes are one of the last remaining European refuges of the black vulture. Inland, the peaks rise to 1,445 metres (4,740 ft); on the coast, the cliffs plunge sheer into the sea.

Improved roads mean it is now possible to cover the entire range in a day, as long as you can cope with switchback bends and tour buses bearing down from above. Far better, though, to put on a stout pair of hiking boots and get out into the mountains on foot. Increasingly there are problems with landowners denying access to traditional rights of way, but many of the best routes remain open – even if only for one day a week – and walking maps are widely available. On foot you can really experience the mountains – you hear the sheep-bells, breathe in the scent of wild herbs, and enjoy the thrill of scaling a summit to be rewarded with a distant view of the sea.

PRECEDING PAGES: peaceful village in the Serra de Tramuntana. **LEFT:** evening in the mountains. **BELOW:** farmer at work, Valldemossa.

Heartlands

The western motorway from Palma fizzles out near Magalluf, from where it is another 15 km (9 miles) on the C719 to **Andratx ⑩**. Like other towns close to the coast, Andratx was built inland from its harbour to protect it from attacks by pirates and Barbary corsairs, once a common feature of Mallorcan life. Formerly the seat of the Bishop of Barcelona, it is now a prosperous county town surrounded by almond groves, whose Wednesday-morning market is one of the island's biggest. The upper town is dominated by the fortress-like 13th-century church of **Santa Maria**.

A road out of Andratx leads after 6 km (4 miles) to the sheltered harbour at **Port d'Andratx ⑪**, once a fishing port but now a glitzy marina with seafood restaurants by the water's edge. From here a twisting coast road passes through the resorts of Camp de Mar and Peguera before rounding the bay to **Santa Ponça**, site of the Aragonese invasion of 1229. A large cross above the marina, the **Creu de la Conquesta**, was erected exactly 700 years after the event.

Sant Elm ⑫, 8 km (5 miles) from Andratx, is the main base for visiting **Sa Dragonera**, a rocky islet which was declared a natural park in 1995. Boats leave regularly all through the summer, and it is possible to spend some time ashore, climbing to the lighthouse at Dragonera's highest point at 353 metres (1,150 ft). Many seabirds can be seen here during the

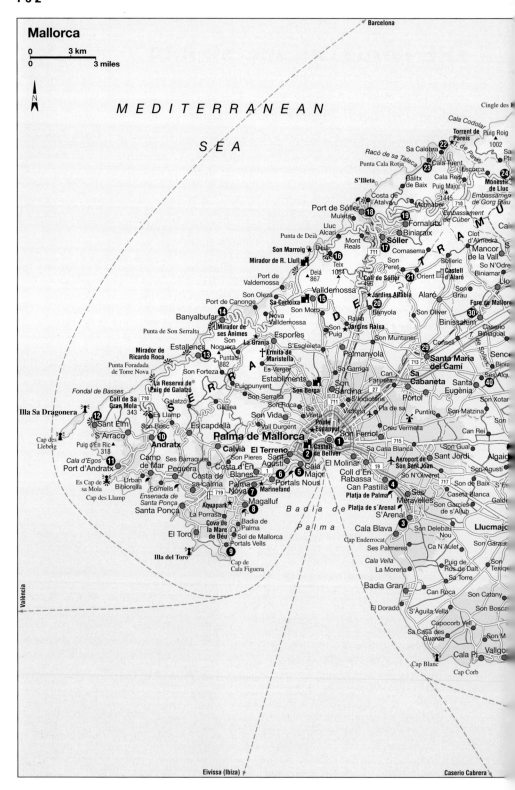

Mallorca

0   3 km
0   3 miles

N

MEDITERRANEAN

SEA

Barcelona

Cingle des

Cala Codolar

Torrent de
Pareis   Puig Roig
1002

Sa Calobra

Racó de sa Taleca

Punta Cala Rotja

Cala Tuent

Escorca

S'Illeta

Bàlitx
de Baix

Cala Reis

Puig Major
1445

Monestir
de Lluc

Embassament
de Gorg Blau

Costa de
l'Atalya

Monnàber

Embassament
de Cúber

Port de Sóller

Muleta

Fornalutx

Lluc
Alcari

Biniaraix

Sóller

Punta de Deià

Mont
Reals

Comasema

Clot
d'Almedrà

Mancor
de la Vall

So N'Odre

Biniamar

Son Marroig

Deià

Teix
1064

Son
Peret

Sóleric

Castell
d'Alaró

Mirador de R. Llull

Deià
867

Coll de Sóller
496

Orient

Son
Grau

Port de
Valdemossa

Valldemossa

Jardins Alfàbia

Alaró

Fore de Mallorca

Son Oleza

Son Moro

Bunyola

Son Oliver

Port de Canonge

Sa Coixa

Nova
Valldemossa

Raixa

Son
Puig

Binissalem

Caseriò
Binagual

Banyalbufar

Mirador de
ses Animes

Esporles

Jardins Raixa

Son Muntaner

Consell

Ses Alqu

Punta de Son Serralta

Son
Noguera

S'Esgleieta

Palmanyola

Santa Maria
del Camí

Senc

Mirador de
Ricardo Roca

Estellencs

Puntals
882

La Granja

Ermita de
Maristella

Sa Garriga

Can
Farinota

713

Sa
Cabaneta

Son
Bini

Punta Foradada
de Torre Nova

Es Verger

Establiments

Son
Sardina

27

Santa
Eugènia

Son Xotar

La Reserva de
Puig de Galatzó

Son Forteza

Puigpunyent

Son Berga

S'Indioteca

Pla de sa

Pòrtol

Fondal de Basses

Coll de Sa
Gran Mola
343

Galilea

Son Serralta

Sor Roca

711

Victoria

Puntiro

Son Matzina

Illa Sa Dragonera

GALATZO

Es Llamp

Son Vida

Sa
Vileta

Creu Vermella

Can Rei

Sant Elm

Son Bosc

Es capdellà

Vall Durgent

Poble
Espanyol

Son Ferriot

Son Gual

Cap des
Llebeig

S'Arraco

Andratx

Calvià

Palma de Mallorca

Castell
de Bellver

715

Algai

Puig d'En Ric
318

Camp
de Mar

Ses Barraques

El Terreno

Sant
Agustí

Cala
Major

El Molinar

Aeroport de
Son Sant Joan

Sant Jordi

Cala d'Egos

Port d'Andratx

Peguera

Son Pieres

Costa d'En
Blanes

1

Portals Nous

Coll d'En
Rabassa

19

So N'Oliveret

Son d'en Baix

Son Agustí

Es Cap de
sa Mola

Urban
Bihiorella

Costa de
sa calma

Palma
Nova

Marineland

Can Pastilla

Platja de Palma

717

Caseta Blanca

Galde

Cap des Llamp

Fornells

719

Aquapark

Magalluf

Badia de

Sol
Meravelles

Son Garcies
de s'Aljub

Ensenada de
Santa Ponça

La Porrassa

Palma

Platja de s'Arenal

Santa Ponça

Cova de
la Mare
de Déu

Badia de
Palma

S'Arenal

Llucmajo

El Toro

Sol de Mallorca

Cala Blava

Son Delebau
Nou

Son Garau

Illa del Toro

Portals Vells

Cap Enderrocat

Ses Palmeres

Ca N'Aulet

Cap de
Cala Figuera

Cala Vella
La Moreria

Puig de
Ros de Dalt

Son
Texiq

Sa Torre

Badia Gran

Can Roca

Son Catany

El Dorado

S'Àguila Vella

Son Bosca

Son M

Capocorb Vell

Sa Casa des
Guarda

Cala P

Vallgo

Cap Blanc

Cala P

Cap Corb

Valencia

Eivissa (Ibiza)

Caseriò Cabrera

Illa de Cabrera

Parque Nacional Marítim-Terrestre de l'Arxipèlag de Cabrera

spring and autumn migrations, while the islet is also home to a large colony of Eleanora's falcons. The success of the Balearic environmentalists in saving Dragonera from development is widely seen as a turning point in Mallorca's move away from mass tourism.

Headlands

Figs ripening in the sun near Estallencs.

A single road, the C710, travels the length of the sierra between Andratx and Pollença. The first part of the route, between the pine woods and the sea, is particularly attractive and there are several *miradors* (lookout points) where you can park your car and get out to enjoy the views. After 19 km (12 miles) the road passes through **Estallencs** ⓭, all ochre houses and cobbled streets, before continuing for another 8 km (5 miles) to the **Mirador de ses Animes**, a former watchtower with stunning views along the coast.

Banyalbufar ⓮, less than a mile further on, is best known for its terraced hillsides, originally developed as vineyards to produce Malvasia (Malmsey) wine. The town's Arabic name means "vineyard by the sea" and after a century of non-production one or two enthusiasts have begun to produce Malvasia once again. Banyalbufar also has a reputation as a hideaway for wealthy foreigners, so much so that British entrepreneur Richard Branson, owner of La Residencia in Deià, has acquired a second *finca* near the town and plans to turn it, too, into a luxury hotel.

BELOW:
Banyalbufar's terraced hillsides were planted with vines by the Moors.

After another 8 km (5 miles) the road divides, with a side turn leading to Esporles and the country house of **La Granja**. The house here has been both a Cistercian monastery and a feudal estate, but it is now a folklore museum devoted to rural Mallorcan life and traditions. Arrows lead the visitor on a tour

of the house and gardens, from the small theatre and family chapel to workshops full of old farming tools. On Wednesday and Friday afternoons a "folk fiesta" features Mallorcan dancing and free samples of local foods as well as displays of lacemaking and embroidery. Many visitors find it all a bit artificial, but go at a quiet time, ignore the tourist kitsch and concentrate on exploring one of the best-preserved mansions on Mallorca (open daily; entrance fee; tel: 971 610032; see also *Traditional Gardens, pages 204–205*).

A narrow road through the olive groves from La Granja returns to Andratx via the mountain villages of Puigpunyent and Galilea. Just above Puigpunyent, **La Reserva de Puig de Galatzó** offers a gentle introduction to Mallorca's mountain scenery. A waymarked path of around 3 km (2 miles) leads past waterfalls, caves and forests, with information panels in several languages interpreting the area's history, ecology and wildlife (open daily; entrance fee; tel: 971 616622).

Artists' quarters

The C710 continues to **Valldemossa** 🄑, Mallorca's highest town and one that will forever be linked with the visit made in 1838 by Frédéric Chopin and his lover George Sand (Baroness Aurore de Dudevant). The couple came to Mallorca to escape the gossip of Paris, hoping that the mild climate would benefit Chopin's health – he had tuberculosis – and that of Sand's 14-year-old son. After a few weeks in Palma, they moved to Valldemossa, having rented a cell in a newly dissolved Carthusian monastery for just 35 pesetas a year.

In a letter to his friend and agent Jules Fontana, Chopin described Valldemossa as "the most beautiful spot in the world" – but it did not take long for disillusionment to set in. The weather was cold and damp (one of Chopin's

Maps: Area 162 City 167

"We could have lived on good terms with the local people [in Valldemossa] had we gone to church ... at least it would have stopped them from throwing stones at our heads from behind bushes whenever we walked by"
– GEORGE SAND

BELOW: tranquil Valldemossa is Mallorca's highest town.

Deià: portrait of an expat enclave

The tile-roofed houses of Deià, hung with bougainvillea and morning glory and surrounded by palm, olive and almond trees, cluster on the slopes of Es Puig, 210 metres (690 ft) above the sea. In 1878, a guidebook noted of the place that "One of its chief characteristics is its collection of strange and eccentric foreigners." Not much has changed.

British poet, novelist and classical scholar Robert Graves was the chief figurehead of the little bohemian colony that gathered at Deià from 1929 until Graves' death in 1985. His presence attracted other artists – including Pablo Picasso, his fellow-painter, Santiago Rusinyol, and the writer Anaïs Nin – who bought houses here or simply hung out.

The myth they generated was a potent one. Today, nearly a quarter of Deià's

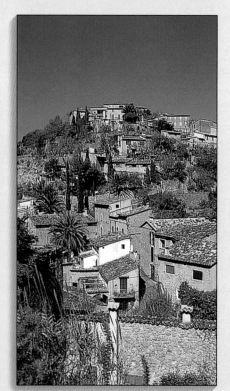

400 inhabitants are expatriates, many of them writers and artists. And after Virgin's Richard Branson bought swish La Residencia hotel here, a stream of celebrities (Princess Diana, Bob Geldof and Sting among them) arrived to rub shoulders with such "local" glitterati as film star Michael Douglas and fashionable dress designer Katherine Hamnett.

But no single name or activity has given Deià and its residents, local or foreign, a new direction or personality to replace Robert Graves. Even in death he continues to draw admirers to the village – his simple burial-place in the local cemetery, marked only by the word *Poeta*, has fresh flowers placed on it almost every day.

The setting remains the same, but the traditional, rural magic that first drew the likes of Graves to Deià is getting harder to find. The village has more than its fair share of galleries, restaurants and smart hotels. Property prices have escalated as foreigners snap up the tiny houses for absurd prices. Local people can no longer afford to buy a house in their native village, and nor can struggling artists afford to live here any more.

The structure of the community has been irredeemably changed – but while locals want to open the village to investment which would provide jobs and livelihoods for themselves and their children, the expatriates see progress and development only as destructive to the idyllic setting they so admire,

Not surprisingly, everything in Deià is relatively expensive, especially during the peak summer season. At weekends, the tiny rock-and-pebble-covered cove is filled, cars line both sides of the street from the beginning to the end of the village, and the cafés, bars and restaurants brim with people.

Yet as long as you do not arrive expecting authentic rustic tranquillity, you may still be charmed by the village of Deià – a sophisticated enclave in the heart of rural Mallorca. ❑

LEFT: struggling artists can no longer afford to live in seductively beautiful Deià.

Map below

few compositions on Mallorca was, appropriately, *Raindrop Prelude*), Chopin's health only got worse, his piano failed to arrive, the relationship deteriorated and Sand had little time to write because she was caring for her invalid lover. The locals disapproved of the adulterous relationship and disliked Sand, an early feminist, because she wore trousers, smoked cigars and refused to go to church. Sand later took her revenge on Mallorca in a vindictive book, *A Winter in Mallorca*, in which she labelled the islanders monkeys, savages and thieves. That does not stop them selling the book to tourists in every shop in Valldemossa.

The **Reial Cartoixa ⓐ**, where Chopin and Sand stayed, was begun in 1399 on the site of a former royal palace. Whitewashed cloisters lead to the old monks' pharmacy and from there to a series of "cells", each with their own garden. Most people head straight for Chopin's cell, containing manuscripts, letters and his Pleyel piano, before going next door to the **Palau del Rei Sanç** (King Sancho's Palace) ⓑ for one of the regular piano recitals. The monastery complex also contains the **Museu Municipal**, whose contemporary art section includes works by Joan Miró and Antoni Tàpies as well as the Mallorcan landscape artists Josep Coll Bardolet and Juli Ramis (open Mon–Sat; closed 1–3pm; also open Apr–Sept: Sun am; entrance fee; tel: 971 612106).

Chopin was forced to use an old village piano for most of his stay in Valldemossa – his own Pleyel was held up by Spanish customs officials.

Nuns and noblemen

Valldemossa was the birthplace of Mallorca's only home-grown saint, Santa Catalina Tomàs, a 16th-century peasant girl turned nun who was canonised in 1935. "Santa Catalina, pray for us," entreat the painted tiles outside virtually every house, and her birthplace **Casa Santa Catalina Tomàs ⓒ**, in Carrer Rectoria near the church, has been turned into a shrine. The *Beateta* ("little

BELOW: Chopin's "cell", which he described as being "like a coffin".

Valldemossa

0   100 m
0   100 yds

One of Valldemossa's many house-plaques commemorating Mallorca's only home-grown saint, Santa Catalina.

blessed one") is remembered each July in a procession through the town, with a local girl playing the part of the saint; the other big summer event is a Chopin festival in the Reial Cartoixa.

Chopin only spent four months on Mallorca; the local hero is another foreigner who devoted his life to the island. Archduke Ludwig Salvator (1847–1915), known simply as *s'Arxiduc*, was an Austrian aristocrat who came to Mallorca to escape the rigid conventions of Viennese court life. An ecologist, explorer, writer and artist, he spent 20 years researching his seven-volume *Die Balearen*, still considered the most comprehensive guide to the Balearic islands.

Local scandal

The Archduke's first house was at Miramar, between Valldemossa and Deià, but he was forever buying up neighbouring estates to protect them from development–it is said that when farmers wanted to fetch a good price for their land, they simply put about a rumour that they were planning to chop down all the trees. In the end he owned over 11 km (7 miles) of coastline, much of which can be explored on the **Camí de s'Arxiduc** from Valldemossa – paths mapped out by the Archduke during tours of his estates by mule (*see box below*).

Like the hippies in Deià a century later, he wore simple peasant clothes to integrate himself with the locals–though occasionally his relationship with local people went beyond mere friendship. The Archduke scandalised local opinion when he fell in love with a carpenter's daughter and bought her the estate of s'Estaca – now owned by the actor Michael Douglas.

Another of the Archduke's estates, **Son Marroig**, 8 km (5 miles) out of Valldemossa on the road to Deià, has been turned into a museum of his life and

BELOW: hikers exploring the Camí de s'Arxiduc.

HIKING THE ARCHDUKE'S PATH

The section of the Camí de s'Arxiduc from Valldemossa to Deià takes about four hours to walk; some parts involve a fairly steep climb but on the whole it is an easy hike. Start at the school which lies just uphill of the small car-park on Valldemossa's north-western boundary. From the steps to the left of the building, turn right, then almost immediately left. The road now dips down slightly; turn right and go uphill until it curves right again and stops at a house. Left from here, a stony track leads over a stile and up into the woods. Follow the path as it winds steeply upwards to reach a gap in a dry-stone wall on the edge of a wooded plain, the Pla des Pouet. Head straight across to an old well, easily visible in a large clearing beside a landmark fallen tree. Now take the path veering off to the right, which bears steeply north-east and then north to lead you up to the Coll de s'Estret de Son Gallard. After you reach several v-shaped stone seats set beside the way, the path broadens out and starts to hug the cliffs, with predictably marvellous views over the rocky, forested coast. As you near Caragolí hill, another path branching off to the left marks the start of the descent to Deià. This is an uncomplicated walk down through woods, terraces and fields, which brings you out at Deià's Es Molí hotel.

work. The gardens contain a white marble rotunda where the Archduke would sit and contemplate views of **Sa Foradada** headland, a jagged rock with a gaping 18-metre (60-ft) hole at its centre. You can walk onto the peninsula, but you must obtain permission from the house first (open Mon–Sat; closed 2–3pm; entrance fee; tel: 971 639158). See also *Traditional Gardens, pages 204–205*.

The high coast road between Valldemossa and Deià is well supplied with viewpoints, each with its own little bar or café. The English writer Gordon West came this way in the late 1920s and feared for the future of this coastline. He wrote: "Gazing down the steep, rock-strewn slopes, across the red soil and the silvery olives to the deep blue of a sea so far below that its wash sounds faintly, like the softest breeze whispering in the pines, one dreads the inevitable day when the passing of some Lord Brougham will change the coast into a place of villas and casinos, of elaborate hotels and fashionable clothes."

Map on pages 162–3

The white marble rotunda at Son Marroig estate.

Hip hangout

West would not like to see **Deià ⓰**, 10 km (6 miles) north-west of Valldemossa on the C710. This small village of green-shuttered houses beneath the Teix mountain is as beautiful as it ever was, but elaborate hotels and fashionable clothes have certainly arrived. In the 1960s Deià developed a reputation as an artists' colony, chiefly because of the presence of the poet Robert Graves, who first moved here in the 1930s and returned in 1946 with his second wife Beryl. For Graves, the attractions of Mallorca were simple: "Sun, sea, mountains, spring water, shady trees, no politics." Not to mention the succession of young women who would arrive in Deià to take up the role of his latest poetic muse.

Graves died in 1985 and is buried in the churchyard of **Sant Joan Baptista**, beneath a simple stone slab inscribed by hand. His son, William Graves, still lives in Deià; his autobiography *Wild Olives* charts the changes in village life over 40 years. One of his early memories is of skinny-dipping in the **Cala de Deià**, a shingle cove reached down a track from the village – a 20-minute walk.

The church is found at the top of the village, on the small hill known as Es Puig. There is a small **museum** attached, whose exhibits include an 11th-century crucifix as well as a collection of Nativity figures (open Fri–Wed; free). Also in Deià, the **Museu Arqueològic** displays the results of the excavations carried out by William Waldren, an American archaeologist who has been visiting Deià for several decades (open Tues–Sun am in summer; free). It was Waldren who discovered the remains of the Balearic antelope, *myotragus balearicus*, in a cave in northern Mallorca in 1962 (*see page 21*).

Gordon West wrote in 1929: "There is nothing to see in Deià, and nothing to do except to be peaceful and dream away the sunny days in the mountains and the lemon groves. The people work on the land, or are engaged in their grey stone houses in the normal pursuits of shoe-making, chair-stringing and hand-weaving." Most visitors still go to Deià in order to be peaceful and to dream, but nowadays the locals are more likely to be engaged in the pursuit of fleecing the tourists who stay in the village's luxury hotels.

BELOW: bathers at lovely Cala de Deià.

The Moorish name for Sóller was Suliar, or sea-shell, for it lies in a shell-shaped valley basin.

Sóller , 10 km (6 miles) from Deià, is a much more down-to-earth place, set in a valley of orange groves which were the source of the town's 19th-century wealth. Sóller was at the centre of the export trade to France, and headstones in the town's cemetery above the station reveal several names of French origin. Some of the tombs are of *Modernista* (Catalan art nouveau) design, with elaborate wrought-iron wreaths and ceramic flowers. There is more *Modernista* architecture in the main square, Plaça de la Constitució; both the bank and the remodelled façade of the church of **Sant Bartomeu** were designed by Gaudí's pupil Joan Rubió.

The **Museu Balear de Ciències Naturals** (Natural Science Museum), in a manor house on the edge of Sóller, has geological and archaeological exhibits including a skeleton of a Balearic antelope (open Tues-Sat and Sun am; entrance fee). Entry to the museum also gives access to the **Jardí Botànic** (Botanical Gardens). Another museum worth visiting is the **Museu de Sóller**, in an 18th-century town house filled with antiques (open Tues–Fri 11am–1pm and 5–8pm; also Sat am; free).

Key route

BELOW:
the vintage train that runs from Palma to Sóller, from where you can catch a vintage tram to Port de Sóller.

A vintage electric train makes the journey over the mountains to Palma, while an assortment of equally antique, bright orange trams trundle through the citrus groves to **Port de Sóller** . From here, you can walk up to the lighthouse for views over the bay or take a boat trip along the north coast to Sa Calobra.

Fornalutx , 5 km (3 miles) northeast of Sóller, is one of the prettiest villages on Mallorca. There are several terrace restaurants that make the most of the view over nearby orange groves.

The climb over the **Coll de Sóller** towards Palma, with its 57 hairpin bends, used to be known as the most terrifying drive on Mallorca; but a new tunnel through the mountains (opened in 1997) has changed all that, bringing the capital within a 20-minute drive. The tunnel emerges at **Bunyola** ❷, close to the Moorish gardens of **Alfàbia** (open Mon–Sat; entrance fee; tel: 971 613123). The key feature here is the spray pergola, or covered walkway, with its 72 columns; there are also lily ponds, bamboo and palm trees, an orange garden and a covered *aljub*, or reservoir; see also *pages 204–205*. The Italianate gardens at **Raixa**, 2 km (1 mile) south of Alfàbia on the Palma road, are also open to visitors (open Wed-Sun; entrance fee).

A twisting road from Bunyola climbs for 11 km (7 miles) to the mountain hamlet of **Orient** ❷, popular with walkers and with day-trippers, who crowd out its restaurants at weekends. From here you can walk up to the **Castell d'Alaró**, a ruined, 15th-century castle. The climb – either from Orient or from the nearby town of Alaró – takes around two hours, passing a farmhouse restaurant where walkers fortify themselves for the final ascent. At the summit there is a small sanctuary, a hostel, a bar serving simple meals, and views all the way to Palma.

Place of pilgrimage

From Sóller the C710 climbs into the high sierra, reaching 1,000 metres (3,300 ft) at the **Coll de Puig Major** pass before dropping to the reservoirs of **Cúber** and **Gorg Blau**, built in the 1970s to provide water for the Bay of Palma resorts. Here you are up among Mallorca's highest mountains, with **Puig Major** (1,445 metres/4,740 ft) a constant presence, easily recognised by the golf-ball radar installations of a military base at its summit.

Just after Gorg Blau, a side road drops 800 metres (2,600 ft) in just 12 km (7 miles) on its way to **Sa Calobra** ❷, where the twin streams of the **Torrent de Pareis** empty into the sea through a narrow gorge. Inevitably, Sa Calobra has become something of a tourist honeypot, and if you are looking for peace and quiet you would do better to make the detour to **Cala Tuent** ❷, with its small sandy beach and 13th-century hermitage of **Sant Llorenç**.

The main road continues for about another 10 km (6 miles) to the monastery at **Lluc** ❷, a centre of pilgrimage for more than 700 years. The story goes that an Arab shepherd boy, newly converted to Christianity, was out walking with a monk when he discovered a statue of the Virgin hidden in a cave. Although the image was placed in the local church three times, it miraculously kept returning to the same spot – and so a chapel was built to house it (open daily; free; tel: 971 517025).

The present Renaissance church dates from the 17th century but La Moreneta ("the little dark one") is still there, now adorned with precious stones and placed in her own chapel behind the church. In the 1980s her crown was stolen, but recovered from the sea by fishermen – another miracle attributed to the Virgin of Lluc. Even today, pilgrims flock to pay homage, especially in August when up to 30,000 people join a special overnight pilgrimage from Palma, covering

Map on pages 162–3

TIP

Look out for the intricately carved Gothic oak chair in the library at Alfàbia. This depicts a tree with owls resting in the branches, shading a prince and a woman playing chess.

BELOW: Fornalutx, a lovely village in a fine setting.

the distance of 48 km (30 miles) on foot. The walk was revived in 1973 by a patriotic bar owner, Tolo Güell, and has grown to become perhaps the largest activity of its kind in modern Mallorca.

The monastery complex includes a hostel for pilgrims, as well as long-term accommodation in the former stable block. There is a **museum** (entrance fee) containing paintings by the Valldemossan artist Josep Coll Bardolet, and the **Via Crucis** (Way of the Rosary), designed at the beginning of the 20th century by Antoni Gaudí. A schoolboy choir, Els Blauets, established in 1531, gives daily performances inside the church before the 11.30am Mass.

Market town

The C710 continues for another 21 km (13 miles) to **Pollença** ㉕, a charming town which bursts into life each Sunday morning for the weekly market, with fruit and vegetables on the main square and artists setting up their stalls in the lanes around the church. A flight of 365 stone steps, soon to be extended, leads from the town centre to the chapel at **El Calvari**. This is the setting for a moving procession on the evening of Good Friday each year, when an image of the crucified Christ is carried down the Calvary steps in silence.

From El Calvari there are good views of **Puig de Maria**, a small hill crowned by an ancient hermitage. A chapel was first built here in the 14th century, when the people of Pollença wanted to give thanks for the ending of the Black Death. For two centuries it was home to Augustinian nuns, before falling into disrepair and eventually being abandoned in 1564. The hermits returned in the 20th century, and the last monks left only in 1987. A small **museum** (admission free) has a collection of *ex votos*, and there are rooms available in the former monks'

Agatha Christie, a frequent visitor to Mallorca, set a Hercules Poirot murder-mystery tale in Port de Pollença. Problem at Pollença Bay *is the title story in a collection of Christie's short stories published by Harper Collins.*

BELOW: Pollença, tucked beneath the eastern slopes of Puig Tomir.

cells should you wish to stay the night. The climb from Pollença to the summit takes about an hour.

Pollença's **Museu Municipal**, in the old Dominican convent, has a fine collection of Gothic art as well as a set of wooden bull sculptures, used in Talayotic funeral rites and dating from the 4th century BC. Among the more unexpected exhibits is a mandala, a Tibetan sand painting created by Buddhist monks on the occasion of the Dalai Lama's visit to Pollença in 1990 (open 10am–1pm daily; also July–Sep: Mon–Sat 5.30–8.30pm; entrance fee). The cloisters of the convent are the venue for Pollença's annual classical music festival, begun by Philip Newman in 1962 and now one of the highlights of the Mallorcan social calendar (*see also The Pulse of Pollença, page 177*).

The **Pont Romà** (Roman bridge) on the edge of Pollença probably dates from the 1st century AD, when the Romans had their capital at Pollentia (now Alcúdia). Directly opposite the bridge, a country lane leads to Ternelles, and the footpath to the ruined **Castell del Rei**, once a stronghold and refuge of the Mallorcan kings. The path is only open on Saturdays and it takes around two hours to reach the castle, 500 metres (1,650 feet) above sea level.

Map on pages 162–3

The Mirador des Colomer is 230 metres (760ft) above the sea.

Northern tip

Cala Sant Vicenç ㉖, 6 km (4 miles) north-east of Pollença, is a laid-back resort set around four beautifully clear coves beneath the jagged limestone ridge of Cavall Bernat. From here, a 45-minute walk over the hills leads to **Port de Pollença** ㉗, long the favoured resort of the British middle classes. Even in the 1920s, Gordon West found "the inevitable half-pay army man and the lonely ageing spinsters whose limited income denies them an existence in England but gives comparative luxury abroad." Perhaps this was because, in this "community of fisher folk" as he described it, "fish may be had for the asking... lobsters and crabs brought wriggling to your door, from the boats whose sails almost shadow your windows".

BELOW: relaxing on Platja de Formentor.

Port de Pollença has changed a great deal since then and is now a major tourist town in summer, though the setting remains idyllic, a horseshoe bay in an amphitheatre of mountains with pine trees leaning into the sea. A narrow road sweeps up the northern side of the bay to the **Mirador d'es Colomer**, with stunning views of plunging cliffs, seabirds and a rocky islet. A short access road then drops down through the pines to the **Platja de Formentor** ㉘, another pretty sandy beach with great mountain views.

It is also the site of Mallorca's first luxury hotel. the Hotel Formentor, opened by the Argentinian Adam Diehl in 1929 (a fact announced to the the world in flashing lights on the Eiffel Tower). It has been playing host to the great and good ever since: Charlie Chaplin, Grace Kelly and Aristotle Onassis all stayed here, and it was the venue for a EU summit in 1995.

From Formentor the road forges on through the pine forest to the end of the sierra at **Cap de Formentor**, 21 km (13 miles) from Port de Pollença. Gaze out to sea from the lonely lighthouse on the edge of the cliffs and you just might be able to see Menorca in the distance. ❏

THE PULSE OF POLLENÇA

*Refreshingly unspoiled by tourism, this tranquil old
market town has a wealth of distinctive architecture
and a beguilingly laid-back pace*

Map
on page
178

Analysing a "typical" Mallorcan town is no easy task, largely because it is almost impossible to find one which is typical. Of course, like many Mallorcan towns Pollença has broad, tree-lined roads and narrow, pavementless side-streets, where the houses give out directly onto the road and the open doorways are draped with beaded curtains. It has the great crumbling church in the *Plaça Major* or central square, where everyone meets at least once a day; it has the weekly market for traders and farmers from the *camp*. Since most Mallorcan towns have these features, Pollença may be said to be typical – but once you begin to get to know it, to stray beneath the surface a little, it becomes a special place, somewhere unique, and somewhere to return to, year after year.

Vital statistics

Pollença lies at the northern end of the island, off the main Inca road, just 7 km (4½ miles) from the bay of Pollença and its sister town of **Port de Pollença** (known locally simply as "Puerto"). It's tucked under the eastern side of Puig Tomir, a great grey mountain that seems to overhang the town to the west.

Pollença's livelihood, once purely agricultural, is now largely dominated by tourism. Tourists have brought considerable prosperity but the industry has had little or no impact on the day-to-day lives of the town's 15,000 inhabitants. They may be better off, but they don't show it, and like all island folk, they are clannish and prefer to keep to themselves. Life goes on chiefly within the family circle – although this, in Mallorca, can be a very large circle indeed.

City hub

For the people of Pollença, life centres around the **Plaça Major** , or to be precise, the little terrace outside the Café Español. From here, you can look out across the square and the rooftops to the sharp, tree-covered peak of Puig Maria, the steep-sided hill matching **El Calvari** hill which rises in the centre of the town (it can be climbed from beside the church up an endless flight of stone steps named the **Via Crucis**). In the Café Español the locals chat to their friends, sip coffee or beer, and simply wait for the day to drift by.

In this activity they are joined by summer residents, many of them long-time inhabitants with villas or flats in the surrounding countryside or in the suburb of **La Font**. Occasionally, there are passing tourists, but except on Sunday (market day in Pollença), few ever penetrate this far into the town centre. Even regular visitors can easily get lost in the inter-linked network of minor streets, most of them one-way and all of them alike. Besides, these casual visitors will speak

PRECEDING PAGES:
Pollença in its
glorious setting.
LEFT: Pollença's
harmonious skyline
includes the
baroque cathedral
bell-tower.
BELOW: a punishing
365 steps lead up
El Calvari hill.

Shops in the narrow side-streets around Pollença's Plaça Major sell locally made souvenir plates in traditional designs like these.

English or German, French or Spanish. In Pollença everyone speaks Spanish, but they prefer to speak Mallorquín.

The roots

Pollença is an old town, and like most Mallorcan towns has its own distinctive history. It retains a Roman bridge, the **Pont Romà**, as a reminder that its roots go back almost to antiquity, though some foreigners say, quietly, that the Pont Romà is simply Romanesque and was probably built by the Moors sometime in the Middle Ages. Much of central Pollença is still medieval, although a good number of buildings date from the classical period of the 17th century. Naturally, there are also new houses and villas on the outskirts – most of them erected since the 1960s.

The town was built inland, well away from its fishing-harbour at Puerto and the sea as a precaution against pirate raids, but the short distance from the coast often proved an inadequate deterrent. Turkish and Barbary corsairs raided the town at will during the 16th and 17th centuries, most noticeably in 1551, when a great raid led by the famous corsair, Dragut, was successfully driven off by the local hero, Joan Mas Ferragut.

This event is celebrated in Pollença every August at a major *festa* called the *Mare de Déu dels Angels*, when e*ls Moros i els Cristianos* (Moors and Christians) engage in mock-battle through the streets of the town for the best part of 24 hours to a backdrop of bands, processions, fireworks and explosions from fire-crackers. Those who do not join in generally try to leave town, while the dogs which usually lie panting in every scrap of shade are conspicuous by their absence. This fiesta is one of a series particular to individual Mallorcan towns.

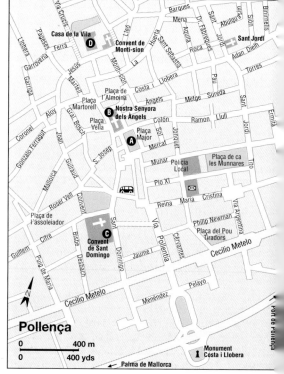

Pollença

0		400 m
0		400 yds

The streets of Pollença

Everything begins in the Plaça Major. In one corner stands the **Club Pollença**, the centre of social life during the winter months, dominated by the vast, dusty Baroque cathedral, **Nostra Senyora dels Angels** . Pollença has many religious buildings, some erected by the Jesuits, who held land here at the end of the 17th century, and others by the Dominicans, who built the **Convent de Sant Domingo** in 1578. This now houses the municipal **museum** (open 10am–1pm daily; also July–Sep: Mon–Sat 5.30–8.30pm; entrance fee).

Some of the town's finest secular buildings are the old houses along Carrer Jesús, many of which have fine carved corbels and Gothic-style pointed windows. The 18th-century **Casa de la Vila**, now the Town Hall, and the **Claustre**, the cloisters of the convent, are employed every year to stage the Pollença Music Festival. This highly successful international event first began in 1962, and has had Doña Sofia, the Queen of Spain, as its patron since 1976.

Pollença is the centre for one of Mallorca's liveliest artistic communities. Many local and international artists, musicians, and writers have homes here, while the town supports several art galleries and produces ceramics, furniture and fine textiles in various small side-street *ateliers*.

As with any other town there are plenty of smaller features worth noticing, like the famous **Gallo fountain**, crowned by a cockerel, at the foot of the stairway which climbs to El Calvari. The graceful 19th-century Via Crucis has 365 wide steps; a fairly exhausting climb gives fine views of the monastery on the top of Puig de Maria outside town. To reach Puig de Maria itself, take the signposted turning off the main road just south of town. After 3 km (1.8 miles), the lane gives way to a steep, winding cobbled footpath.

Back in town, after the obligatory stop for a refreshing beer at the Café Español, you can visit the 15th-century churches of **Roser Vell** and **Sant Jordi** (St George), or make a longer excursion to the medieval **Castell del Rei** in the Ternelles valley, two hours' walk from town. There's variety aplenty in Pollença.

Local pace

It's a fairly accurate guess that most visitors or summer residents will put off such excursions until tomorrow, or maybe until the day after that, or perhaps next year… or sometime… Instead, there is the drift into town about four o'clock to get the foreign papers from the kiosk in the *Plaça* and scan them over a cup of coffee. This is the time to chat to friends who come strolling by, and stop, and sit down. Slowly, afternoon turns into evening and another long, hot day has floated pleasantly by.

Of course, for the younger folk in this age of affluence, life is more eventful than that and more exciting than it used to be. Less inhibited, or perhaps less shy than the older people, they mix more easily with the newcomers and look forward to the annual arrival of the summer visitors, with its promise of excitement and pretty girls. Even so, everyone admits that while the summer is livelier and that's the time when the money rolls in, Pollença is much nicer in winter, when the summer people have gone. ❏

Map on page 178

TIP

You can stay in a monk's cell at the monastery on top of Puig de Maria. Contact the Ermita de Nostra Senyora del Puig in advance on 0034-971-530235.

BELOW: antique door-knocker, Carrer Jesús.

THE MALLORCAN PLAIN

Much of it is overlooked by visitors, yet the
fertile central region of Mallorca has much to offer, from
beaches and wildlife to castles and caves

Map on pages 162–3

etween the northern sierra and the south and east coasts lies the agricultural and industrial heartland of Mallorca: a fertile region of farmland known as *es pla*, the plain. Yet it is not entirely flat; the mountains of the Serra de Llevant stand guard over the east coast, while hills rise out of the central plain – some of which are crowned with historic sanctuaries.

To many people, this area is not just geographically, but visually plain; the prevailing vistas are of dusty fields and long, narrow streets with shutters closed to the outside world. The towns conform to a familiar pattern – an oversized church with a bare sandstone façade dominating a central *plaça,* with streets leading off – and most of them only really come alive on market day. This, however, is where the soul of Mallorca lies, where the traditional festivals are still celebrated with gusto and the markets more than just another excuse to take money from the tourists.

This is also the best part of Mallorca to observe the impact of the seasons. In February the plain is carpeted with the blossom of 7 million almond trees, covering the island in a layer of delicate, low-lying white cloud. Jacaranda and bougainvillea dominate in summer, joined in autumn by flowering vines. The dilapidated windmills which dot the landscape – some of which have been restored to working use – only add to the appeal.

Much of the plain remains little-visited by tourists, merely something to be glimpsed from the air-conditioned coaches which whizz visitors from the airport to the east coast resorts. In fact, there are three main routes from Palma across the plain, passing through the towns of Inca, Manacor and Llucmajor on their way down to the coast; this chapter will look at each of them in turn.

Old roads, new roads

The new motorway from Palma to Inca has relieved pressure on the old main road, the C713. From the outskirts of Palma, the road bypasses the potters' villages of Marratxí and Pòrtol on its way to **Santa Maria del Camí** ㉙. This was once the first road on the island, connecting the Roman cities of Palmaria (now Palma) and Pollentia (now Alcúdia) – hence the name of the town as "St Mary of the road", where weary travellers could find rest.

Step through the large entrance portal of the Can Conrado, a 17th-century mansion on the town's main street, and enter the peaceful cloisters of the **Convent dels Mínims**. The museum upstairs is open by appointment only; if you do manage to get in, seek out the fascinating document room, with old newspapers, marriage certificates, tax demands and a 1518 bill of sale for a 22-year-old slave called Ali.

PRECEDING PAGES: Montuïri lies at the heart of Mallorca's central plain. **LEFT:** a carpet of almond blossom covers the plain in February. **BELOW:** the cloisters, Convent dels Mínims.

If you're interested in good craft-work, give the ceramic workshop **Ceràmica Can Bernat** (Carrer Bartolomeu) a try; **Textiles Bujosa** at Carrer Bernardo de Santa Eugenia 77, on the main road back to Palma, is also worthwhile. And look out for the 17th-century fountain with a wooden water-sheel (*sini*), formerly turned by a mule with blinkers, which lies near the turn-off in the direction of Bunyola. It makes a good photo-stop.

Binissalem ㉚, 8 km (5 miles) from Santa Maria, got its name from the Moors; it means "Son of Peace". The town is at the centre of the island's wine industry, and ranks second only to Palma in the number and splendour of its historic mansions, most of them built in the 18th and 19th centuries on the profits from the wine trade. A good time to visit is on Sunday mornings, when an art and crafts market is held beneath the plane trees on the church square. The church itself, **La Asunció**, dates from the 13th century and contains a fine Madonna by Adrià Ferran; there is also a memorial in honour of the local vintners outside. Binissalem's cemetery is worth a visit, too – it's one of the oldest on the island.

The third-largest town on the island, **Inca** ㉛, is heavily promoted to tourists as "the city of leather", with a visit to a factory outlet a compulsory feature of organised coach tours. These invariably take place on Thursdays, when Inca becomes the setting for Mallorca's biggest street market. Local produce is still sold outside the market hall and the main square, Plaça d'Espanya, is taken over by flowers and plants, but most of the market is little more than a tourist trap. The presence of the ubiquitous Senegalese traders, with their cheap jewellery and "ethnic" art, suggests that these days Inca, Mallorca is not that far removed from 5th Avenue, New York or Covent Garden, London.

BELOW: Inca hosts the biggest street market in Mallorca, held every Thursday.

MALLORCA'S WINELANDS

Devastated by a *phylloxera* plague in the 1890s, Mallorca's vineyards are only now starting to recover. Today, the wine region – centred around Binissalem and its neighbouring towns of Consell and Santa Maria – covers some 600 hectares (1,480 acres) in total. **Bodega Ferrer** in Binissalem is the best-known producer; opened by José Luis Ferrer in 1931, it's now run by the third generation of his family (actually, the original *bodega* was lucky to last a year – during the first harvest, the wine tanks burst open, spilling 60,000 litres of crude wine onto Binissalem's streets!). You can visit the *bodega* (on the right as you enter the town from Palma) by prior appointment to buy and taste the wines (tel: 0034 971 511050).

Most of the production is *tinto* (red wine), based on the local Mantenegro grape with small amounts of Cabernet Sauvignon and Tempranillo. The best red wines, aged in oak, are labelled *crianza*, *reserva* and *gran reserva*. Pick of the Binissalem whites is the fruity *blanco* made by Herederos de Ribas; it makes a good accompaniment to a seafood meal. The end of September is a fine time to visit the winelands, for this is when the big wine festival known as the **Festa de sa Verema** takes place, with float-processions and oodles of free wine.

Inca is also known for its *cellers*, restaurants serving traditional Mallorcan cuisine in former wine-cellars. Ca'n Amer, beside the covered market, is one of the more adventurous and was chosen to represent Balearic cooking at the Expo 92 fair in Seville.

The parish church of **Santa Maria la Major** and its accompanying **museum** are open on Thursday mornings to coincide with the market; the museum includes a 15th-century crucifix and a large collection of altar robes. There is another small museum at the monastery of **Sant Bartomeu** (open daily, am only; donation), which the nuns will show you round on request. The monastery houses the most complete collection of the works of Llopis the Elder and Llopis the Younger, two masters of 16th-century painting in Mallorca.

Windmills and wetlands

The views from the hermitage of **Santa Magdalena ❸❷**, 6 km (4 miles) north-east of Inca at a height of 300 metres (1,000 feet), are alone worth the detour from the C713. In the distance is the spine of the *serra,* with the bay of Palma visible to the south and Pollença bay to the north. Across the plain you can see some of the 12 "new towns" which were created by Jaume II in 1300. The people of Inca still make a *romeria* (pilgrimage) to the hermitage on the first Sunday after Easter each year.

The C713 continues towards Campanet, where another short detour leads to the **Coves de Campanet** (open daily; entrance fee), the smallest and least-visited of Mallorca's underground caves. Nearby is the oratory of **Sant Miquel**, one of the few Christian churches to have been recognised before the Catalan conquest of 1229.

Map on pages 162–3

Inca's Ca'n Amer is one of Mallorca's top restaurants (cellers)*.*

BELOW: fine local produce for sale in Inca.

Junípero Serra

Miguel José Serra was born in 1713 in a humble house in Petra, Mallorca, which still exists and which is open to the public. He was baptised in the nearby parish church and began his religious studies at the Convent of San Bernadino, just across the road from his birthplace. From this constrained background – even a visit to Palma, 35 km (22 miles) away must have seemed an adventure – came the man whose statue stands today in the American Hall of Fame on the Capitol in Washington DC.

Serra was received into the order of St Francis in 1730 and changed his name to Junípero. For a time he was Professor of Theology at the Llulliana University of Mallorca. Then his application to become a missionary was granted, and he arrived at the Mexican port of Veracruz on 7 December 1749.

He spent about 18 years preaching and converting at the Mission of Sierra Gorda and in Mexico City and its dioceses, and was already 54 when he was given the task that would occupy him for the rest of his life – the task which led, in effect, to the creation of the state of California.

Britain, Spain and Russia had all become interested in the west coast of the North American continent. There had been some early exploration of territories here by Sir Francis Drake and various Spanish navigators, but it had never been consolidated. in 1768 Carlos III decreed that Spain should establish herself in the area; accordingly, the well-tried formula of the Cross of Christ and the Crown of Spain – missionaries and military working together – was once again employed. Father Serra carried the Cross, and Don Gaspar de Portolá, Governor of the Californias, and Captain Fernando Rivera y Moncada represented the Spanish Crown.

From 1769–82 nine Missions, from San Diego de Alcalá to San Francisco de Asís, were founded and established under Serra's presidency; 12 more were built after his death in 1784. But by 1822 California was part of Mexico, and both had been lost to Spain. The Crown had not triumphed but the Cross most certainly had. Today the Missions and their influence remain.

There is still a question mark over Father Serra's attitude to the Californian Indians he sought to convert. It was undoubtedly paternalistic (in both a religious and non-religious sense – they were taught simple agricultural and construction techniques as well as the Bible) and it was probably also insensitive and even cruel in that he gave little importance to the Indians' indigenous culture and beliefs and religious contexts. However, these are attitudes in missionary work which are still troublesome even today.

Serra's beatification was achieved in 1988 and owed much to the advocacy of the American Catholic Church. ❑

LEFT: statue of Junípero Serra outside the Basílica de Sant Francesc, Palma.

Map on pages 162–3

Sa Pobla ㉝, 6 km (4 miles) south-east of the caves, is variously known as the "Garden of the People" and the "Land of a Thousand Windmills". Much of the farmland here has been reclaimed from the Albufera swamps, and is now used to grow strawberries and potatoes.

Muro ㉞, a further 5 km (3 miles) south, is dominated by its Catalan-Gothic church of **Sant Joan Baptista**, with a free-standing campanile connected to the main church by a bridge. A substantial town house, Ca N'Alomar, has been converted to accommodate the **Museu Etnòlogic de Mallorca**, the ethnological section of the Museu de Mallorca in Palma. The museum houses furniture and equipment typical of a country house, together with a series of recreated blacksmith's, cobbler's and jeweller's workshops. Upstairs there is a fine collection of *siurells*, the distinctive Mallorcan toy whistles made out of plaster and fashioned into curious shapes (open Tue–Sun; closed 2–4pm and Sun pm; entrance fee).

The wetlands of **S'Albufera** (open daily; free; tel: 971 892250), between Muro and Alcúdia bay, support more than 200 species of resident and migratory birds in 800 hectares (2,000 acres) of reed and sedge marshes. In the 1860s a British firm, the New Majorca Land Company, endeavoured to drain the marshes but went bankrupt after completing 400 km (250 miles) of irrigation channels and more than 50 km (30 miles) of road. Rice was grown here in the early 20th century, and a paper-making factory existed until the 1950s; it was only in 1985, as rapid development in the bay of Alcúdia threatened the area's ecology, that S'Albufera became a protected nature reserve.

Access is from the C712 coastal road, where you are encouraged to leave your car (this is compulsory at weekends and certain times during the breeding

Sa Pobla's main church is dedicated to Sant Antoni Abat, patron saint of pets. On the saint day (10 January) each year, the town's pets are led in a procession through the streets and then ritually blessed.

BELOW: the S'Albufera marsh is a protected nature reserve.

Ramon Llull

Ramon Llull's claim to be Mallorca's most famous son is based equally on his profound scholarship and his zeal for the conversion of Arabs and Africans to the Christian faith. He studied and wrote extensively, founded a School of Oriental Studies near Valldemossa and journeyed great distances through Europe, the Middle East and Africa.

Yet for the first part of his life Ramon Llull was nothing more than a rich young man-about-town whose father held office at the court of Jaume II of Mallorca. He married and had two children, but then scandalised 13th-century Palma society by falling in love with a married woman and – so legend has it – pursuing her on horseback into Santa Eulàlia church.

It is not reliably established what caused his sudden commitment to the Church but once the decision was made he implemented it with clear-minded determination. Having decided that the conversion of infidels and unbelievers should henceforth occupy his life, he began systematically to prepare himself. He visited many holy places in Europe, spent time at the universities of Montpellier and Paris and then returned to Mallorca – to a hermitage on the Puig de Randa – to study Arabic with the help of a Moorish slave he had bought specifically for that purpose.

At the age of about 60, Llull considered himself ready for his great work and began a series of journeys to the Middle East and to Africa as far as Ethiopia and the Sudan. It is believed that on one of these missions some 20 years later, in 1315, he was stoned to death by a mob near Tunis – although more recent evidence suggests he actually died in Mallorca of old age.

It is not altogether clear from accounts of Llull's life how deep-rooted and long-lasting any of his conversion successes proved to be. What is not in doubt, however, is the range of his scholarship. His subjects included metaphysics, astronomy, physics, chemistry, anthropology, law, statecraft, warfare and horsemanship, in Latin, Catalan and Arabic. He also found time to write novels, which chart urban middle-class life in medieval Mallorca, and a book of proverbs.

Lull's tomb lies in the 14th-century church of Palma's Convent of Sant Francesc, close to the church of Santa Eulàlia which he desecrated as a young man. His imposing statue stands on a small traffic island on the Passeig Sagrera at the main entrance to Palma from its great bay.

Llull's statue properly belongs to this remarkable Mediterranean setting for he was, indeed, a remarkable man of whom Mallorca is rightly proud. Professor Allison Peers, who has studied the man's life and work, writes that: "In his own country Llull receives the simple homage of a Saint." Llull is beatified already, but sainthood is still to come. ❑

LEFT: Ramon Llull, Mallorcan polymath of the 13th century.

seasons). Inside the reserve, there is a small visitor centre and a network of footpaths and cycle trails with several bird-watching hides. Birdwatchers come here from all over Europe, but it remains a haven of quiet right on the edge of Mallorca's longest beach.

By contrast, the 9-km (6-mile) stretch of golden sand between **Port d'Alcúdia** and Can Picafort has become an ever-expanding concrete jungle of high-rise hotels, with only the dune-covered shore behind S'Albufera managing to resist the trend. Port d'Alcúdia is an example of mass tourism gone mad; one of its avenues is so dominated by foreign restaurants and fast-food joints that the locals have taken to calling it "Dollar Street".

Can Picafort ㉟, with its small marina and beachside promenade, is equally touristy but slightly more restrained. A 30-minute walk south of town, crossing the Son Bauló torrent, leads to the **Necròpolis de Son Real**, a prehistoric burial ground with tombs dating back to the 7th century BC. A second necropolis has been discovered on the **S'Illot des Porros** ("Leek Island"), just offshore.

Map
on pages
162–3

Alcúdia's medieval city walls.

Along the east coast

South of Can Picafort, the C712 continues its broad sweep around Alcúdia bay towards Artà, with side roads leading to the exclusive resorts of **Son Serra de Marina** and **Sa Colònia de Sant Pere ㊱**, with their yacht clubs and still-deserted beaches. To the north, the road ends at **Alcúdia ㊲**, where you can finally rejoin the C713 from Palma. This medieval walled town was built on the site of the old Roman capital of Pollentia ("power"), destroyed by the Vandals in the 6th century AD. Excavations into Roman Pollentia continue, but signs point the way to the **Ciutat Romania** (Roman city), where the remains of

BELOW: windsurfing in Alcúdia bay.

several houses can be seen, and the **Teatre Romà**, the only known Roman theatre in Mallorca, built in the 1st century AD. A number of finds from the excavations, including pottery, jewellery, coins and surgical instruments, are on show in the one-room **Museu Monogràfic de Pollentia** (open Tues–Sun; closed Sat–Sun pm; entrance fee) beside the parish church of **Sant Jaume**. The church also has its own museum containing religious relics and Gothic art (open Easter to Christmas: Tues–Fri am and Sun am; free). The compact old town, inside the medieval walls, is reminiscent of Palma's Arab quarter, with its heavily restored palaces and cobbled streets.

From Alcúdia, a narrow road snakes across the headland on the southern shore of Pollença bay, towards the military zone at Cap des Pinar. After 5 km (3 miles), a side road leads up to the **Ermita de la Victòria**, a fortress-like sanctuary overlooking the bay. A 15th-century wooden statue of Victoria, Alcúdia's patron saint, is kept inside the church; each July, residents of the town make a *romeria* (pilgrimage) to her shrine. The views from the terrace of the restaurant above the hermitage are some of the finest in Mallorca.

The central plain

The main road across the centre of the island is the C715, which traverses the plain on its way from Palma to Manacor. After 20 km (12 miles) it reaches **Algaida ⊕**, and one of Mallorca's strangest tourist attractions: the **Can Gordiola** glass museum and factory, housed in a mock castle (open daily; closed Sun pm; free). Gordiola blown glass, coloured a distinctive pale blue and green, has been manufactured in Mallorca since 1719, building on a tradition which dates back to Roman times. You can watch it being made in the open-plan work-

Gordiola blown glass has been manufactured by the same family firm in Algaida since 1719.

BELOW: Alcúdia's Roman theatre dates from the 1st century AD.
BELOW RIGHT: at work in the glass factory at Gordiola.

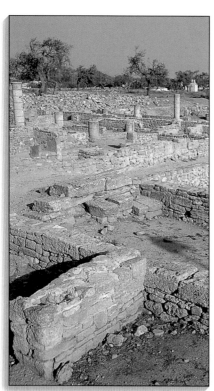

shop; if you like what you see, there's plenty for sale in the showroom next door.

Just outside Algaida on the C715 are several old-fashioned restaurants known for their traditional Mallorcan cuisine. This is where the people of Palma come for Sunday lunches of roast suckling pig, washed down with the local red wine. **Montuïri** 🕙, 8 km (5 miles) further on, is easily recognised by its old stone windmills, climbing up the hillside on the edge of the village. The inhabitants of Montuïri cling solidly to local traditions such as the Easter Sunday procession, the "song to the Easter pies", and the *cossiers* dances, performed to the accompaniment of flutes and bagpipes at the Sant Bartomeu fiesta on 24 August.

North of Montuïri are several small towns and villages (including Santa Eugènia and Sencelles) where life goes on almost untouched by tourism. Here you can still find carpenters and stonemasons, *xeremiers* (bagpipe-makers) and chair-stringers, farmhands and vineyard owners, and a genuine sense of village identity. Increasingly, though, as work opportunities in the countryside decline, the houses in this area are becoming second homes for the people of Palma – and beyond. The tiny hamlet of **Ses Alqueries** 🕙, near Santa Eugènia, has just 40 residents, mostly foreigners who have restored its older houses with care. There are no shops, no cafés and no video library, and as the locals move out for the want of such facilities, the foreigners eagerly move in for the lack of them.

A royal road

Costitx, 5 km (3 miles) east of Sencelles, has been given a new lease of life by the opening of Mallorca's first astronomic observatory in 1991 (visits by appointment only; tel: 971 876019). Also in Costitx, the **Casa de la Fauna Ibero-Balear** is a natural history museum created by an amateur taxidermist,

Map on pages 162–3

TIP

Montuïri's 17th-century church of Santa Maria has a magnificent interior, including a 16th-century retable by the Valencian painter Mateu Llopis.

BELOW: fertile agricultural lands of the central plain.

Francisco Ruiz Bort. The museum contains examples of almost all Mallorca's native species and would be a good place to visit before going birdwatching in the S'Albufera marshes (open Tues–Fri am; also 2nd and 4th Sat and Sun of each month; entrance fee; tel: 971 876070).

Although there is evidence of Talayotic, Roman and Arab settlements in the area, the modern town of **Sineu** ⏏, 7 km (4 miles) south-east of Costitx, was founded by Jaume II in 1309, when he built a royal palace – now a convent – on the foundations of a Muslim *alcàsser*. It was his successor, King Sanç, who declared Sineu to be the centre of Mallorca, establishing the town as his rural headquarters and strengthening the *camí vell de Sineu*, the "royal road" between Sineu and Palma. Nowadays Sineu is best known for its weekly market, held on Wednesdays and the only one on the island where livestock are still traded. Afterwards, farmers gather in the town's celebrated cellar restaurants for plate-fuls of *frit de porcella*, a fry-up of vegetables, potatoes and pork innards.

The parish church of **Santa Maria** is open on market days; its small museum (donation expected) contains a collection of ceramic bowls, discovered during extension work to the church in the late 19th century. Also in Sineu, **s'Estació** is an offbeat contemporary art gallery based in the old railway station, with a small permanent collection and a changing programme of exhibitions (open Mon-Sat; closed 1–4pm and Sat pm; free).

The plaque from the Museu de Junípero Serra in Sineu, which commemorates the Mallorcan missionary who helped found the state of California.

Famous son

The road from Sineu to **Petra** ⏢, criss-crossed by the old railway track from Inca, threads its way through a cultivated valley of almond and apricot groves. Petra, 10 km (6 miles) south-east of Sineu, is a small town with a big claim to fame. This was the birthplace of Fray Junípero Serra, the Mallorcan missionary who founded the Californian missions which grew into the cities of San Diego, San Francisco and Los Angeles (*see page 186*); his statue stands in the main square.

Serra's birthplace in Carrer Barracar Alt has been conserved much as it would have been in the 18th century (open daily; free). To get into the **Museu Junípero Serra** in the same street, follow the directions to the keyholder's house; the museum contains models of his various missions and memorabilia of his life and work (open daily; donation expected; tel: 971 561149). A series of ceramic plaques depicting Serra baptising native Indians lead from here to the convent of Sant Bernardí (open Mon-Sat; closed 1–4pm; free), where Serra first studied.

Serra preached his final sermon in Mallorca at the **Ermita de Bonany**, 4 km (2½ miles) above Petra. According to legend, the villagers of Petra made the pilgrimage up here in 1609 to pray for rain; when two years of drought were followed by an abundant harvest, they named their chapel *bon any* ("good year"). The present church dates from 1925; there is a simple hostelry attached where you can spend the night in a whitewashed cell. The views from the terrace extend right across the plain.

Sant Joan, 6 km (4 miles) southwest of Petra, is a pig-farming village famed for its traditional sausages, celebrated each October in an annual sausage festival. Just outside Sant Joan is **Els Calderers**, an 18th-century manor house filled with period furnishings and family portraits as well as a collection of 19th-century toys (open daily; entrance fee; tel: 971 526069). The house is reached from Vilafranca de Bonany, a small town where strings of sun-dried tomatoes, garlic and peppers hang from the shopfronts along the main road.

Artà Peninsula

Now you are back on the C715. **Manacor** ⓭, 10 km (6 miles) east, is Mallorca's second city and the nearest the island has to an industrial town. There is really only one reason for stopping here: pearls. The prinicipal manufacturer is the world-famous **Majorica**, whose factory and showroom is signposted from the main road. Simulated pearls are not cheap – they are a high-quality product, with prices to match – but they last for ever and are impossible to distinguish from the real thing. At the peak of the tourist season, thousands of people visit the factory every day. The perfunctory tour is easily missable and gives away few of the secrets of pearl manufacture, said to be based on powdered fish scale.

The C715 swings north to **Artà** ⓮, a hilltop town on the site of a Moorish fortress. A long avenue of cypress trees leads from the Catalan-Gothic bulk of the church of **Transfiguració del Senyor** to the sanctuary of **Sant Salvador**. Inside the chapel is a portrait of Ramon Llull being stoned to death by a Muslim mob in Tunisia – although there is now some doubt as to whether this actually took place (*see page 188*).

Just outside Artà, the Talayotic settlement at **Ses Països** is entered through a massive stone portal, built into a Cyclopean wall (open Mon–Sat; closed

TIP

Perlas Majorica is Manacor's largest pearl manufacturer. The factory is open for tours on weekdays from 9am–1pm, then 3–7pm, and on Sat– Sun from 10am–1pm.

BELOW: Sineu, now a serene country backwater, was once a royal town.

The medieval fortress of Capdepera was built by Mallorca's King Sanç as a protection against pirates.

1–3pm and Sat pm; entrance fee). A number of the archaeological finds from Ses Països are on show in the **Museu Regional d'Artà** in the town centre (open Mon–Fri am; entrance fee).

The crenellated walls and towers of the medieval fortress at **Capdepera**, 8 km (5 miles) east of Artà, are visible from afar. The castle battlements (open daily; entrance fee) offer good views of **Cala Ratjada ㊺**, Mallorca's easternmost town and a crowded resort in summer. There are several good beaches and coves both north and south of here; the area is particularly popular with water-sports enthusiasts. Above the resort, set among hibiscus bushes, are the **Jardins Casa March**, the grounds of the former country home of one of Mallorca's richest sons, the banker Joan March. The gardens contain modern sculpture by Rodin and Henry Moore among others, and can only be visited by prior arrangement with the tourist office (tel: 971 563033; *see also pages 204–205*).

Coastal caves

The large beach at **Canyamel**, 8 km (5 miles) south of Capdepera, is set in an attractive bay backed by high cliffs. Just above the bay, the **Coves d'Artà** are the most spectacular of the various limestone caves along this eastern seaboard. During his 13th-century conquest of Mallorca, Jaume I found 2,000 Arabs hiding inside them with their cattle. Rediscovered by the French geologist, Edouard Martel, in 1876 at the instigation of Archduke Ludwig Salvator, the caves are said to have inspired Jules Verne to write *Journey to the Centre of the Earth*; one of the stalagmites is a full 22 metres (70 ft) tall.

BELOW:
exotic lighting in the Artà caves.

The guided tour lasts about an hour and comes complete with sound and light effects to illustrate the caves' more unusual features. Some of the paths can

be slippery, so wear sensible shoes (open daily; entrance fee; tel: 971 841293).

Mass tourism rears its ugly head at **Cala Millor** ⊕ ("the better bay"), where a magnificent 1.8-km (1-mile) stretch of sand is backed by hotels, restaurants and bars. **Cala Bona** ("the good bay"), to the north, is more restrained, set around a small fishing harbour. From Cala Millor, a 30-minute walk leads to the headland at **Punta de N'Amer**, a haven of peace in a ribbon of over-development. There is a small bar beside the 17th-century watchtower at the summit.

South of Cala Millor, the coast road passes the drive-through **Safari-Zoo** (open daily; entrance fee) on its way to **Porto Cristo** ⊕, an ancient fishing port and now a family resort which was the site of Mallorca's only Civil War action. The Republican battleship *Jaime I* landed 12,000 men here in August 1936; they took the town and advanced 10 km (6 miles) inland but were driven back by the Nationalists, aided by Italian warplanes based near Palma.

Crowds of summer visitors are attracted to the **Coves del Drac** (Dragon Caves), where the visit includes a boat trip across Lake Martel, Europe's largest underground lake (open daily; entrance fee; tel: 971 820753). Mallorca's small **aquarium** (open daily; entrance fee) is nearby, and there are more caves on the outskirts of town at **Coves dels Hams** (open daily; entrance fee). From here it is another 10 km (6 miles) to return to Manacor and the C715 to Palma.

The south-eastern route

The third route out of Palma, the C717, runs south-east towards the shoemakers' town of **Llucmajor** ⊕, site of the 1349 battle in which Jaume III died at the hands of Pedro IV of Aragón, bringing to an end the short-lived kingdom of Mallorca. The beginnings of Mallorcan history are visible at **Capocorb Vell**, 13 km (8 miles) south of Llucmajor on the road to Cap Blanc. This lonely, romantic spot contains five Bronze Age talayots (circular stone watchtowers) and the walled outlines of an ancient village.

North of Llucmajor, **Puig de Randa** is, at 543 metres (1,780 ft), the highest point on the Mallorcan plain. This is where Ramon Llull retired, chastened (so legend has it) by a failed seduction attempt, to found his first hermitage in the late 13th century. In total, there are three monasteries on the mountainside; the **Santuari de Cura**, where Llull lived, is at the summit, beneath a forest of radio masts. The 16th-century grammar school here contains a collection of Llull memorabilia, and from the terrace there are views as far as the island of Cabrera.

A country lane from Llucmajor leads through the apricot groves to the workaday town of **Porreres**, 13 km (8 miles) away. The town hall here contains a small **art gallery**, open on Tuesday mornings to coincide with the weekly market; among the mostly modern works are two by Salvador Dalí, both hanging in the council chamber. Just outside the town is the **Santuari de Montesió**, a hilltop sanctuary with a five-sided cloister and great views out to sea.

Campos ⊕, 13 km (8 miles) from Llucmajor on the C717, was founded by Jaume II in 1300 on the site of a Roman settlement; according to legend there are still several Roman ships lying on the sea-bed off

Map on pages 162–3

Randa produces one of the island's most potent liqueurs.

BELOW: sleepy Porto Cristo waterfront.

Map
on pages
162–3

the coast here. Campos today is a pleasant, if uninspiring place, at the centre of an agricultural district filled with wind-machines scooping up water for irrigation. Worth a visit, though, is the town's church of **Sant Julià**, originally built in 1248 although the present structure dates only from the 19th century. Inside is the famous painting of **Sant Crist de la Paciència** by the 17th-century Sevillian artist, Bartolomé Murillo. Permission to visit the church and its small museum must be obtained from the nearby *rectoria*.

The town's port, **Colònia de Sant Jordi** (where boats leave for Cabrera), lies some 14 km (9 miles) to the south, a mass of hotels and apartment complexes. Just inland from here are the **Salines de Llevant**, an area of saltpans known for its migratory birds, and the **Banys de Sant Joan**, a thermal spa whose hot waters are used to treat rheumatism and arthritis. A side road leads down to the sea at Ses Covetes, from where you can walk onto the long **Platja ses Covetes**, a perfect, unspoiled beach of white sand and wild dunes. The name means "small caves", and refers to the numerous caverns in the area, used by the Romans as burial-chambers.

Coves and crosses

BELOW: threshing machinery and tools at the Santuari de Sant Salvador.
RIGHT: windmills are a common sight on the central plain.

Northeast of Campos, the C714 leads to **Felanitx**, dominated by the huge Baroque church of Sant Miquel, poised majestically above a long flight of stone steps. Felanitx has a reputation for producing the best brains in Mallorca, and certainly a long list of island politicians, writers, architects and intellectuals are proud Felanitxers; it was also the birthplace of Miquel Barceló, the Mallorcan artist who became the darling of the New York art world in the 1980s (*see also Miró on Mallorca, pages 156–57*).

High above the town, at the summit of the Serra de Llevant (500 metres/1,650 ft), the **Santuari de Sant Salvador** looks down over the Mallorcan plain. This is the grandest of Mallorca's hilltop hermitages, flanked by a huge stone cross and a massive statue of Christ, both visible for miles around. The monastery church contains a fine 16th-century alabaster retable; there are also 13 spartan cells here in which pilgrims and visitors can be accommodated.

East of Felanitx, the coast is studded with tiny *cales* (coves), each with their own character: Both **Porto Colom** and **Porto Petro** retain a fishing-village atmosphere, while **Cala d'Or** is all champagne and expensive yachts. The white-washed, flat-roofed holiday apartments and hotels here are in the cube-shaped Ibizan style; the oldest date from the 1930s and were designed by the architect Pep Costa Ferrer. **Cales de Mallorca** has been blighted by insensitive hotel developments, but pretty **Cala Mondragó**, south of Cala d'Or, is definitely worth the detour, with a pair of sandy beaches on the edge of a nature reserve.

From the town of Santanyí, where the C717 runs out, a minor road drops down to the sea at **Cala Figuera ㊿**. Whitewashed cottages reach down to the water's edge; waterfront restaurants serve up sublime seafood. During the long summer evenings, fishermen sit on the steps mending nets. Sit here and remind yourself: this is what you came to Mallorca for. ❑

Map on pages 162–3

CABRERA

*The fifth Balearic island, which is now
almost entirely uninhabited, is a haven for wildlife. Its
diminutive size belies an eventful history*

The designation of **Cabrera** ❺ as a national park in 1991 opened a new chapter in the history of this rocky archipelago, lying just 10 km (6 miles) off Mallorca's south-east coast. The islets that sheltered Barbary pirates and became a death-camp for Napoleonic soldiers are now protected for future generations as one of the last remaining wilderness areas in the Mediterranean.

Until the beginning of the 19th century, the history of Cabrera and the islets surrounding it had been much like that of any other Mediterranean island lying in the shade of a much larger neighbour. In good years the island was occupied by various generations of farmers, who cultivated its fields and shepherded flocks of goats and sheep. Fishermen came to its fertile waters to fill their nets. It also served as a base for pirates planning raids on Mallorca, and for those trying to protect her coasts, lying such a scant few kilometres to the north.

Prison island

The early years of the 19th century were difficult ones in Europe. Napoleon marched towards the four corners of the continent followed by a proud army, but they were unprepared for the humiliation of their first full-scale defeat by the Spanish at the Battle of Bailén.

In 1808, thousands of defeated soldiers were confined in eight prison ships anchored in the bay of Cádiz. Weakened by disease and threatened by a hostile local population, plans were made to transfer them to a safer keep. The original idea was to send them to Mallorca, but the island had no facility for such a large contingent of officers and men. A year later, they stepped ashore onto tiny, uninhabited Cabrera.

What actually happened to "Prisionier N130", who carved his inscription high on the castle wall, and his 9,000 companions will probably never be truly known. But we do know that when they arrived on this harsh island, their first inventory must have been no more than a short list of one or two ploughed fields, a small pine forest, a few goats and fig trees, a well with little water and a ruined 14th-century castle.

The castle became the centre of their first improvised camp. At first, no one thought of Cabrera as being more than a short-term stay; Charles Frossard, an imprisoned officer, tells how "we lived in grottos and caverns" until crude barracks were erected.

Rats for tea

The soldiers' plans looked ahead only as far as the next provision boat, which arrived from Mallorca every four days carrying sparse rations. Rats as well as robbers made it necessary to distribute the rations immediately. As was to be expected, the hungry

PRECEDING PAGES:
Platja L'Olla,
Cabrera.
LEFT: Cabrera's
14th-century castle,
a former prison.
BELOW: a perfect
approach to the
island.

The island's bleak scrubland is home to a surprisingly rich wildlife.

soldiers ate the meagre food supply of a pound of bad bread, a quarter-ounce of beans and half an ounce of oil within hours of its arrival. The officers fared better with an additional half-pound of goat meat and a quart of wine.

An account by chronicler Abate Turquet tells of how, in the desperation for food, "a mouse could be bought for seven or eight beans, a rat for 25 or 30." With poor rations and almost no water, wrote Charles Frossard, "sickness became the biggest enemy. We hoped for a remedy (by drinking) salt water. But the cure is worse than the disease, and those who drink it die quicker."

In May 1814, five years after they arrived, the 3,600 survivors were taken by boat to the south coast of France. Most of them remained in Marseilles until their deaths, unwanted by a French government embarrassed both by its debacle at Bailén and its own lack of care. Thirty years later a monument was erected on a hillside overlooking the port of Cabrera, in remembrance of the 5,000-odd prisoners who never returned. It reads: "*A la memoire des Français Morts à Cabrera*" and is signed "His Royal Highness the Prince of Joinville".

Wilderness status

The tragedy of the Cabrera prisoners has been all but forgotten in debates over the island's more recent history. In 1916 the archipelago was expropriated by the Spanish government and converted into a garrison. During the Civil War, it served as a bleak place of exile for Franco's opponents. But it was a series of military manoeuvres – using live ammunition – during the 1970s and 1980s which led to repeated calls for the army to abandon the islands. The campaign was backed by the Balearic government, and in April 1991 the Spanish parliament declared Cabrera a national park.

BELOW:
Port de Cabrera.

A handful of soldiers remain on Cabrera, but these days they are outnumbered by park wardens and day-trippers. A tour boat leaves from Mallorca's Colònia de Sant Jordi every day in summer, giving visitors time to swim, snorkel and hike up to the castle above the port. A museum has opened inside an old wine cellar, not far from the monument to the French prisoners. There is also a two-hour walk to the **lighthouse** on the N'Ensiola peninsula, at the island's south-west tip, or you can climb to **La Miranda** for distant views of Mallorca.

Map on pages 162–3

Isolated rarities

Cabrera is a small island, measuring less than 7 km by 5 km (4 miles by 3 miles) and only 170 metres (560 ft) at its highest point. Geologically, it is an extension of Mallorca's Serra de Llevant, an outcrop of submerged mountains with their peaks rising out of the sea. The dominant vegetation is maquis, or thick scrub-land, with large numbers of wild olives as well as juniper and giant fennel. Since the demise of farming in the 1950s, the pine forests have grown in size and wild flowers, including bee orchids, asphodels and Balearic peonies, have taken over once more.

The unpolluted skies over Cabrera attract such bird species as peregrine and Eleanora's falcons; both types, as well as ospreys, build their nests on the cliffs. Migrating seabirds include Cory's and Manx shearwaters, storm petrels and an important colony of Audouin's gulls. Four-fifths of the world population of Balearic lizards live on Cabrera, including a number of sub-species that are not known to exist anywhere else; their survival is due to the absence of snakes and other predators which have wiped out the population on Mallorca.

Thanks to restrictions on commercial fishing, the waters around Cabrera teem with marine life. The concentration of grouper and red mullet is far greater than anywhere else in the Balearics, and there are a number of crustacean species not seen elsewhere. Dolphins and sea turtles swim just off the coast, while biologists continue to search for traces of the Mediterranean monk seal, once common around Cabrera but not seen for 50 years. Elsewhere in the Mediterranean the seal is threatened with extinction, and there is a long-term proposal to reintroduce it to Cabrera.

According to Pliny, Cabrera was the birthplace of the legendary Carthaginian general, Hannibal.

BELOW: wild flowers flourish on Cabrera.

Out of bounds

Visitor numbers are strictly controlled to prevent dam-age to the archipelago's fragile wildlife. All fishing for sport is prohibited, and scuba-divers must have a permit from the park authorities. Overnight stays on Cabrera are not allowed, while the smaller islands remain totally out of bounds to visitors. Anyone arriv-ing on a private boat needs to obtain permission before attempting to moor, and in high summer this permission will be granted for only one night.

The authorities are well aware that there is a potential conflict between the two aims of the national park: conservation, and public access and enjoyment. In one sense, the Mallorcans have finally regained their little island from the military. It must now be hoped that Cabrera's delicate ecosystem can survive the influx of tourists. ❑

TRADITIONAL GARDENS ON MALLORCA

Rooted in the island's three centuries of Moorish rule, the history of the Mallorcan garden has now passed its 1,000th birthday

Traditionally, Mallorca's Arab gardens combined a flower garden, made up of native plants, with a vegetable garden and an orchard. Reservoirs were another important feature, included for both decorative and productive purposes. Although the Christian conquerors who arrived in the 12th century moved swiftly to destroy much of the island's Muslim heritage, they recognised the value and simple beauty of these ornamental gardens. Many of them, including the ones at Raixa and La Granja (*above*), were consequently handed out among Jaume I's followers in reward for their services during the conquest. They continued to be developed in Hispano-Arab style until well into the 17th century.

During the 1700s, the aristocracy began to desert their country estates in favour of settling in Palma. The *finca* became less a way of life and more a symbol of prestige and wealth; as a result, many of the gardens were redesigned according to the latest European fashions, in baroque or neo-classical style. The Italianate staircase at Raixa (*see page 171*) is perhaps the grand-est example from this period.

The combination of natural and man-made beauty in Mallorca's gardens still makes them marvellous places in which to relax, even today.

▷ **SON MARROIG**
This white marble rotunda, imported from Italy, is the centrepiece of Archduke Ludwig Salvator's Romantic 19th-century garden near Deià.
(*See pages 168–9.*)

▷ **A JAR OF OLIVES**
The Moorish gardens at Alfàbia (the name means "jar of olives" in Arabic) were redesigned in baroque style in the 18th century. Its most notable feature is an unusual pergola of spraying water.

△ **LIGHT AND SHADE**
Palm trees soar above the gardens at Alfàbia, a sign of their Arab origins. These lush gardens also contain orange and lemon trees as well as lily ponds, jasmine and honeysuckle.

▽ **LA GRANJA**
The country house at La Granja, near Esporles, began as a Cistercian monastery and is now a museum of rural life. The Romantic garden here is one of the island's finest.

SCULPTURE GARDENS

The modern sculptures in the S'Hort del Rei gardens in Palma (*above*) continue a long Mediterranean tradition of embellishing the natural landscape with art. Mallorca's best-known example used to be the fine collection of classical statues that was gathered by the Cardinal Antoni Despuig to adorn his Italianate garden at Raixa in the 18th century – sadly, these have now been moved to the Bellver Castle museum in Palma, but the gardens are still very much worth visiting.

More recently, the banker Joan March assembled a superb collection of modern sculpture in his garden at Cala Ratjada, including works by Rodin, Henry Moore and Barbara Hepworth. You can visit by arrangement with the local tourist office, or for one of the classical concerts held here in summer.

◁ THE KING'S GARDEN
The former royal gardens beneath the Almudaina palace, restored in the 1960s, are a popular lunchtime retreat for the people of Palma.

▷ BOUGAINVILLAEA
Brightening gardens all over the Med, this was first imported from Brazil by a French explorer, Louis de Bougainville.

MENORCA

A detailed guide to the island, with principal sites cross-referenced by number to the maps

The Spanish have a partiality for christening their tourist areas with catchy names. Menorca is commonly known as the *isla verde y azul* ("green and blue island"), although the locals know it as the windy isle. Unlike bold and brash Mallorca 34 km (21 miles) to the southwest (and visible on a clear day), Menorca is understated both in its landscape and its people.

Indeed, the island has a quite unfounded reputation among Mallorcans for being dull (by way of retaliation Menorcans have their own saying: *Mallorquí – lladre fi* – "a Mallorcan is an elegant thief"). The truth is not that the island is wrong for the people who visit it, but that visitors' expectations may be wrong for the island. If you're looking for lively Ibizan-style nightlife, for example, you will be disapppointed. Instead, Menorca's low-key resorts with their pristine coves and bays make it ideal territory for family holidays.

The main highway which bisects the island from north to south also provides a geological dividing line. In the north, the island is mainly sandstone, with a barren coast exposed to the frequent tempestuous winds blowing in off the Golfe du Lion. To the south, limestone predominates, sliced into beautiful, sheltered coves and inlets at the coast.

This means that the landscape, too, requires a patient eye. The over-hasty will miss the subtle changes from red-soiled stone-walled agricultural land to gently undulating forests, from barren *macchia* reminiscent of Scotland to pine woods smelling like Switzerland.

Away from the urban areas and the coastal resorts, lonely baronial *fincas* dominate the landscape, but despite the atmosphere of mild decay, residents here enjoy one of the highest levels of income in Spain, and prices can be surprisingly high. The Menorcans prefer quality to quantity. ❏

PRECEDING PAGES: Menorcan folk-dancers celebrate the spring; Georgian façade in the British-built Es Castell.
LEFT: pretty Cala Morell, northeast of Ciutadella.

MAÓ AND EASTERN MENORCA

Maps:
Area 214
City 217

The island is greener and flatter than its larger neighbour, and less developed. This is where you'll find historic ports, pristine coves and beaches, and a wealth of prehistoric remains

I f Mallorca is the biggest and eldest of the Balearic brothers, and Ibiza the youngest and trendiest, then Menorca is the quiet one in the middle who actually proves rather interesting when you draw him into conversation. The island has been likened to an open-air museum, thanks to its huge concentration of megalithic monuments – many of which have been discovered by farmers turning over their soil. In most cases these *talaiots* and *taules* still stand, unannounced and unadorned, in the middle of farmland; an evocative link between the present and the roots of Balearic history.

Just 48 km (30 miles) long and an average of 16 km (10 miles) wide, Menorca is a gently sloped plateau stitched together with dry-stone walls. Slightly cooler and wetter than its larger neighbour, in winter it is scarred by the chilling *tramuntana* wind, whipped up in the snowy peaks of the Pyrenees. The north coast, where the wind strikes, is jagged and barren, carved by deep inlets; the milder south coast, meanwhile, is dotted with coves and the island's main beaches.

LEFT: festivities in Maó's Plaça Constitució.
BELOW: copper gin-still at Maó's Xoriguer distillery.

Tourism here is on a human scale, with few high-rise resorts and many of the best beaches accessible only on foot. Menorca is less dependent on tourism than its neighbours; dairy farming is still an important industry, along with the manufacture of shoes, gin, cheese and ice-cream. This economic diversity has been enhanced by Menorca's status as a UNESCO biosphere reserve, with the aim of sustained tourism development within a framework of conservation and support for local industry.

Even so, Menorca has not been immune from the Balearics' tourist explosion. In 1950, the island had just 200 hotel beds; now there are 40,000, and almost a million visitors a year. Perhaps as a result of the island's colonial history, the majority of these visitors are British.

Island capital

Maó ❶, the Menorcan capital – still widely referred to by its Spanish name, Mahón – has always been at the centre of the island's turbulent history. Its long, deep harbour has provided protection for the city's rulers, but also borne the brunt of numerous invasions. The result is a city whose influence is greater than its size. Maó has given its name to a cheese (*queso de Mahón*, one of Spain's finest cheeses, ironically no longer produced in the city) and to a sauce (*salsa mahonesa*, or mayonnaise), but at heart it remains a provincial town of some 24,000 people, with a reputation for serious-minded intellectualism in contrast to the flamboyance of Ciutadella.

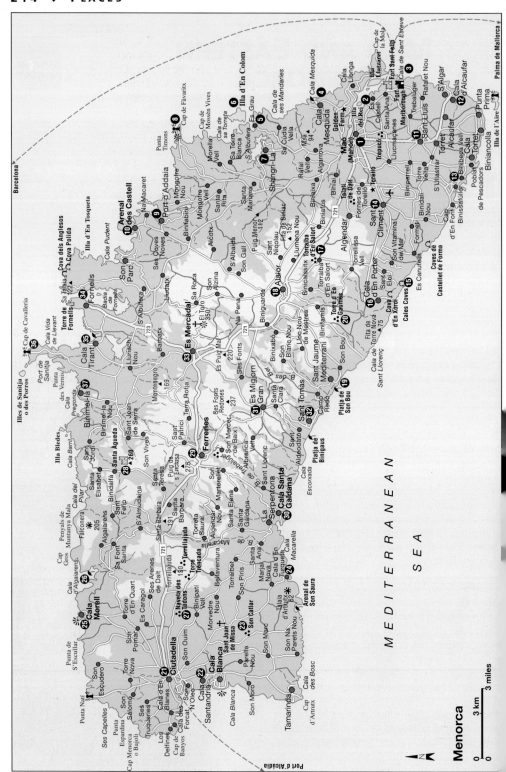

Menorca

Most people arrive in Maó at **Plaça de s'Esplanada** , the terminus for the island-wide network of buses. This former parade-ground is the city's main meeting point, the setting for markets, fiestas and the early evening *passeig*. Old men play bowls beneath the palm trees while children have fun on the nearby swings. The obelisk in front of the old British barracks honours the victims of the Spanish Civil War.

Just behind the square in Carrer Cifuentes, the **Ateneu de Maó** is the focus of Maó's intellectual life. This scientific, literary and artistic association was founded in 1905 and continues to keep alive the tradition of scholarship on the island. The small museum contains watercolours of 18th-century Maó, as well as a collection of paintings by Joan Vives Llull (1901–1982). The natural history section is so comprehensive that an old folk song relates: "Maó has three things that no other town has; a good port, beautiful women and even Noah's ark" (open Mon–Sat; closed 1–4pm; free).

City of culture

Carrer ses Moreres (also known as Carrer Dr Orfila) is the main street connecting Plaça de s'Esplanada with the heart of the old town. A bust of Mateu Orfila (1787–1853), the founder of forensic medicine, stands outside No. 13, the house where he was born. At the foot of this street, and a few metres to the right in Costa de Deià, is the city's opera house, **Teatre Principal** . This was the first opera house in Spain when it opened in 1829; for many years it was chosen by the leading Italian companies as the opening venue for their Spanish tours. After decades of neglect, it is being restored to its former glory and will once again soon be hosting Maó's spring opera seasons.

Map on page 217

BELOW: sun-bathed Maó harbour.

Carrer ses Moreres leads into Carrer Hannover, Maó's smartest shopping street. The name dates from the period of British rule when Menorca had close links with the Hanoverian dynasty, and houses on the street clearly belie the British influence, with their brass door-knockers and elegant bow windows (*boinders* in Menorquín). The boutiques here and in the other pedestrian streets nearby are a good place to shop for Menorcan leather shoes and bags.

Prehistoric artifacts in the Museu de Menorca in Maó.

At the foot of Carrer Hannover, Plaça Constitució is dominated by the barn-like church of **Santa Maria** Ⓒ, founded by Alfons III in 1287 after the Catalan conquest of Menorca. The present, neoclassical structure dates from the 18th century. The massive organ, built in 1810, was shipped from Barcelona during the Napoleonic wars under the protection of the British Navy. Organ recitals are held here every morning except Sundays in summer, and the Chinese symphony orchestra performed in this church on their first ever visit to the West.

In the same square is the **Ajuntament** Ⓓ, or Town Hall, with the clock presented by the much-loved British governor Sir Richard Kane mounted in its façade. You can wander inside during office hours, to see the portraits of former governors on the walls and a stone tablet from the 1st century AD (which confirming that Maó was a Roman settlement).

Opposite the town hall, Carrer Sant Roc leads to **Port de Sant Roc**, the only remaining section of the medieval city walls.

A blend of styles

Carrer Isabel II, beyond the town hall, is lined with grand 18th-century houses, built in the Georgian style with fanlights, sash windows and wrought-iron balustrades. The street ends at the monastery church of Sant Francesc, whose cloisters have been converted to house the **Museu de Menorca** Ⓔ, with archaeological finds from the island's many Bronze Age sites (open Tues–Sun; closed 1.30–5pm, Sat–Sun pm; entrance fee). The church itself is a curious blend of late Gothic and Churrigueresque (Spanish Baroque), the latter style seen to most spectacular effect in the florid chapel of the Immaculate Conception. From the terrace outside the church there are good views over Maó harbour.

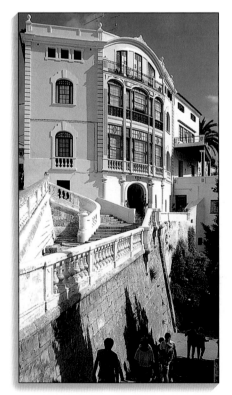

There are more harbour views from Pont des Castell, a narrow alley beside Plaça Conquesta. The statue at the centre of the square commemorates Alfons III, the young king who drove the Moors out of Menorca at the tender age of 21. From here, Plaça d'Espanya leads into Plaça del Carme, and the bare stone walls of the **Església del Carme** Ⓕ, begun as a Carmelite convent in 1751 but heavily restored in 1941 after the Civil War. The cloisters have been extensively remodelled to house the city's covered market, with fruit and vegetable stalls beneath the whitewashed arches. Also in the cloisters, the **Collecció Hernández Mora** Ⓖ displays the permanent archives of a local historian and author who left his entire collection of island maps to the city of Maó (open Mon–Sat am; entrance fee).

The busy fish market, **Mercat del Peix** Ⓗ, occupies a circular building in nearby Plaça d'Espanya; from here, steps leads down to the waterfront.

Undoubtedly the best way to approach Maó is from the sea, sailing into the harbour where the city occupies a commanding position on the cliffs. Maó was built around its harbour, the second-largest natural port in the world. Castles have been built and demolished at its mouth, where the La Mola promontory, Spain's easternmost point, still houses a military base.

"The tides affect it very inconsiderably, as they observe no regularity, ebbing and flowing a foot or two, as they are influenced by the wind. The land on the north side is extremely barren... the south side assumes a better aspect, being in a good state of cultivation." Thus wrote the cartographer to the British Admiralty in 1813. On the town side the harbour is very deep, shelving to shallow water on the far, northern shore, where millionaire celebrities have their villas. There is an oft-quoted but little understood 16th-century rhyme praising Maó, attributed to the Genoese admiral Andrea Doria: "*Junio, julio, agosto y Mahón, los mejores puertos del Mediterráneo son.*" Roughly translated, it means that the safest place to moor outside the summer months of June, July and August, is in the port at Maó.

Around the harbour

In summer, glass-bottomed boat tours of the harbour depart regularly from Maó and Es Castell, passing three small islands on their way to the harbour mouth. The first, **Illa del Rei**, was used as a bridgehead by Alfons III for his conquest of the city in 1287. The ruins of a 6th-century church have been discovered here; there are also the remains of an 18th-century British military hospital, which gave the island the popular name of Bloody Island. Further out is **Illa Plana**, a former quarantine island, and finally **Illa Llatzaret**, the largest of the

Map below

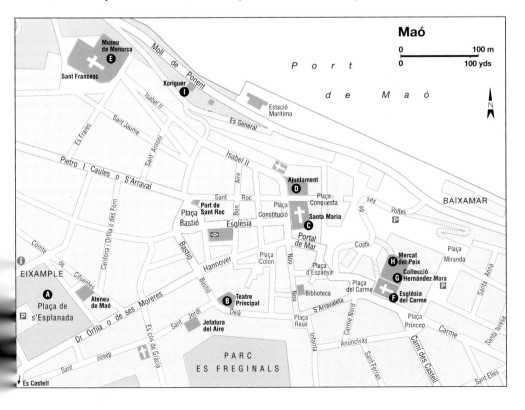

Gin has been produced on Menorca for over 200 years and is now famous all over the world.

three, which was separated from the mainland in 1900. Llatzaret was the site of an isolation hospital for infectious diseases, including leprosy; the tall, double-thick walls around the island were designed – somewhat optimistically – to prevent germs from being carried by the wind down to Maó. Nowadays the island is used as a holiday centre by employees of the Spanish health service.

Beside the water's edge, close to the harbour steps, the **Xoriguer distillery ❶** turns out gin and various gin-based liqueurs from old-fashioned copper stills. Gin has been produced on Menorca since the late 18th century, but its popularity with British sailors certainly helped to ensure its survival. Visitors are encouraged to taste and buy; the gin-and-lemonade mix, *pomada*, a Menorcan version of gin-and-tonic, is more palatable than many of the herbal concoctions on sale here (open daily; closed 1–4pm; free).

This waterfront area, known as **Baixamar**, is where Maó's limited late-night action takes place. From the ferry terminal, where boats leave for Palma and Barcelona, a long quayside road, lined with restaurants and souvenir shops to serve the growing number of cruise passengers, leads to the yacht moorings at **Cala Figuera**. This deep cove has become one of Maó's most fashionable spots, with numerous restaurant terraces perfectly placed to catch the lunchtime sun.

Myths and military zones

Further out, on the road to Es Castell, is the wine-red **Hotel del Almirante**, formerly the home of the British Admiral Collingwood. This elegant Georgian building has been filled with antiques and paintings from the period of British rule. Across the harbour, on the north side, is another colonial mansion, Sant Antoni, popularly known as **Golden Farm**. This is the setting for perhaps the

greatest of many myths in the history of Maó. The story is that Lord Nelson and his mistress, Lady Emma Hamilton, spent time here together in 1799, but historians have found no evidence to back up the claim. Indeed, Nelson is thought to have made just one brief visit to Menorca – alone. Golden Farm is privately owned and visitors are definitely not welcome, but its ochre-coloured façade dominates the northern shore.

Es Castell ❷, 1.5 km (1 mile) from Maó along the harbour's southern side, has previously been named Georgetown (after an English king) and Villacarlos (after a Spanish one). The town was built by the British in 1771 as a garrison for their troops, and the main square, Plaça de s'Esplanada, is lined with handsome Georgian buildings. On one side is the Ajuntament (Town Hall), with its very British clock tower; on the other, the old British barracks, still used by the Spanish army. The barracks contain an interesting **Museu Militar** (Military Museum), with period English furniture and displays on the history of **Fort Sant Felip** (open Sat–Sun am; free).

This 16th-century fortress, at the southern entrance to Maó harbour, was enhanced by the British using the latest military engineering techniques to create one of the most formidable defensive systems in Europe. An entire garrison of soldiers lived underground here, in what amounted to a sizeable military village, its different parts connected by a labyrinth of tunnels. The fort was dismantled by the Spanish in 1782, apparently to make the island less attractive to Britain; the result was that the British were able to retake Menorca without a single loss of life. It was stone from Fort Sant Felip that was used to build the 19th-century stronghold across the harbour at La Mola, a barracks which served as Spain's most dreaded military prison during the Civil War and the Franco era.

Facing the ruined fortress across the pretty creek of **Cala de Sant Esteve ❸** is the seven-sided **Fort Marlborough**, built by the British to provide extra cover for Fort Sant Felip. For some reason Fort Marlborough was ignored when Fort Sant Felip was destroyed; it has now been carefully restored and opened to visitors. Slide and video displays recall the various battles for Menorca, and the walk through the tunnels is punctuated by loud explosions and other special effects. If this all gets too much, you can climb up to the grassy roof for peaceful views of the surrounding landscape and out to sea (open Tues-Sun am; free). Above the fort, the **Torre del Penjat** is a circular watchtower constructed by the British in 1798.

To the north

The less populated northern side of the harbour, known to the locals as s'Altra Banda ("the other side"), is largely given over to a Spanish naval base. There are two deep coves here, Cala Rata and Cala Llonga, the latter occupied by exclusive villas offering some of the best views of the harbour and the city. Between the two, the **Cementiri dels Anglesos** (English cemetery) in fact contains the graves of American sailors, stationed in Maó during the 19th century. North of here, and still remarkably untouched by tourism, is **Cala Mesquida ❹**, Maó's

---

Maps:
Area 214
City 217

The legend which pinpoints Golden Farm as the love-nest of Nelson and Emma, Lady Hamilton rests on nothing more than a few words carved into a desk in the mansion's library – "remember of me E".

BELOW: good spirits in Maó harbour.

Mahón Cheese

Quite how long Mahón cheese has been made in Menorca nobody can be sure; legend claims that it goes back further even than the Greeks.

Despite its pedigree, the Menorcan product remained a purely seasonal farmhouse cheese for much of the 20th century. Every day from September to June, twice daily after the cows had been milked, the women of the *fincas* would laboriously work the curds, squeezing out the whey from 10 litres of milk for each kilo of cheese and then pressing the curds into squares. (For rennet they traditionally used the juice from *carxofes d'herbes*, a special variety of artichoke, now usually replaced by bottled vegetable rennet). Once the cheese was shaped, it was placed in a wooden press to squeeze out the remaining whey, then unwrapped and floated in mild brine until it had sucked in enough salt to preserve it.

From this came the four types still sold today: mild *fresco*, or *tierno*, eaten after as little as eight days, smooth and white with bubbles in the centre, used to stuff Christmas turkeys and fill small, sweet pastries; *semi-curado*, sealed with yellow cheese with a creamy consistency; *curado*, matured for longer until it is firm at the edges with a deep, nutty flavour and orange rind; finally, *viejo* or *añejo*, resealed and turned for a year or more till it has a granular texture, rock hard rind and a powerful kick for the nose and throat, similar to that of Parmesan.

Although all farmhouse Mahón shares a particular flavour from the island's salty pastures – in recognition of which it carries a *denominación de origen* label – no two cheeses are ever the same. The local soil, warmth of the makers' hands, the addition of a little goat's or lamb's milk for flavour, and the maturing process – all add individual character.

Inevitably, as with nearly all other farmhouse cheeses, traditional Mahón now competes with industrial versions. Avoid the El Caserio brand, which can only be described as a plastic, foil-wrapped travesty; Coinga, made by a farmers' co-operative in Alaior, is closer to the original but with a blander flavour.

There is also now a third alternative: an unpasteurised cheese made traditionally, but under controlled hygienic conditions and with a mould and press to replace the labour-intensive, costly work of squeezing by hand. The results, close to farmhouse cheese but with the necessary guarantees of uniform quality for commercial buyers (80 percent of production is exported from the island) offer a way forward not only for Mahón, but also for Spain's fifty other excellent regional farmhouse cheeses.

If you are lucky enough to be on the spot, however, savour the taste of the really splendid genuine article. Try a chunk of fine *añejo* – eaten the local way with red wine, figs and grapes – before it is a thing of the past. ❑

LEFT: the best place to buy Mahón cheese is in Alaior, centre of the dairy industry.

nearest beach, overlooked by yet another British defence tower as well as by the headland known as Es Pa Gros ("the big loaf").

North of Maó, a minor road, the PM710, threads its way towards Fornells, with several opportunities for diversions onto the rugged north coast. Just 1 km out of the city, shortly after the roadside monument to Sir Richard Kane, a country lane travels the 7 km (4 miles) to **Es Grau** ❺, a peaceful seaside village well-stocked with fishing boats. The village was founded in the early 20th century as a weekend retreat for the people of Maó, and still serves much the same function today.

Separated from the beach by pine woods and dunes, **S'Albufera** is a freshwater lake that looks remarkably like a Scottish loch, complete with midges. The water echoes to the sound of birds, and especially the splashing of ducks. Cormorants and herons are frequently seen here; in winter the lake attracts a migrant colony of ospreys. After much debate, S'Albufera was finally declared a nature reserve in 1995.

Imaginary paradise

The park extends to the **Illa d'En Colom** ❻, 400 metres (1,300 ft) offshore and the largest island off the Menorcan coast. The island is home to an endemic species of lizard, *lacerta lilfordi*. Traces of early habitation have been found here, including the remains of a Byzantine church. In summer you can visit the island by boat from Es Grau and spend time on its two sandy beaches.

S'Albufera owes its protected status to the failed development at **Shangri-La** ❼, an unfinished *urbanización* on the lake's southern shore. This was the brainchild of a German property developer, conceived during the 1970s when

Map on page 214

Es Grau has a Blue Flag beach.

BELOW: the freshwater lake of S'Albufera is now a nature reserve.

The lighthouse at Cap de Fàvaritx.

the tourist boom was at its height. A golf course – now heavily overgrown – was built and more than 60 houses were completed before the whole project froze in the face of local opposition. After years of wrangling, environmental campaigners succeeded in getting any further development declared illegal. In many ways, this was a defining moment for Menorca, as the realisation hit home that tourism had to be controlled. Some of the houses have been destroyed, others are still lived in, but the whole resort has a desolate air. The developers must have foreseen what would happen; why else would they name their village after an imaginary paradise?

Not far after the Es Grau turn-off, another minor road, **Camí d'En Kane**, heads inland through a pastoral landscape of meadows, cattle and dry-stone walls. The road has its origins in the British conquest of Menorca, when the first governor, Sir Richard Kane, had a new road built across the island from Ciutadella to Maó. With the opening of the C721, the old road fell into disuse, but the eastern section has now been restored and dedicated to its creator.

Diverse resorts

The next detour, to **Cap de Fàvaritx ❽**, crosses a barren, lunar landscape, culminating in a promontory of crumbling slate cliffs, lashed by the *tramuntana* wind. From the headland above the lighthouse it is just possible to make out a pair of wide sandy beaches to the south. A footpath, beginning at a wooden gate 1 km back along the road, leads to these beaches and even in summer they are usually deserted.

The PM710 continues through the pine woods for another 6 km (4 miles), reaching a crossroads where a broad highway runs down towards the sea. At the

BELOW: the landscape en route to Cap de Fàvaritx is bleak, but there are fine sandy beaches nearby.

end of this road are three very different resorts. **Port d'Addaia ❾** lies at the mouth of a 3-km (2-mile) inlet, chosen by the British as the bridgehead for their final invasion of Menorca in 1798. The natural harbour here provides excellent anchorage and the marina is usually full of yachts. **Na Macaret** is a charming, low-rise seaside village where the Menorcans take their summer holidays. By contrast, **Arenal des Castell ❿** is one of the few places on the island to have succumbed wholeheartedly to mass tourism. Two ugly hotels tower over the beach, and the streets of the new town are home to numerous timeshare developments. The beach is perfect – a wide arc of golden sand, more than 600 metres (2,000 ft) long – but it is difficult not to try to imagine what it must have been like before the tourist industry moved in. From the west end of the resort, a coastal path leads to another major *urbanización* at Son Parc and from there across a herb-scented headland to the quiet cove at Cala Pudent.

The southeastern tip

In the southern outskirts of Maó, just off the road to Sant Lluís, are a *taule* and *talaiot* that have stood for 3,000 years. At 4 metres (13 ft) high, the *taule* is the tallest yet discovered. Not far from here is Maó's **hippodrome**, the closest Menorcan equivalent to a bull-ring. The entertainment here consists of trotting races, in which a jockey sits in a small cart behind a horse and tries to make the horse move as quickly as possible without breaking into a gallop. The races are held on most weekends throughout the year.

Sant Lluís ⓫, 5 km (3 miles) south of Maó, is a dazzling town of white-washed houses, founded by the French in 1761 and named in honour of Louis IX. During the French occupation, Sant Lluís was briefly the seat of government of the island. The windmill at the entrance to the town, **Molí de Dalt**, houses a small folk museum, with a collection of old farm tools (open Wed–Mon, am and evenings; am only in winter; entrance fee).

This southeastern corner of Menorca, once the island's wine-growing region, is dense with holiday villas and small, attractive beaches. East of Sant Lluís, **Cala d'Alcaufar ⓬** is a tiny resort set around a fishermen's creek. A restored section of the coastal bridleway, **Camí de Cavalls** – which once ran around the entire Menorcan coast – connects the *cala* with the larger *urbanización* at S'Algar.

The resort of which the Menorcans are most proud is the "fishing village" of **Binibeca Vell ⓭**, 5 km (3 miles) southwest of Sant Lluís. Designed by Antonio Sintes in 1972, it was Binibeca that paved the way for a new style of vernacular coastal architecture, favouring low, whitewashed cottages instead of faceless, concrete hotels. It is easy to mock Binibeca – the *poblat de pescadors* has few fishermen and the village has a steeple but no church – but it has profoundly affected the way Menorca has viewed its subsequent tourist development.

West of Maó, the PM704 passes through the more genuine village of **Sant Climent ⓮** on its way to Cala d'En Porter. Just outside Sant Climent, beside the airport runway, is one of Menorca's most fascinating ancient sites. The 6th-century church of **Torelló** was

Map on page 214

CAMÍ D'EN KANE

ZONA D'ORDENACIÓ DE EXPLOTACIONS DE MENORCA CONSELLERIA D'AGRICULTURA I PESCA
GOVERN BALEAR

The eastern section of the old Camí d'En Kane road has now been restored; it's well worth driving for its beautiful views.

BELOW: Binibeca Vell, designer "fishing village".

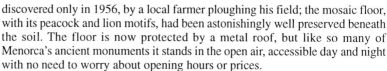

Map
on page
214

discovered only in 1956, by a local farmer ploughing his field; the mosaic floor, with its peacock and lion motifs, had been astonishingly well preserved beneath the soil. The floor is now protected by a metal roof, but like so many of Menorca's ancient monuments it stands in the open air, accessible day and night with no need to worry about opening hours or prices.

Cales Coves ⓯, 7 km (4 miles) southwest of Sant Climent, is even older; some of the caves here, carved out of the cliff face, were occupied 3,000 years ago. In Talayotic times they were used both as burial chambers and dwellings, with the dead and the living housed in adjacent caves. The more modern caves, dating from the 4th century BC, are quite sophisticated in design, with windows, patios and separate cubicles for different family members. Roman inscriptions on the walls suggest that these continued to be lived in even after the end of the Talayotic period. In fact, a few are still lived in today, by modern-day troglodytes, whom the authorities seem unable to dislodge.

Cales Coves is only accessible down a long and arduous track, but **Cova d'En Xoroi**, barely 1 km along the coast, is visited each day in summer by coachloads of tourists. The cave, halfway down a sheer cliff on the edge of **Cala d'En Porter** ⓰, has been imaginatively converted to house a disco, with dance floors perched above the sea, open to the night sky. Legend has it that the cave was home to Xoroi, a Moorish pirate shipwrecked at Cala d'En Porter; when he fell in love with a local girl, he abducted her and took her to his cave. The couple brought up four children in complete secrecy until their footsteps in a fresh snowfall gave away their hiding place. When they were discovered, the Moor supposedly leapt into the sea and drowned, but his wife was rescued by her family and accepted back into island life. Cala d'En Porter itself was one of Menorca's earliest beach resorts, in a magnificent setting where tall cliffs surround a wide sandy bay.

BELOW: Cova d'En Xoroi near Cala d'En Porter houses a disco in summer.
RIGHT: fiesta time in Es Castell's Plaça s'Esplanada.

Ancient settlement

Five kilometres (3 miles) back from Cala d'En Porter on the PM704, a minor road runs north, past the prehistoric site of **Torralba d'En Salort** ⓱ (*see page 227*), to **Alaior** ⓲. Menorca's third-largest town, Alaior produces shoes, ice cream (the popular La Menorquina brand originated here) as well as the famous Mahón cheese (*see page 220*). Founded by Mallorca's Jaume II in 1304, it is a pleasing jumble of sloping streets which all seem to converge on the huge parish church, Santa Eulàlia.

The largest beach on the island is at **Son Bou** ⓳, 8 km (5 miles) south of Alaior. The eastern end is dominated by two vast hotels; there would have been more if environmentalists had not won a battle to stop further development. As you move east, the beach gets quieter and the scenery wilder.

Long ago, Son Bou may have been the capital of Menorca. One of the island's biggest Talayotic settlements, **Torre d'En Gaumés**, lies just a few kilometres inland (*see page 227*). On the beach itself, only discovered in 1953, a 5th-century North African church squats beneath the two giant hotels. What will the archaeologists of the future, you wonder, make of the tourist *urbanizaciones* of today? ❑

Map
on page
214

Menorca

Palma
Mallorca
Eivissa

BELOW: a *naveta*,
a burial chamber
cum dwelling, at
Biniac L'Argentina.

PREHISTORIC MENORCA

*The mysterious Talayotic villages and monoliths
scattered all over the island are still being
investigated by archaeologists today*

M enorca is often referred to as an archaeological museum without walls. Whether you travel the island's back routes or its main roads, the truth of this statement soon becomes clear. You're never far from the sight of some kind of megalithic ruin – some as impressive as Stonehenge, and nearly comparable in age.

It is estimated that there are more than 5,000 prehistoric sites on Menorca and Mallorca, dating back as early as 6000 BC. Menorca, however, has as many as three times the number of sites found on its sister island.

On both islands, the prehistoric mother culture is known as the **Talayotic Culture**. The term "Talayotic" was coined at the turn of the 20th century by two prehistorians, the Spaniard Jose Colominas Roca and the Frenchman Emile Cartaillac, who based it on the Arabic word *atalaya,* meaning "watchtower". It refers to the single most characteristic structure of the period: a circular or square building with a single entrance and a large centre pillar made up of three to six increasingly massive stone elements, placed one upon the other.

In ancient times, the *talaiots* probably served as meeting-places for the elders of the community, very much like the *kiva* of the southwestern American Indian. However, the Talayotic culture is believed to be most closely related in age and social organisation to the Nuraghic and Torreanos cultures of Sardinia and Corsica respectively, where similar architectural structures can be found.

In Menorca, the culture is chronologically divided into three periods: the **Pretalayotic Period** or culture of the caves, *circa* 2000 to 1300 BC; the **Talayotic Period** of the Bronze Age, *circa* 1300 to 800 BC, and the **Post-Talayotic Period** of the Iron Age, *circa* 800 BC up to Roman colonisation in 123 BC.

Geographical features

To understand how Talayotic Culture developed, it is necessary to consider a few important geographic and geological factors.

At 702 sq. km, (271 sq. miles), Menorca is smaller than its sister island of Mallorca (3,740 sq. km 1,444 sq. miles), and has none of that island's extremes of landscape, of mountain and plain. On the whole, the terrain is rather monotonous, thanks to continual exposure to winds from various directions, particularly the prevailing north wind.

The main highway, which divides the island from north to south between the capital city of Maó in the east and the town of Ciutadella westward, also bisects the island's two most important geological formations. These have shaped the pattern of man's settlement on Menorca from prehistoric right up until modern times.

North of the highway, the coast is exposed to tempestuous winds which blow in off the Golfe du Lion; in bad weather, it can be inaccessible by sea for days at a time. The south coastline, by contrast, is marked by deep gorges (locally called *barrancs*) which slice the island's limestone bedrock into beautiful coves and inlets; there are also a number of sandy beaches which run for several miles. Scores of caves – most with fresh water sources – pockmark both sides of the *barrancs*; most have signs of prehistoric occupation and some are still occupied even today. It is in this southern region that about 90 percent of Menorca's Bronze and Iron Age open-air settlements can be seen.

Settlements to explore

Menorca's largest and most elaborate open-air Talayotic settlement is the fortified prehistoric town of **Son Catlar**, lying just southeast of Ciutadella near Son Vivó farm. Built around 1800 BC inside a Cyclopean wall system with inner chambers, over 800 metres (2,624 ft) of the ramparts remain. Within them lie the entire range and variation of Talayotic architecture, including five *talaiots* and a *taule*. The latter, peculiar to Menorca alone, is an immense rectangular monolith, up to 4.5 metres (915 ft) high, with a huge tapered capstone set on top. This one stands at the entrance to a horseshoe-shaped religious sanctuary dating from 1000 BC. There are over 30 such sanctuaries on Menorca – very much like the Temples of Malta, but of considerably younger age. Son Catlar is roughly as old as ancient Troy, although it is some nine times larger.

You can visit another such settlement complex in the Talayotic village of **Torre d'En Gaumés ❷⓪** which extends all around a large commanding ridge on the road from Alaior to Son Bou. It also consists of a range of buildings, with its own *talaiots* and *taule*.

Other well-preserved *taulas* are at **Talatí de Dalt**, a few miles west of Maó on the south side of the Maó-Ciutadella road, and **Torralba d'En Salort**, lying along a minor road running north to Alaior from just outside Cala En Porter. Here, archaeological excavations have shown the *taule* was used for ritual offerings of animals. Bronze statuary of a bull, a horse and terracotta statues of the Carthaginian goddess Tanit at Torralba, along with human effigies of foreign household gods like the Egyptian Imhotep found at Torre d'En Gaumés, suggest a mixed pantheon of gods in the *taules'* latter stages of use.

Another common Talayotic architectural landmark is the *naveta*, a building shaped like an overturned boat. Perhaps the oldest of the Talayotic architectural forms, the *naveta* dates from 1500 BC. It served a dual purpose on Menorca and Mallorca, being used both as communal living quarters and as a burial chamber. The best example of the form is the **Naveta des Tudons**, which lies just off the Maó-Ciutadella road, 6 km (3½ miles) east of Ciutadella. You can actually enter the *naveta* here, gaining access to both the upper and lower levels.

Most of the monuments are open to the public, for no fee, but remember that some are also on private property, and permission should be asked at the nearest farmhouse before visiting them. ❑

TIP

The biggest and best-preserved *taula* on Menorca lies just 20 minutes' walk south of Maó's Plaça s'Esplanada. Follow Es Cós de Gràcia to the ring road, then take the track that leads past the cemetery to the site at **Trepucó**.

BELOW: the *taule* at Trepucó, the biggest on the whole island.

CIUTADELLA AND WESTERN MENORCA

Maps:
Area 214
City 232

*Despite a plethora of busy resorts, there are still plenty
of unspoilt beaches to explore here – along with historic
Ciutadella, the island's most Catalan town*

Maó and **Ciutadella** ㉑ may be only 45 km (28 miles) apart but they face in different directions, turning their backs on each other as they look out to sea. The rivalry between the two cities goes back to the 18th century, when the first British governor, Sir Richard Kane, moved the capital across the island. The power base shifted but the clergy and the aristocracy stayed put, safely ensconced in their Renaissance palaces. The result is that Ciutadella remains the most Catalan town on the island, with little of the Georgian architecture which distinguishes Maó. It was the Spanish governor of Menorca, the Count of Cifuentes, who endeared himself to the citizens of Ciutadella with a saying which many believe still holds true today: "Maó may have more people, but Ciutadella has more souls."

As the crow flies, Ciutadella is less than 50 km (30 miles) from the Mallorcan coast; at dusk the mountains of Mallorca turn pink on the horizon. So perhaps it should come as no surprise that the old town, with its Gothic churches and honey-stone façades, is rather like a miniature Palma. This is, after all, what the city's name implies. Palma's alternative name is Ciutat de Mallorca; Ciutadella de Menorca is "Menorca's little city".

PRECEDING PAGES:
midday serenade at
the Molí des Recó,
Es Mercadal.
LEFT: a simple
courtyard.
BELOW: Ciutadella's
Plaça des Born.

Route march

The best way to explore Ciutadella is to walk, with an accurate map but no fixed route, at different times of the day and night. Inevitably you keep returning to the streets around the cathedral, home to jewellers, antique shops and outdoor cafés. When night falls, history comes alive here, with small architectural details – sundials, saints in niches, coats of arms – spotlighted by old-fashioned street lamps. By this time the fish restaurants beside the port are starting to fill up, but if you walk back along the creek and look up at the old wall, you can imagine past centuries, when the gates were locked from sunset to sunrise.

At the heart of Ciutadella is **Plaça des Born**, the old Arab parade-ground, now a shady square of trees and cafés. A pair of handsome 19th-century palaces, Palau Torresaura and **Palau Salort** Ⓐ (open Apr–Oct: Mon–Sat am; entrance fee), stand symmetrically to one side, facing the crenellated town hall, built on the site of the Moorish citadel. The obelisk in the square's midst commemorates the victims of a Turkish raid on Ciutadella in 1558, which devastated much of the city.

The main street of the old town is now an attractive pedestrian thoroughfare linking Plaça des Born to the palm-lined **Plaça Alfons III** (also known as Plaça de ses Palmeres, or "palm tree square"). The different

This mythical creature embellishes Ciutadella's Palau Torresaura.

segments of the street each have different names, but the whole thing is commonly known as **Ses Voltes ⓑ** after the Moorish-style arches at its centre – a reminder of the days when Ciutadella, known as Medina Minurka, was the Arab capital of the island.

The fortress-like **cathedral of Santa Maria ⓒ**, with its splendid Gothic buttresses, was built on the site of the old mosque soon after the Christian conquest, with the ancient minaret incorporated into the belfry (open 9am–1pm, 6–9pm daily; free). The nearby bishop's palace, Ca'l Bisbe, dates from the 18th century, when Ciutadella lost its status as capital but regained the bishopric (after a gap of 1,300 years) as compensation. It is usually possible to peek into the bishop's courtyard, with its stone staircase and galleried arcade. The **Museu Diocesà** (Diocesan Museum) ⓓ, in an Augustinian convent on Carrer Seminari, has a large collection of prehistoric artifacts as well as landscapes by the Catalan painter Pere Daura (1896–1976), who was born in Ciutadella (open Tues–Sun am in summer; Sat am in winter; entrance fee).

City festival

Where Carrer Seminari meets Ses Voltes, glance up to see a small, modern statue of a ram, mounted on a column. The ram carries a flag bearing the cross of St John, a symbol of Ciutadella's festival, **Festa de Sant Joan**, which takes place each year on 23–24 June. On the previous Sunday, a live ram is carried around the town on the shoulders of a man dressed in sheepskins, representing John the Baptist. Then, for two days, the citizens of Ciutadella go wild, with horseback processions, firework displays and jousting tournaments in Plaça des Born. Like all the great Spanish fiestas, Sant Joan has its own vocabulary

BELOW: Menorcans put a lot of effort into their festivals.

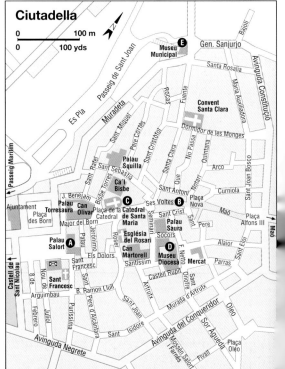

Ciutadella

and rituals, based above all on the Menorcan passion for horses; the *caixers*, or horsemen, who represent the medieval social classes, ride among the crowds, prancing and circling on their horses' hind legs (*see also pages 60–61*).

Facing Carrer Seminari, Carrer Santa Clara leads to the convent of the same name, founded by Alfons III in 1287. The church was destroyed during the Turkish assault in 1558 and again during the Civil War, but has been rebuilt over and over again. A community of recluse nuns still live here. At the end of this street, the fortress of Bastió de Sa Font now houses the **Museu Municipal ⑤**, with displays on the history of Menorca from Talayotic through to Muslim times. Some of the ancient skulls show wounds caused by trepanning, or cranial surgery, which indicate that the Talayotic culture must have developed advanced surgical techniques. In some cases the wounds have healed over, proving, somewhat remarkably, that the patients survived (open Mon–Sat 10am–1pm and 7–9pm in summer; Sat am in winter; entrance fee).

Harbour promenade

Ciutadella's port squats beneath the medieval walls at the end of a long, narrow inlet, though for many years there have been plans to extend the harbour into the sea. The port is at one end of the **Passeig Marítim**, a seafront promenade which is a popular sunset stroll. From here, Mallorca appears as two separate islands, the flat central plain invisible between the mountains of the Serra de Llevant and Serra de Tramuntana.

Halfway along Passeig Marítim, beside the 17th-century **Castell de Sant Nicolau**, is a bust of Admiral David Farragut, a hero of the American Civil War. This son of a Menorcan emigrant paid a brief visit to Ciutadella in 1867,

Map on page 232

TIP

When you visit the Museu Diocesà, be sure to take a look at the Neoclassical portal in the building's boundary wall. It is crowned by an odd sculpture of the Virgin Mary, threatening a dragon-devil with a hammer and cudgel.

BELOW: the Castell de Sant Nicolau in Ciutadella.

when he was awarded honorary citizenship; a huge crowd lined the streets to welcome him home.

It takes about 30 minutes to walk to the end of the Passeig Marítim at **Cala Degollador**, Ciutadella's tiny beach. Strangely, despite its proximity to the city, this is the least developed beach on the entire west coast. North of Ciutadella, the rocky creeks at Cala d'En Blanes, Cala d'En Bruc, Cala des Forcat and Cales Piques have merged remorselessly around the *urbanización* of Los Delfines; it is difficult to tell where one ends and the next begins. To the south, **Cala Santandria** (where the French landed during the invasion of 1756), **Cala Blanca** and especially **Cala des Bosc** have become busy resorts, the latter based around a decidedly chic marina.

Coves and stones

East of Cala des Bosc, the coastline still fits the image of Menorca the unspoilt island, with a handful of lovely beaches protected by the lack of easy access roads. **Arenal de Son Saura**, 10 km (6 miles) southeast of Ciutadella, can be reached only by following a track which passes through six gates, several fields and a farmyard – plus, you usually have to pay a toll to cross private land. There are two beaches here, both backed by pine trees, although many pines were uprooted when a whirlwind swept through the area in 1992. The road to Arenal de Son Saura passes the prehistoric village at **Son Catlar** ❷, built around 1800 BC and surrounded by a Cyclopean wall (*see page 226*).

To get to two more unspoilt beaches you have to pass the 15th-century hermitage of **Sant Joan de Missa**, which is unlocked just once a year when the *caixers* ride out here during the festival of Sant Joan. Its square bell-tower,

TIP

The little cafés around Ciutadella's colourful market (Plaça Llibertat) are a good place for fresh coffee, *ensaimadas* and a spot of people-watching.

BELOW: the pretty cove of Cala d'En Turqueta is popular with families.

starkly white, stands out above walled fields dotted by farmhouses and the occasional *talaiot*. **Cala d'En Turqueta ㉔**, a further 6 km (4 miles) southeast, is a beautiful cove, popular with local families at weekends. A coastal path connects it to Arenal de Son Saura. Another bumpy track across farmland leads to **Cala Macarella**, from where you can walk to the more secluded, and largely nudist, beach at Cala Macarelleta. Both of these can also be easily reached on foot from Cala Santa Galdana.

North of Ciutadella, stretching towards the lighthouse at **Punta Natí**, is a wild and barren landscape punctured with *ponts*, the uniquely Menorcan cattle shelters made out of stones built into the shape of a pyramid. Another road from Ciutadella leads to **Cala Morell ㉕**, 8 km (5 miles) northeast, where an upmarket villa development has been added to a cluster of prehistoric caves. The levelled rock platforms below the cliffs here are jokingly referred to as sunbeds. The woods and farmland to the east of Cala Morell, in an area of legendary beauty known as La Vall, are largely private, though it is possible (by paying a toll) to drive most of the way to **Cala d'Algaiarens ㉖**, where twin beaches are set in a horseshoe bay. From the end of the road, a short walk through the woods leads to the dunes; from here you can clamber down to the beach.

The Bronze and Iron Age caves at Cala Morell are surprisingly refined, decorated with classical carvings and with windows cut into the rock.

Ancient sites

A single main road, the C721, crosses the island between Ciutadella and Maó, giving access to the main south coast beaches as well as to the inland towns. Four km (2½ miles) out of Ciutadella, the boat-like outline of the **Naveta des Tudons ㉗**, dubbed the oldest roofed building in Europe, is clearly visible from the road. This remarkable Bronze Age burial chamber, built on two storeys,

BELOW: prehistoric caves, Cala Morell.

*The Bronze Age
Naveta des Tudons.*

BELOW: the stately
home of Binisues,
near Santa Agueda.

was fully excavated in the 1950s, when more than 50 bodies were discovered inside along with a number of bronze ornaments. The finds have been removed to the island's museums, but the *naveta* still stands in the middle of a field. It can seem mundane when swamped by a coachload of tourists, but caught in solitude in the early morning or evening light it is quite magnificent. A notice warns visitors not to climb on the ruins, but there is nothing to prevent you from crawling inside. As far as anyone knows, *navetes* are unique to Menorca and of those that have been discovered, this is in by far the best condition (*see page 226*).

Two other ancient sites, **Torrellajuda** and **Torre Trencada**, have *taules* hidden among the olive trees and are much less visited than the *naveta*. Both are signposted from the C721. Close to Torre Trencada, on the old road from Ciutadella to Maó, **S'Hostal** is a disused limestone quarry which has been turned into an unusual open-air museum. Workmen give demonstrations of quarrying techniques and you can walk right down into the quarry, beneath the sheer limestone walls. It was from quarries such as this that the stone for monuments like Naveta des Tudons was probably extracted.

Highest town

Just after Castillo Menorca, a mock castle and souvenir emporium beside the C721, a side road leads to the conservation area at **Cala Pilar**, reached by a 30-minute walk through the oak woods. From the beach, a 10-minute scramble over the headland will bring you out at the next cove, Es Macar d'Alfurinet, where the pebbles have been sculpted by the sea into giant boulders.

Another worthwhile detour is to **Santa Agueda** ❷❽, a ruined Arab fort reached by a steep paved Roman path. The governors of Medina Minurka had their

summer palace here, and it was the final Muslim stronghold to surrender following the Christian invasion. The views from the summit, at 260 metres (850 ft), stretch along the north coast and as far west as Ciutadella. On the road to Santa Agueda, **Binisues** is a stately home belonging to one of Ciutadella's noble families, with original furnishings and a museum of rural life (open Apr–Oct: daily; entrance fee).

At 140 metres (450 ft) above sea level, **Ferreries 🔞** is the highest town on Menorca, surrounded by terraced *tanques* in the shadow of S'Enclusa mountain. Founded by Jaume II of Mallorca at the beginning of the 14th century, it remained a small village known mainly for its blacksmiths until it developed furniture and shoemaking industries in the 20th century. Now, it has grown into a prosperous new town, with wide avenues and a spacious feel. A popular farmers' market is held in the main square on Saturday mornings.

Map on page 214

Glizy altar in the church of Sant Bartomeu, Ferreries.

Resorts and hideaways

Just outside Ferreries, and signposted from the road to Es Migjorn Gran, the prehistoric village of **Son Mercer de Baix** is perched high above a ravine with dizzying views of the valley floor. This is one of several *barrancs* (limestone gorges) which carve up the southern half of Menorca, attracting birds, butterflies and wild flowers to their lush grasslands and seasonal streams. The best known, **Barranc d'Algendar**, has its source close to Ferreries and parts of the gorge can be explored on foot.

The stream empties into the sea at **Cala Santa Galdana 🕥**, 10 km (6 miles) south of Ferreries and perhaps the best example in Menorca of a beauty spot spoiled by thoughtless development. The perfect oyster-shell bay, known as the "queen of the coves", is dominated by two highrise hotels, one at either end of the beach. Villas and apartment blocks climb up the hillsides, and in the summer the beach is packed with bodies. Motorboats and jet-skis shatter whatever peace remains. Older Menorcans remember Cala Santa Galdana as a virgin cove, reached by donkey cart down a bumpy track. The closest you can get to that atmosphere now is by walking east through the pine woods to **Cala Mitjana**, or west over the herb-scented cliffs to Cala Macarella – though even these are liable to get crowded in summer.

The village of **Es Migjorn Gran 🗓** (formerly San Cristóbal) was founded as an offshoot of Ferreries in the 18th century. As the only one of Menorca's municipalities that does not lie on the main road, it retains a sleepy, provincial feel, with plenty of traditional rural architecture. The simple whitewashed houses along the Carrer Major have balconies and wooden shutters, and the parish church of Sant Cristòfol, its square bell-tower topped by a cockerel, is satisfyingly proportioned.

On the edge of the village, a farm track leads to the Binigaus gorge, where you can walk along the valley floor to the **Cova des Coloms**, a limestone cave the size of a cathedral. The nearest beach is 5 km (3 miles) south at **Sant Tomàs 🔢**, a low-key resort set around a single main street between the pine woods and the

BELOW: Cala Santa Galdana – and hotel.

dunes. The beach was devastated by a freak storm in 1989; all the sand you see today had to be imported to replace what was lost.

Es Mercadal , at the centre of the island, was founded in the 14th century as a market town on the Maó to Ciutadella road. This is another town that tourism has largely ignored; besides farming, the main local industries are the manufacture of *avarques* (sandals with soles made out of tyres) and almond macaroons. The town has a reputation for its excellent Menorcan cuisine; one of the better restaurants is to be found inside an old windmill at the top of the main street. Es Mercadal also contains an 18th-century reservoir, Cisterna d'En Kane, built on the orders of the first British governor.

The unmistakable bronze statue of Christ at El Toro.

Patron saint

Standing proudly above Es Mercadal at a height of 350 metres (1,150 ft), **El Toro** is the highest point on Menorca and an ancient centre of pilgrimage. A convent has stood here since medieval times, and is still inhabited by nuns today. Inevitably, there is a legend about the origins of the sanctuary, and equally inevitably, it involves a statue of the Virgin and a cave. In 1290, three years after the Moors were expelled from Menorca, monks walking on the mountainside were led by a wild bull towards the summit, where they found a figure of Mary hidden in a cleft. Following this miracle, a chapel was built to house the statue, and La Verge del Toro, as it is known, became Menorca's patron saint.

BELOW: an old windmill, home of the Molí des Recó restaurant.

The present baroque church dates from the 17th century; the Madonna inside the chapel now has a bull at her feet. Outside, a bronze statue of Christ is dwarfed by the aerials of a modern radar station. The views from the terrace are tremendous, extending right across Menorca to the sea on all four sides.

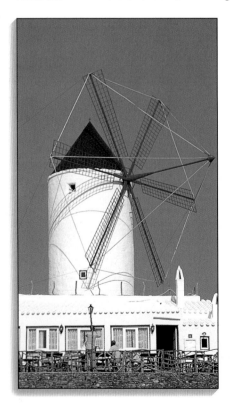

THE ENGLISH INFLUENCE

Dominated by the British for most of the 18th century, it is not surprising that an enduring colonial legacy lives on in Menorca – in the architecture, the customs, and, most intriguingly, in the local dialect. Menorquín is peppered with Anglicisms at every level, from the most superficial to the most profound. Some, like *vermell com un Jan* (red like an Englishman) and *ball des cosil* (Scottish dances), are colloquialisms which have worked their way in; others are direct Menorquínisations of English words. For example, *tornescru* and *bech* are the islanders' versions of the words "turnscrew" and "back" – totally unconnected to their Spanish equivalents of *destornillador* and *respaldo*. According to the British historian D.W. Donaldson, there are at least 50 commonly used words such as *beguer* or beggar (Spanish: *mendigo*), *bifi* or beef (Spanish: *carne*), *tibord* or tea board (Spanish: *bandeja*) and *chel* or shell (Spanish: *concha*) which fit this category. Then there are the marks left on the language by the island's first British governor, Richard Kane. According to legend, the locally grown *prunes de neverso* are named after his response to seeing a type of plum which, up until that moment, he had "never saw". Kane's favourite apple, meanwhile, is still known as a *poma de Kane*.

In the courtyard is a memorial to Father Pedro Camps, who led a group of Menorcans to Florida in 1768 in protest at the persecution of Catholics by successive British governors. It is Camps who is widely credited with keeping alive the Catholic faith in Florida during the British occupation (1763-83). Descendants of those original Menorcan emigrants still live in and around the town of St Augustine in Florida.

Map on page 214

Fit for a king

The C723 runs north from Es Mercadal to the fishing village of **Fornells** ❸, built at the edge of a long, shallow bay. For Spaniards, Fornells is synonymous with lobster, said to be particularly good here. King Juan Carlos certainly thinks so; he has frequently sailed his yacht over from his Mallorcan summer home to eat *caldereta de llagosta* (lobster stew) at the waterfront restaurants.

The ruined 17th-century fortress of **Sant Antoni**, destroyed by the Spanish in 1782, stands at the water's edge. The fort saw a heavy exchange of gunfire during the first British invasion of 1708, but Fornells quickly surrendered; afterwards, the commander of the invasion force, James Stanhope, wrote to his superiors in London that Maó and Fornells were the two best ports in the Mediterranean. Not far from the ruined citadel, a British defence tower stands at the mouth of the bay on the headland of Cap de Fornells. The nearest beaches are at **Ses Salines**, where the sheltered waters of the bay offer excellent conditions for windsurfing, and **Cala Tirant** ❸, dominated by the "country club" development at Platges de Fornells.

The rugged coastline west of Fornells harbours some of Menorca's most unspoilt coves. A rough track across a rocky spit leads to the island's northernmost point, **Cap de Cavalleria** ❸, where a lighthouse stands on top of cliffs that drop a sheer 90 metres (300 ft) into the sea – it can be frightening up here when the *tramuntana* blows. The road to the cape passes the small jetty at **Sanitja**, Menorca's third port in Roman times but now a quiet creek with a handful of boats. Near Sanitja, a dusty lane, just passable by car, drops down to the beaches of Cavalleria and Ferragut, popular with local families at weekends. There are no facilities, so take a picnic and plenty of water.

A coastal footpath (45 minutes each way) leads to the beach at **Binimel·là** ❸, which can also be reached by car. A small stream flows into the sea here beside the sand dunes. Although once earmarked for tourist development, the authorities have decided to preserve Binimel·là's natural beauty; a moratorium on new building has now been declared.

From the west end of the beach, it takes around 30 minutes to walk over the headland to **Cala Pregonda**. Many people consider this the most beautiful spot on the entire Menorcan coast. Pine woods reach down to the sand; the dunes are carpeted with wild flowers; you can swim out across transparent waters to a small island with its own tiny beach. There are no tourist facilities here, and the few villas were built by the owner of the neighbouring land before the restrictions came in. If you think this is idyllic, just remember – once upon a time, all of Menorca was like this. ❏

BELOW: inquisitive goats at Cap de Cavalleria.

IBIZA AND FORMENTERA

*A detailed guide to these two islands, with principal sites
cross-referenced by number to the maps*

The collective name *Pitiüses* applies to the islands of Ibiza, Formentera and the small rocky islands around them (Sa Conillera, Illa des Bosc, Es Vedrà, Es Vedranell, S'Espalmador, S'Espardell, Tagomago and a host of other even smaller ones); this probably derives from *pityussai*, the name given to the islands by the Greeks. The Roman naturalist and geographer Pliny the Elder traced the name back to an ancient Greek word for thick pine forests.

Mallorca is only 80 km (50 miles) away from Ibiza, while Denia, the nearest harbour on the Spanish mainland, is around 90 km (56 miles) away. Even the coast of North Africa is just 180 km (110 miles) away, the same distance as Barcelona. This strategically favourable position turned Ibiza and Formentera into desirable military bases for centuries.

After struggling to make ends meet for so many hundreds of years, **Ibiza** (population 50,000) has done well to finally become as successfully young and trendy as it is now. The island is a summer magnet for ravers, clubbers and dance music-lovers, who party all night and stretch out on the beaches during the day to sleep off their excesses. Here originates the Balearic beat, a disco mix concocted in the clubs at the height of the summer and played throughout Europe by the autumn. Rock and pop stars holiday here, in a surprising number of exclusive hotels that have no need to advertise their existence. In Ibiza it is the night that matters.

In the past, **Formentera** (population 4,000), which along with Cabrera is one of the two little sisters of the Balearics family, often was not quite strong enough to be firm about its own identity. Holidaymakers from the bigger island, revved up and raring to go, would cross the 4-km (2½-mile) strait that separates the islands and go tearing around, looking for something that really grabbed them and not finding it. This, after all, was where the police made their first drug raids on the Sixties hippies on bicycles, or later in a hired taxi. Now, however, this same unspoilt quality draws an ever-growing stream of discerning visitors. ❏

PRECEDING PAGES: Ibiza's Sa Caleta beach lies near Ses Salines in the southwest of the island; chilling out in Sant Antoni.
LEFT: young girl in traditional Ibizan costume.

IBIZA, WHITE ISLAND

*In the south of the island lie salt-pans, long sandy
beaches, the major holiday playground of Sant Antoni –
and, of course, those legendary clubs*

Maps:
Area 248
City 253

Once the ultimate European getaway for both the hippies and the jet-set of the 1960s, Ibiza is now better known as club capital of the Med. Smaller than neighbouring Menorca (Ibiza's coastal circumference is just 210 km or 130 miles, as opposed to Menorca's 286 km/177 miles), it nevertheless receives the same number of visitors, most of whom are British or German.

An island of excess, Ibiza – or Eivissa, as it is called in Catalan – attracts two very different types of sun-and-fun lovers. On the one hand, you'll see the worst of cheap package tourism around the bay of Sant Antoni; on the other, the liveliest and most colourful nightlife in Europe is to be found in and around the island's capital, **Eivissa** ❶ (Ibiza town).

One of the reasons the island has garnered such status on the European and American club scenes is the extraordinarily tolerant attitude of the locals – there is very little that they haven't seen before. "Live and let live" and "Don't worry, be happy" could be Ibizan mottos. Having suffered at the hands of pirates and invaders throughout the centuries, the Ibicencos now welcome tourists with open bars and happy smiles. After all, throughout a long history of foreign dominance, it's the first time they've had visitors who actually pay for the privilege of being there.

LEFT: backstreets of Sa Penya quarter in Eivissa.
BELOW: Easter procession in Dalt Vila, Eivissa.

Origins

Ibiza and Formentera have far fewer megalithic monuments than the other Balearic islands of Mallorca and Menorca, and there are hardly any clues to prehistoric life here. We do know that the ancient Greeks used the islands as a staging-post, calling them *nesari pityussai,* or the "pine-tree islands".

Apart from the Greeks, other early visitors included the Phoenicians. They were followed by their distant cousins, the Carthaginians from North Africa, and later, of course, by the Romans.

The Carthaginians named the island after one of their gods, Bes, from which the present-day name developed. Bes was one of the more pleasant Punic deities – a kind of Bacchus-figure, responsible for merry-making and happy love-matches. A good thing, perhaps, that they didn't name the place after one of the less friendly gods like Baal or Melkart, both of whom preferred the blood of human sacrifice to mere offerings of wine and flowers.

The Carthaginians are also said to be responsible for the introduction of the long-eared, stretch-snouted *podenc eivissenc*, or Ibizan hound. Bearing a striking resemblance to Anubis, the jackal-headed Egyptian god charged with guarding the tombs of the pharoahs, these creatures are notoriously unfriendly – yet locals say they make good hunters.

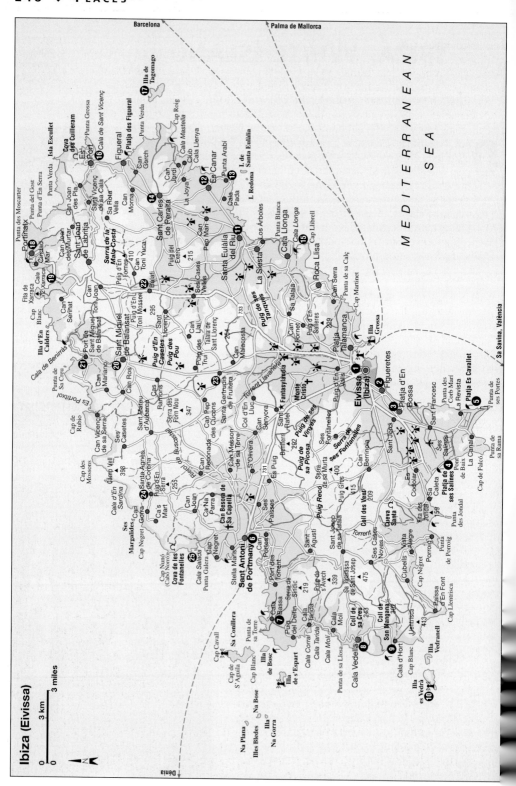

Ibiza (Eivissa)

Barcelona

Palma de Mallorca

MEDITERRANEAN SEA

Sa Savina, València

Dénia

0 3 km
0 3 miles

N

Maps:
Area 248
City 253

Burial ground

The fact that there are no poisonous plants, insects or animals on Ibiza could well have been why the Carthaginians brought their dead all the way from the other side of the Mediterranean and buried them here – to them, the island's rich, non-toxic soil would have guaranteed a happy afterlife. Ibiza has extensive Carthaginian, or Punic, necropoli and and is particularly rich in artifacts and archaeology from that era. Indeed, there are two Punic museums, one within the walls of the capital's old quarter, by the cathedral the **Museu Arqueològic Dalt Vila ⓐ** (open Tues–Sun; closed 2–4pm and Sun pm; entrance fee), and the other just outside town at the ancient burial ground of **Puig des Molins.**

Ibiza's strategic position halfway between the continents of Africa and Europe also meant that under the Carthaginians and the Romans it became a great centre for trans-Mediterranean trading. Its vast natural *salines*, or salt flats, were heavily exploited – not only for export (salt was the most expensive white powder of its day), but also to help preserve much of the food-stuffs of passing ships (*see page 154*).

A bust of the all-powerful Punic goddess Tanit, in the Museu Arqueològic Dalt Vila.

Roman relish

Maó in neighbouring Menorca might have given its name to the locally invented mayonnaise, but Ibiza was the birthplace of the far more ancient delicacy of *garum*, a sticky, gloopy ketchup made of fish gut (if the Romans and the Carthaginians had eaten hamburgers, this would have been their relish). Apart from this historical footnote, there is very little evidence of Roman occupation on the island, except for the original roads – and they fan out from Ibiza town like a handful of long, narrow rulers.

BELOW: Dalt Vila by night, Eivissa.

Doing the *Passeig*

Siesta and fiesta apart, an integral part of Spanish life-style is strolling the squares or promenading the parks in that most essential of trivial pursuits: doing the *passeig*.

Somewhere between a pastime and a profession, the point of the *passeig* is to meet, chatter, mix and mingle. In the old days, this was an important couple of hours of lubrication that kept the wheels of the week turning, providing endless topics for conversation, speculation and scandal. Indeed, thanks to the country's hot climate, street meetings were essential simply for reasons of hygiene. Houses tended to be cramped, strictly the domain of the family, built small and dark to keep the costs down and the heat out. Being outside meant air to breathe as well as space to move.

Modern Ibizans are still avid participants in the *passeig*, daily in summer

and – during the quiet winter months – every Sunday. By 6 o'clock everyone is out on the stroll; Eivissa's aptly named Passeig Vara del Rey square becomes the centre of the universe as far as the town is concerned. Look and be looked at; dress up, eye up, be eyed up.

Three, maybe four, generations move around the square in a ritualistic routine of meetings and greetings. Widowed grannies looking rather like polished black beetles push perambulators. Contented parents idle arm-in-arm alongside. Well-scrubbed children do their utmost to mess up their Sunday best by playing "Havoc and Scream" the length of the Passeig. Even the birds chip in.

Also included, and part of the rites of the *passeig*, is a stop at an ice cream vendor for the kids, an aperitif or two on a street-side terrace and the purchase of a bag of *pipas* (sunflower seeds) to consume at a bar or on a bench.

But once the square served a purpose rather more significant than just amicable strolling. Before the loosening of social attitudes, this was the official cruise centre. Here you'd hope to catch the eye of someone you fancied even if you were out under the watchful gaze of promenading parents.

For young clubbers, doing the nightly *passeig* in Eivissa is just as ritualistic. Dressed in full party regalia (anything from a silver sheath dress to a leather bikini), revellers prowl the narrow streets around the port, calling in at the loudest bars. From their ringside seats they cruise both the crowd and the nightclub PR teams, keeping an eagle eye out for "talent" – or at least free tickets.

After an early-evening siesta followed by sundowners on board, the yachties then emerge to join the fray. Around ten, it's time for dinner before a second, alcohol-fuelled *passeig*, this time taking in the shops as well as some more bars. By 2am, it's time to hit a club. Grandmother probably wouldn't approve, but at least the ritual endures. ❏

LEFT: it's doubtful whether grandma would approve – but at least the *passeig* endures.

Like the rest of Spain, Ibiza didn't escape Moorish invasion. Muslim rule lasted almost uninterrupted here for 300 years (from the 9th to the 12 centuries) but the Moors were a reasonably tolerant people, and during their stay, synagogues, mosques and churches existed quite harmoniously side by side.

Traditional dress, music and customs were all heavily influenced by Arab culture, and to this day Moorish traces can still be discerned. The hamlet of Balafia, near Sant Llorenc, is perhaps the best-known architectural example: here, the buildings are all flat-roofed, key-windowed and white-washed, with rooms built to functional order in the shape of cubes; if more rooms were needed, more cubes were simply added. Plenty of architects have subsequently copied this cubist style – indeed, Ibiza is said to have influenced the biggest cube-maker of the twentieth century, Le Corbusier. Some of the smartest modern homes on the island have also been built along these lines.

After the reconquest of the island by the Spanish in 1235, the Moors were sent packing. The Catholic church with its regal representatives now began the lengthy, and at times, literally tortuous process of bringing the Ibicencos back into the fold.

Maps:
Area 248
City 253

Long-eared and stretch-snouted, Ibizan hounds make good hunters.

Christian Conquerors

Ever since 1235, when Catalan crusaders acting on King Jaume and the church's behalf invaded the island in the name of Christianity, Ibiza has been a Catalan island as well as a Catholic one. Loyalty to the mainland, however, did not always pay dividends. Once Columbus discovered America, Spain's Mediterranean lands and islands were left to fend for themselves against attacks from pirates and exiled Muslims. Although the king of Spain, Felipe II, ordered the construction of thick walls around Ibiza town in 1554 in an attempt to protect the capital, Spain was by now devoting most of its men and resources to protecting the plunder-ships returning from the New World. As a result, the legendary Balearic corsairs came into their own, out-pirating the pirates, patrolling the coastlines and getting rich as a result. But thereafter the island's fortunes slid into decline as it became a pawn on the chessboard of European politics. In 1715, during the Spanish War of Succession, Ibiza ended up backing the loser and suffered the consequences by having its precious salt-fields taken over by the victor. With their main source of income gone, the islanders were left practically bankrupt – and they were to stay that way for the next 250 years.

BELOW: the Portal de ses Taules is adorned with Eivissa's coat of arms.

Ibiza entered the 20th century as a poor, neglected Spanish outpost. Yet when the flower-children of the 1960s discovered this tolerant "White Island", all that began to change. Against the odds, the Ibicencos had stumbled across a new and exceedingly lucrative source of income which did not depend on the political whims of a Madrid government too far away to care and too confused to interfere.

New arrivals

So the tourist boom began. The easy-going 1960s led into the packaged summer 1970s. Ibiza's laid-back reputation had already spawned an exotic nightlife,

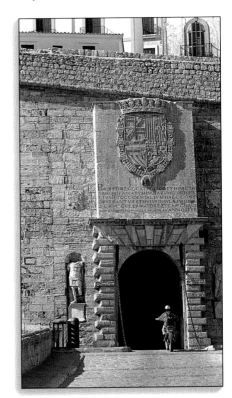

This angel adorns a statue in the Passeig Vara del Rey. It commomorates an Ibizan-born soldier named del Rey, who died fighting US forces in Cuba at the turn of the century.

BELOW: imposing colonial houses line Eivissa's Passeig Vara del Rey.

but the island really captured the imagination of hedonistic holidaymakers in the late 1980s, when a new kind of music, acid house, started being played in its clubs. The island quickly became a magnet for young Brits and Germans who would dance all night to the Balearic beat (often fuelled by the new feel-good drug, Ecstasy), and then sleep off their excesses on the beach.

By the late 1990s, this club scene had become highly sophisticated. Where Ibiza dared, others would follow; DJs from top London clubs now took to spending the summer season on the island, attracting huge crowds of fans.

At the same time, thanks to its reliably hot summers and low-cost lifestyle, and the gently-shelving beaches of resorts like Es Canar and Platja d'En Bossa, the island matured into a pleasant family holiday destination – a world apart from the excesses of the night-time scene.

Since the 1970s, regional identity and autonomy have become very important cultural and political issues in the Balearics – as indeed they are in many other parts of Spain. While Spain was still under the jackboot of Franco, only Castillian Spanish was allowed to be heard on the streets. Nowadays, most of the road-signs and street-names on the island have been altered to the local dialect, *Eivissenc* – a version of Catalan. If you're driving in from the airport, the signs for **Eivissa** will take you into Ibiza Town.

Eivissa (Ibiza Town)

There are four parts to the main town of the island: the old walled city, Dalt Vila, on high; the Sa Penya, or old fishing quarter; Sa Marina, along the waterfront, and the new town, which spreads out for some distance from the **Passeig Vara del Rey** ❸, the large square by the port.

The **Dalt Vila** makes use of the natural defences afforded by the high cliffs on which it is built, the other three sides being well protected by a wall of massive and seemingly unassailable proportions. And yet this is the citadel which was supposedly stormed by Jaume I in 1235, when he recovered the island from Arab control (actually, tradition has it that Jaume's troops were allowed to enter secretly in the middle of the night by the ruling sheikh's brother, in revenge for the sheikh having stolen his wife).

Spain has declared Eivissa's old town a national monument. Following the country's admission into the European Community in 1986, a Euro-funded renovation project was set up to restore Dalt Vila to its former imposing splendour.

There are two principal gates into Dalt Vila—the **Portal de ses Taules** ❻ (so named because of the huge slabs, or *taules*, that used to serve as the drawbridge) and the **Portal Nou** (new) ❼. Traffic nowadays circulates by entering by the former and leaving by the latter. Within the walls there are the ruins of the old **castle** ❺, the cathedral and **Ajuntament**, or Town Hall, the **Museu d'Art Contemporani** ❻ (open Mon–Sat; closed Sat pm; entrance fee), and some excellent open-air restaurants. These are somewhat quieter than those packed into the "Ibiza Triangle" of bars down by the harbour, and the views from here over the bay are quite magnificent – as indeed they should be from a position almost 91 metres (300 ft) above the sea.

The **Cathedral of Santa María de las Nieves** ❻ is built on well-hallowed ground on the site of a mosque, a Roman temple and – more than likely – a Carthaginian shrine (open Mon–Sat; closed Sat pm; entrance fee; free on Sun am for Mass).

Maps
Area 248
City 253

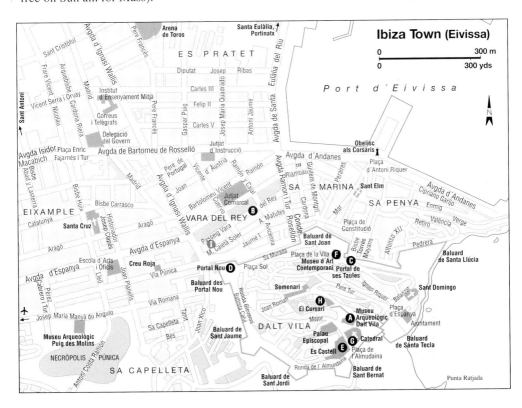

Ibiza Town (Eivissa)

Ses Salines

A traditional Ibizan curse runs "Go and haul salt" – which was the fate once endured by captured pirates and criminals alike. There are nearly 1,000 acres of productive *salines* (salt flats) between Eivissa's airport and the sea – flats which have played a key role in the island's history.

In the past, before tourism, Ibiza's one lucrative commodity was its abundance of natural, sea-farmed sodium chloride, a valuable resource. Used for preservation purposes, salt was vitally important to sailors on long journeys. Salt beef, salt fish, salt pork – salt with everything.

As a result, everybody journeying the Mediterranean from North Africa to mainland Europe used and abused the island's strategic position and stocked up with salt on their way through. The salt-pans were absolutely central to Ibiza's economy. Indeed, it was from the

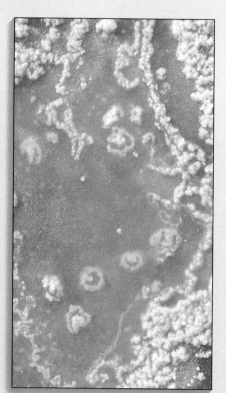

proceeds of salt sales that the fortification of Eivissa town was made possible and the walls of Dalt Vila built in 1554.

At the time of the wall-building, all of the islanders owned a share of the *salines,* and survived quite profitably on trading the salt for foreign grain. However in 1715, following the Spanish War of Succession, the *salines* were appropriated by the state as punishment for Ibiza having supported the losing faction.

Nonetheless, the Ibizans received an annual rent on the pans right up until the middle of the last century, when the *salines* were sold to a private company. Then, finally, the islanders lost all rights, including the right to free salt.

The present owner of the rights and the salt-pans themselves, Salinera Española SA, has improved and mechanised the methods of panning and collecting so much that nowadays the work of 600 is done by only 20.

The extraction process is slow but effective: centuries of practice have seen to that. First, two electric pumps allow two and a half thousand cubic metres of sea water into the below-sea-level flats. It then takes about three months for the water to evaporate and the salt to precipitate, and after that there remains a 10-cm (4-inch) layer of fine white salt, ready for collection (Ibizan salt is of such high quality because there are no poisonous plants nor creatures on the island, and the ground itself is non-toxic).

Of the 1 million tonnes of salt produced annually in Spain, Ibiza's *salines* contribute 60,000. Spain consumes 400,000 tonnes in total, and the rest is exported – much of it to Scandinavia and the Faroe Islands for salting fish.

From an ecological point of view, the *salines* are very important, for they have made Ibiza a popular stopping-point for migratory birds. Herons, storks and even flamingoes rest over here en route to the winter resorts of North Africa, feasting on the abundant food trapped in the shallow water. ❑

LEFT: until tourism took off in the 20th century, salt was Ibiza's most lucrative commodity.

Within the walls lies a maze of impossibly tiny streets which sneak in and out of each other – it's an ideal place for hide and seek. Here too is **El Corsari ⓗ**, once a pirate family mansion, now a hip hotel favoured by visiting DJs and music business celebrities. Eivissa's many gay visitors frequent the Anfora disco here and the bars along the **Sa Carrosa**, just inside the walls. There are plenty of other popular gay bars outside Dalt Vila, too, particularly above the Sa Penya quarter.

Tucked away under Dalt Vila at the end of the harbour, **Sa Penya** was once the fishermen's quarter and still is the poorest and shabbiest part of town. The small, cramped houses here are home to many of Eivissa's gypsy families, who on hot nights usually sit outside chatting, knitting or shelling peas till well beyond midnight. Then they retire indoors to bed, with doors and windows fully open to benefit from any odd breeze. Yet only a few metres down the street along the harbour, you'll see Wealth out shopping.

Night moves

Everything happens at night in the **Sa Marina** district. The shops are here, most of the bars and nearly all of the popular restaurants. In fact, it is easy to forget that it is night-time as you walk through the brightly-lit streets (more like alleys), weaving amongst stalls, bar stools and restaurant tables. After sunset, the crowd around the "Ibiza Triangle" (formed by the bars **Zoo**, **Tango** and **Vogue**) swells and the public relations teams of the major clubs begin their evening's work. As most venues (**Privilege**, **Amnesia** and **Pachá** are the best-known) have party nights two or three times a week, they send out exotically dressed and highly competitive "press gangs" to convince passers-by that their night would not be

Map on page 253

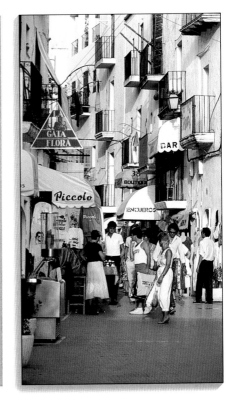

BELOW: shopping along Eivissa's Carrer Major.

F IS FOR FAKE

One of the most intriguing characters to wash up on Ibiza's shores was the master-faker of the 1960s and '70s, Elmyr de Hory. Born into an upper-class Budapest family, de Hory studied under Fernand Léger in Paris and survived a wartime concentration-camp in Transylvania. Back in Paris after the war, he began to churn out, and sell, quantities of Great Works – by "Matisse", "Dégas" and "Dufy", amongst others. By 1969, he had netted himself a cool $60 million on the international art market. Everyone was fooled, including Japan's National Museum of Western Art, which bought a "Dufy" and a "Modigliani".

Aged 55, Elmyr de Hory arrived in Ibiza, where he built a plush villa, drove around in a red Corvette Sting Ray convertible and hung out with the beautiful people. Alas, the bubble burst when a Texan oil millionaire who had purchased no fewer than 44 paintings from de Hory's front man, Fernand Legros, discovered he had been duped. The French authorities soon began pressing for de Hory's extradition. He was never arrested, as Legros was, but after several years spent worrying that the French would get their way, de Hory finally committed suicide in 1976. He had, however, already been immortalised in Orson Welles's 1973 film of his curious life, *F is for Fake*.

complete without a visit to their particular venue. They usually try to stick little badges on passers-by which display their club logo, just so you won't forget – and they sometimes hand out free entrance passes (*see Nightlife, page 95*).

Beyond the Passeig Vara del Rey is the **Eixample**, or new town – a badly designed sprawl thrown up in recent years to house the overspill from Dalt Vila. It is to new apartments here that the locals moved with the money earned from tourism. The new covered *mercat* (market) is here, too, as are the major bus stops from whence you can reach almost every corner of the island. One good thing about this area is that the ordinary family restaurants tend to be exceptionally good value compared to those on the main tourist circuit.,

Close at hand

The nearest beaches are to be found at **Figueretes** ❷, a mile-long stretch of holiday homes and hotels, which also boasts some smart places to stay, including **Los Molinos** with its own pool and beach access. The bay goes beyond to **Platja d'En Bossa** ❸ which is, if not quite The Last Resort, very near to it. The package holiday was delivered here and it is doubtful that the postman will ever come back to take it away again.

The most fashionable beaches are at Es Cavallet and Ses Salines. Both are on the road signposted La Canal, off the airport road and at the end of the salt-flats. **Ses Salines** ❹ has the sea-fun stuff – windsurfer boards, mono-skis, kayaks and so on – some good food huts and even some beach boutiques. **Malibú** is the most chic *chiringuito* (beach bar) at which to hang out and sip Sea Breezes, and the *only* way to pitch up at lunchtime is by power-boat. Although the beach is sandy and quite clean, raffia-type seaweed does collect at the water's edge.

TIP

To find out what's on in Eivissa, look out for the local daily newspaper, *Diario de Ibiza*, which has a supplement in English and German during the summer months.

BELOW: locally made crafts are on sale all over Ibiza.

Set beyond an ancient watch-tower, **Es Cavallet** ❺ is probably the most popular nude beach on Ibiza (families linger around the *chiringuito* at the beginning of the long sandy stretch). Other facilities here include rudimentary ball courts, a massage table (complete with masseur) and even, at times, a hairdresser. Further along, and catered for too, is a fairly outrageous gay section. Local buses to La Canal from Eivissa save a long walk to either beach.

Inland, along the Eivissa-Sant Josep road is the **Cueva Santa**, a small cave open to the public. A little further along this road you'll see signposts for **Casa Juana**, one of the island's better restaurants.

Map on page 248

You'll find this odd-shaped monument to Colombus in Sant Antoni.

Acquired taste

As you set out from Eivissa to explore the island, keep a look-out in bars and cafés for the local brand of *herbes*, a delicious, aromatic mixture of herbs stewed in alcohol. The taste varies from recipe to recipe; some versions are heavily biased towards anise, while others owe much to carob. On Ibiza, carob beans – which look rather like black, flattened bananas – are most commonly used as pig-food, but they also have a high syrup content, rather similar to maple, and are thus a good choice for distillation into alcohol. Some versions are sold with fresh sprigs of herb submerged in the liqueur, but whichever you choose, a bottle of *herbes* is a good way to remember an island holiday.

Sant Antoni

The island's second town **Sant Antoni** ❻, 15 km (9 miles) from Eivissa, may as well be planets away. It was called Portus Magnus by the Romans because of its sizeable natural harbour and is nowadays referred to as Portmany by the

BELOW: on the beach at Sant Antoni.

Map
on page
248

island authorities. The town has a stunning setting along the side of a large, beautiful bay, and could still be extremely romantic (you can watch the sun set here beyond a dozen small islands dotted off the shore) were it not for the fact that it has become a favourite destination for Europe's cheapest all-inclusive package holiday-makers. Sadly, it has ended up looking like a very grubby all-night drive-in supermarket.

The harbourfront and the pedestrianised streets behind, dubbed the "West End", heaves with clubs, pubs, boat trip touts and discos. There are souvenir shops stuffed with straw-hatted donkeys, bars serving pints of beer, shandies and knickerbocker glories and restaurants which specialise in those very Ibizan dishes – baked beans, bacon and chips. Chic it isn't, but it is certainly fun. There are a few redeeming features – a sunset viewed from the Café del Mar, for instance, or the huge seafood platters at Can Pujol, an overgrown beach shack on the opposite side of the bay. Generally, though, the entire place is geared exlusively for young people out to have a good time. And if your idea of having a good time is getting extremely sunburnt, drinking oceans and bedding legions, then this is the place for you.

The **Parish Church** of Sant Antoni stands out in this bedlam like an oasis of tranquillity. Built in the 14th century on the ruins of a mosque, it is a white-washed architectural mixture of fortress and Persian palace.

Just outside Sant Antoni, at Sa Vorera, is **Pike's**, a hip hotel which has been home to some of the island's most outrageous rock 'n' roll parties; Grace Jones and George Michael have been two of the regular celebrity guests. It also has a very good restaurant.

RIGHT: Ibizan *campesina.*
BELOW: counting sheep.

Along the coast – by sea

If you tire of the cheek-to-cheek roasting on the beach at Sant Antoni, join the sun-seekers who take a boat ride instead out to the inlets and coves beyond the bay. To arrange a trip, head for the waterfront **Passeig de ses Fonts**, where the ferry and excursion boats are berthed.

At the Blue Flag **Cala Bassa** ❼, directly across the bay, there is a lot of tourist development, but if you head further south beyond the family time-share holiday lets and the busy resorts of **Cala Vedella** ❽ and **Cala d'Hort** ❾, you will come across a little bit of the South Pacific: the offshore islet, **Es Vedrá** ❿, featured as Bali Hai in the 1950s film *South Pacific* (*see also Magic Ibiza, page 99*). **Cala Carbó**, not far from Cala d'Hort but rather more intimate, is worth a visit for its stretch of sandy beach.

There is a wide choice of boat trips further afield as well, some of which are in glass-bottomed boats. You could try one of the excursions linking the resorts along the southwest coast, some of which include a circuit of Es Vedrá. For a glimpse of the largely untouched northwest coast, sign up for the two-hour journey to Portinatx, which will give you views you'd never be able to see otherwise. Then there's the Wednesday hippie market at Punta Arabí (*see page 264*), a day-trip to little Formentera, or even the mainland. Bon Voyage! ❑

SANTA EULALIA AND THE NORTH COAST

Map on page 248

With its sleepy rural interior still relatively untouched by tourism, the northern part of Ibiza suits those who prefer getting off the beaten track

Ibiza is almost two different islands, separated by a straight line running from Sant Antoni to Eivissa. To the south are the clubs, the packed resorts, the beautiful people, the salt pans and the long, sandy beaches. The north is another story altogether – jagged cliffs, tiny, undeveloped rocky coves only accessible by boat, sleepy, whitewashed *finques* and orchards of almond trees which turn the parched fields pink and white in spring.

What tourist development there is in the north could have been better done. Much of it is characterless, 1970s-style five-storey hotels and many a remote *cala* has been scarred by an apartment complex on its pristine beach. But with a mountain bike, car or a boat, or a good hiking map, there are plenty of untouched places. Inland, dirt tracks criss-cross the almond and olive groves and tiny hamlets cluster around their squat village churches. A few ageing hippies still potter around the village of Sant Carles de Peralta, but much of the island's interior simply dozes in the sun, oblivious to the tourist boom nearby.

PRECEDING PAGES: Cala Conta, just a boat trip away from Sant Antoni. **LEFT:** Puig d'En Missa church, Santa Eulàlia. **BELOW:** fun in the sun, Santa Eulàlia.

A river runs through it

Santa Eulàlia ⓫ is Eivissa's third town and the only one in the whole of the Balearics to be graced with a river. A Roman viaduct, the Devil's Bridge, is just visible from the bridge which crosses it.

Puig d'En Missa, the hill behind the town, is topped with a domed and whitewashed 14th-century church, built (like the town) in the name of the saint. Next to it, but hardly ever open, is a small museum containing paintings of a Catalan artist named Barrau, and surrounding it are some typically square, flat-roofed Ibizan houses. The steep climb up to the church is worthwhile when the weather's not too hot for the impressive views up and down the hazy coast. From here, you can follow the signs to the worthwhile **Museu Etnològic** nearby, housed in a traditional *finça*, whose displays on the island's rural past include traditional clothes and jewellery and an old oil mill (open Mon pm, Tues–Sat; entrance fee)

In Santa Eulàlia itself, there is a busy fresh-produce market and some lively shopping to be done along its main streets, including a small *rambla* imitating the famous promenade in Barcelona. The pedestrian **Carrer Sant Vincenç** is packed in the evenings with holidaymakers looking for something more than the sausages-and-chips on offer in the surrounding resorts, mingling with locals on their nightly *passeig*. Every other whitewashed building is a restaurant or a *tapas* bar, from **Maharba**, where patrons lounge on

big floor cushions and feast on Arabic *mezze,* to **Rincón de Pepe**, a busy *tapas*
emporium with a massive selection, including several vegetarian items.

East of Santa Eulàlia is the beach resort of **Es Canar** ⑫, very busy, very
English and indeed, developed from scratch by an English family in the 1970s.
Apart from a couple of low-key nightclubs, this is a family-and-older-couples
kind of resort, and there's plenty of Yorkshire pudding and fried breakfast on
offer for the homesick. The crescent-shaped harbour is pleasant enough but
there's not much else to see, and the only clue that local people live here too is
the painted fishing boats moored against the low harbour wall.

Hippie hangouts

A little further around the bay is **Punta Arabí** ⑬, site of a weekly hippie market.
Started in the late 1960s to raise money for a local school, the market soon
became a useful outlet for bohemian wanderers who had amassed vanloads of
silver trinkets during the winter season in Goa. It was also a timely project, as
by this stage even the most tolerant islanders had begun to make complaining
noises about the lack of contribution the hippies were making to island life.
Nowadays, the market is a big attraction; every Wednesday, special boats run to
it from Eivissa and Sant Antoni, as well as fleets of coaches.

The goods on sale are a mixture of trash and kitsch: woven bracelets, lurid,
embroidered waistcoats, leather and the ubiquitous silver jewellery. Some stalls
sell souvenirs from the clubs and Balearic beat dance-mix CDs; there are sand
pictures and fake Rolexes. But are these real hippies? Not likely. Most of the
genuine-looking characters smoking joints and strumming *California Dreamin'*
are simply out to make a fast buck – they even charge for photographs.

BELOW: brightly
coloured beach-
ware for sale at
Punta Arabí's
hippie market.

Sant Carles de Peralta , the village where the first hippie settlers lived in communal *finques*, is so tiny and sleepy you'd hardly know you'd just passed through it. Just inland from Es Canar, it's in a lovely position between olive groves and pine woods – the so-called "herb gardens" of the 1960s are long gone. The legendary **Anita's Bar** is still here, though, serving *herbes*, the local liqueur, along with hearty traditional dishes.

Anita's Bar was a popular hippie hangout in the 1960s.

Clifftops and coves

There are numerous *cales* (coves) forming the jagged coastline north and south of Santa Eulàlia, however the scenery varies considerably. Some coves, like **Cala Llonga** , have been sadly over-developed, with the pine forests on either side of a deep fjord cleared to make way for ugly hotels. The best *cales* are those accessible only by dirt track, on foot or by boat.

Walking trails along the clifftops are erratically marked, with many paths simply ending in a tangle of undergrowth. A notable exception is the one-and-a-half hour trek from Santa Eulàlia to Cala Llonga along an old mule-track. You'll pass some exquisite scenery as the path climbs through the pine-woods over two mountains, **Puig d'En Pep** (240 metres/785 ft) and **Puig Marina** (205 metres/670 ft). The route, clearly indicated by waymarkers, ends on the outskirts of Cala Llonga.

A hearty lunch washed down with buckets of chilled rosé is a classic way to spend an Ibizan Sunday, especially in summer. As always, the best restaurants are the most inaccessible, and you certainly can't get much more remote than **Cala Mastella**, a tiny cove east of Sant Carles at the end of another dirt track. Leave the car and follow a trail on the left-hand side of the cove over a pile of rocks and around the headland to a tiny bay, shaded by trees, with a solitary *chiringuito* built on stilts above the water. There's only one dish on the menu, brewed in a large pot, and everybody eats together at long benches. With no traffic, no jetskis and no beach umbrellas crowding the miniature strip of sand, it's pretty near perfect.

BELOW: village church, Sant Carles de Peralta.

Some 15 minutes' drive south of Santa Eulàlia, at **Roca Llisa**, is Ibiza's only golf complex. It's not exactly St Andrews; while there are nine-hole and 18-hole courses, some of the holes are a trifle bizarre, crossing what appear to be private gardens and even a small quarry. However, the atmosphere is friendly and you don't need a handicap to play.

Offshore wilderness

Heading north from Santa Eulàlia, the coast grows wilder and less developed. Rocky, pine-topped headlands separate hidden bays, some with an immaculate, sandy beach, others lined with glistening rocks giving way to the turquoise depths. That said, busy **Cala Sant Vicenç** is hardly worth the trek. Better beaches and more enthralling scenery can be found nearby; there's no need to suffer the bland charmlessness of this holiday high street.

Cala Sant Vincenç is, however, the starting-point for boat trips to the islet of **Tagomago** , Ibiza's own offshore wilderness with an unusual Pacific island

Map on page 248

Pa amb oli (*bread moistened with tomato and olive oil) forms the centrepiece of this tasty Ibizan snack.*

name. A solid chunk of rock rising 100 metres (330 ft) out of the sea, it is guarded by a lighthouse although inhabited only by seabirds. Fishing and diving are the only pursuits here, but there are also a couple of tiny *cales* where yachts moor for lunchtime picnics.

Portinatx ⑱, in the far north of the island, was the unlikely setting for some of the scenes from the film *South Pacific*, the legacy of which still sustains several local bars and restaurants. Portinatx is essentially a beach resort, and coastal scenery aside, not a particularly attractive one at that, with boxy hotels lining the waterfront. There are, however, some beautiful sunbathing spots on broad, flat rocks at each end of the resort's three beaches, and some breathtaking hikes along the cliffs. Various wealthy locals have built spectacular homes here, which means the clientele at the *chiringuito* in **Cala d'En Serra** is often distinctly glamorous. **Cala Xarraca ⑲** makes an excellent spot for a lingering lunch, followed by a gentle potter around the rocks on a pedalo.

Helium and Hacienda

Inland from Portinatx, the route between the two charming villages of **Sant Joan** and Sant Miquel is one of the island's prettiest. A hippie collective called Helium can be found along this road, easily identified by the inventive array of tin-can sculptures on display in the garden.

Like many Balearic villages, **Sant Miquel ⑳** was originally located inland, safe from marauding pirates. A solid little church dating back to the 14th century provides the backdrop for regular Thursday evening *ball pagès*, or country dancing displays, after which there's a chance to sample the local *herbes*. Sadly, **Port de Sant Miquel ㉑** has not escaped the developers' heavy hand quite so

BELOW LEFT:
luxurious Hacienda hotel, near Port de Sant Miquel.
BELOW RIGHT:
antique shop, Santa Gertrudis.

lightly. although the town's pretty cove is nonetheless a good place for a swimming stop. On the cliffs to the right is a bar affording wonderful views, while down below the illuminated **Coves de Ca Na Marça** make a popular – if rather overrated – excursion (open daily, mid-May–Oct; entrance fee).

If bars and restaurants aren't a prerequisite, head for **Cala de Benirràs** instead, a breathtaking little inlet where sheer cliffs plummet into the turquoise depths and the tiny beach has no facilities at all. Be warned, though, that the dirt track leading to the beach is rather punishing on the average rental car.

Hidden under the pine trees on a cliff-top round the hairpin bend from Port de Sant Miquel is the island's best and most beautiful hotel, the **Hacienda**.

Heading inland

Some of Ibiza's inland villages are worth a special trek. On the road from Portinatx to Eivissa, tucked away along a dirt track near Sant Llorenç is beautiful **Bàlafi 22**, the island's only surviving Moorish hamlet. Further down the road on the way to Sant Rafel is **Santa Gertrudis de Fruitera 23**, a sleepy little place with no less than four art galleries, all featuring work (of varying quality) by resident expatriates. The village bar, Can Costa, is a popular arty hangout.

The alternative route from Sant Miquel to Sant Antoni is via **Santa Agnès de Corona 24**; it's one of the most spectacular drives on the island. Make time to explore the small dirt roads trickling down to the coast from here, and you'll come across some enchanting, and quite deserted, small, sandy *cales*, like Punta Galera and **Cala Salada 25**. At **Cabo Norró**, off the main road to the left, you can also visit a cave covered in what are allegedly Bronze Age paintings – look out for the signpost for Ses Fontanelles just before reaching Santa Agnès. ❑

Map on page 248

TIP

On the menu at the Hotel Hacienda are some interesting Carthaginian dishes, including swordfish with *garum*. It also produces a fine *herbes*, flavoured with lemon, tarragon and mint.

BELOW: the Coves de Ca Na Marça, below Sant Miquel.

The Hippie Era

Just as the west coast of California became a sanctuary for almost every American mama and papa dressed in a kaftan in the 1960s, so Ibiza became the European summer home for every flower-child who could get it together to make the crossing from Barcelona. Back then, the hippie circuit consisted of Goa for the winter and Ibiza for the summer, with North Africa and Turkey en route.

At the time, Spain was hardly a beacon of liberalism; after all, General Franco ruled with iron fists rather than open arms. But artists and bohemians drawn to Ibiza's scenic beauty found that the locals were extraordinarily tolerant. As the island was at this stage little more than a neglected outpost, this attitude was probably as much a product of its isolation as anything else; it also helped, of course, that a good deal of foreign money was suddenly pouring into local bars, shops and businesses.

In the 1970s, the rich and famous also started visiting this hip centre of summer "happenings". Joni Mitchell, for example, sang about the island on her 1971 album *Blue*: "So I bought me a ticket, I caught a plane to Spain/Went to a party down a red dirt road/There were lots of pretty people there/Reading Rolling Stone, reading Vogue ..." (*California*). The jetset had arrived.

Eivissa then was an unassuming provincial harbour town. Everyone stayed at Dalt Vila and went to the beach at Figueretes, where they made music, smoked joints and simply hung out.

In Santa Eulàlia, meanwhile, the "in" (or rather, the only) place to see and be seen was Sandy's Bar, while all the action in Sant Carles de Peralta, the sleepy village at the heart of the hippie community, was at Anita's bar, still going strong. Back then, Amnesia was just a sprawling *finca* with a barbecue-stand, while Privilege was a mere country bar equipped with a stereo and a pool.

Although these days most of the hippies have grown up and moved on, their tradition has become firmly entrenched in island life. Hippie style, for example, spawned Ibiza's famous fashion label Ad Lib, with its distinctive designs in finely-embroidered white lace and cotton. Local icon and founder of the label, the late Smilya Mihailovitch, claimed Ad Lib was a backlash against the rigidity of Parisienne *haute couture*.

Some old hippies continue to come back every summer, although now it's usually with a Volvo, designer labels and children of their own. Others – about a dozen families – remain on the island all year round, living communally near Sant Carles and producing arts and crafts for another long-standing hippie venture, the Punta Arabí market near Es Canar. Ironically, this is now one of the island's biggest commercial successes – and tourist attractions. ❑

LEFT: long-legged attractions at Punta Arabí.
RIGHT: Ibiza's interior is remarkably unspoilt.

FORMENTERA

*A lack of modern development is what draws
discerning visitors to the tiny island of Formentera, but
for how much longer can it remain unspoiled?*

Map
on page
276

Formentera, a ragged sliver of rock in the Mediterranean 4 km (2½ miles) south of Ibiza, contains little of the obvious scenic or cultural interest found in the other Balearics. As the 4,000 islanders themselves put it, *hi ha molt poca cosa que veure*, there is little to see: a handful of ruined watch-towers, a few windmills and three fortress churches. But the uncluttered simplicity, sometimes even raw harshness, of the landscape and the absence of distracting human grandeur have given the island other rare qualities: a sense of timelessness and of space, despite its small size. And, when the light softens in the early morning and evening, an almost abstract beauty of colour and form. It comes as no surprise to learn that the islanders have the longest life expectancy in Spain.

How long Formentera will retain these qualities is hard to know. Sometimes called a miniature Ibiza of yesteryear, there are still areas of quiet farmland and hardly any glitziness, but it takes little to swamp such a small area. In summer the population doubles and the island teems with hired bikes, cars and safari jeeps. Tourism has brought addictive economic dependence and the lure of large-scale development may become increasingly difficult to resist.

PRECEDING PAGES:
view to La Mola;
Formenteran
grande dame.
LEFT: traditional
bread oven.
BELOW: Formentera
offers quiet farm-
land rather than
glitzy nightclubs.

Port link

One important protection remains to preserve the isolation: there is no airport. The island's main link with the outside world remains a small port, **Sa Savina ❶**, named after the Phoenician juniper trees which grow all over the island. Its straggling, modern appearance, an unpromising first impression when you come off the boat, belies its considerable historical importance. Limestone, dried fish, fruit and sea-salt have all been exported from here to Ibiza, although until recent times heavy seas and storms could cut winter communications for weeks at a time.

These days the increasing numbers of ferries and boats and a hydrofoil carry mainly tourists. The harbour is the focus of local life only twice a year: in January, when the Three Kings bring in the children's Christmas presents by boat, and in July, when the fishing boats gather here and sail out as a fleet to be blessed on the feast of Our Lady of the Sea. This is Formentera's principal annual fiesta.

Smells and salt

From Sa Savina a road runs south past the **Estany des Peix**, a lake with sandy shores said to be well stocked with trapped sea-fish, and another loops east, skirting the larger **Estany Pudent** – literally Smelly Lake, an honest enough name at low tide thanks to its mass of weed. The surrounding country is flat and somewhat featureless except for hillocky dunes and

the abandoned salt-beds, bleakly beautiful walled sheets of pink and yellow water or sparkling beaten earth, a solitary salt heap and an old railway track with small freight trucks nearby. A question-mark hangs over the salt-beds' future; the owners planned to sell them for development, but were frustrated by local opposition. Now there is a campaign for a national park to protect the area and the birds of passage – over 250 species – who come through here every winter.

Quiet metropolis

The road south leads past the only petrol station on the island to **Sant Francesc Xavier ②**, sometimes called the capital of the island but in reality little more than a swollen village. If you sit for a while in a café on the miniature *plaça* here, opposite the 18th-century fortress church (built without windows for better protection) and the shabby but gracious library, you can catch something of the feel of life here before electricity, the telephone and tourism arrived in one fell swoop in the late 1950s.

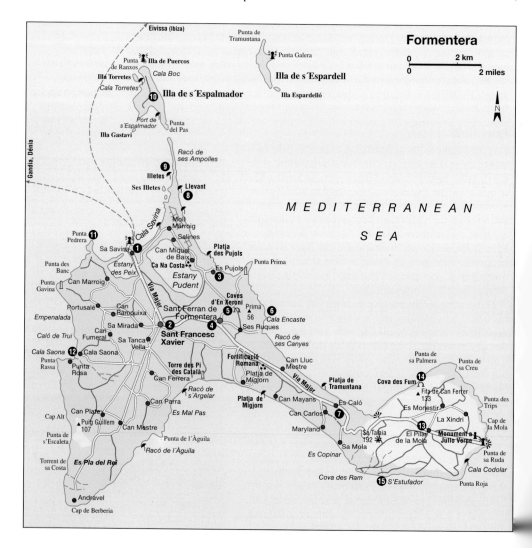

The church, modern inside except for the lovely font, was built as a shelter from piracy, which plagued the island until the arrival of steamboats and the telegraph; the library used to be the town hall. In the side-streets there is everything from a health food store to a chapel dating back to Formentera's 14th-century Catalan conquest by the Archbishop of Tarragona – which confirmed the island's link to Ibiza as one of the Pityussai (*see page 245*) rather than to Palma as one of the Balearics. Other shops include fishmongers and a co-operative where farmhouse sheep and goat's cheeses are sold in spring and early summer.

Map
on page
276

Hand-made sweaters in traditional Formenteran designs are a good buy.

Tracks and trees

South and west, down networks of dirt tracks called the *carreteres del camp*, are lovely unspoilt patches of farmland criss-crossed by dry stone walls, now occasionally replaced by breeze-blocks, a sign of more hurried times. The fields, bald and brown in summer after the April harvest, are dotted by prickly pears, giant fig trees, (their branches supported by a ring of smaller trees) and carob trees, now the most important crop for export.

The modesty of the geometrical farms which are fronted by unexpectedly gracious flowery porches and with wells, circular threshing grounds and domed ovens nearby, spell out the centuries of poverty and simplicity of life here which gave rise to the famed longevity of the small number of islanders.

The road east loops round to **Es Pujols** ❸, a fully fledged resort – small by some standards but not for Formentera, and rapidly spawning discos, beer gardens and apartments. Ugly club-hotel bungalows engulf the watch-tower on **Punta Prima**, the rocky eastern headland. Only the fine view of Ibiza, with the island of Es Vedrà rearing up like a sphinx and the fishermen's ramshackle

BELOW: the 18th-century fortress-church of Sant Francesc Xavier.

boat houses, suggest the unspoiled bay where the island's first beach hotel was built 30 years ago. Nonetheless, Es Pujols is within easy walking distance of Formentera's best beaches and is also the liveliest place to be at night, so it can make a good base for a short stay.

There's no shortage of time to catch up on the gossip on Formentera.

Stone ring

Ironically, the oldest known human monument on the island, a *dolmen* dating from 1600 BC, stands unsignposted and rarely visited just down the road at **Ca Na Costa**, a promontory into the Estany Pudent. The ring of upright stone slabs—discovered in 1976 with human remains, ceramics, jewellery and axes typical of a sophisticated Bronze Age culture – is the best of such 40 sites on the island. It also suggests that Formentera once had a more fertile landscape which was destroyed by deforestation some time before the Phoenicians, Greeks, Romans and Moors arrived; they all found the rocky environment suitable only as a strategic military outpost.

The third main settlement on the island, **Sant Ferran ❹**, is traditionally the centre of the island's vineyards and, more recently, of its alternative culture. It is said that the hippies first gravitated here not so much because of **Fonda Pepe**, its now legendary bar, but because they would be out of easy reach of the *guardia civil*, who at the time operated only by bicycle; the first drug arrests were eventually made by police in hired taxis. Fonda Pepe survives as a living museum of post-sixties European youth culture, and is still packed to the gills in the high season, yet at the same time it is very Spanish, with loud music and local barflies of all ages.

BELOW: soaking up the sun on Llevant beach.

Unexpected, but slotting happily into local life in Sant Ferran, are an excellent privately run library and a workshop making guitars and other musical instruments. Nearby, the **Coves d'En Xeroni ❺**, the only caves on the island open to the public, were found by a farmer making a well. Decorated by fibrous roots from the kitchen garden, they have disco lights and even a bar.

Herbal tipple

The main road runs east down the spine of the narrow central isthmus, past a ruined Roman fortress (up an unmarked track near the 10 km marker). The northern side is rocky, primitive landscape, sloping down from steep red cliffs at **Cala Encaste ❻**, where you can swim off slippery boulders, to **Es Caló ❼**, a little fishing village open to the road. According to local tradition this was the birthplace of *herbes*, the local and variable herbal brew, first made here in an illegal distillery in the early 19th century.

To the south curves the **Platja Migjorn**, a sweep of narrow sandy beach, clogged with seaweed in places and backed by a number of tourist developments such as the Hotel Formentor, a chunky white blot with Anglo-German timetables for organised sports, and Maryland, a holiday village in the same mould. Beyond here are some good small coves and rocky bays reached by footpath. Otherwise, the quiet stretch of sand near Torre des Català in the east is a good bet for undisturbed sea bathing.

Map on page 276

Best beaches

Popular since the 1960s but able to absorb the crowds, and undeveloped except for small beach cafés, are the beaches on the finger of land north of the salt-beds, reached by sandy track or boat. **Llevant ❽**, an open shoreline, has ocean-like breakers on windy days; on the other side **Illetes ❾**, sometimes nicknamed Tahiti for its atoll-like offshore islands and milky-blue waters, is sheltered and has windsurfers for hire. Strip totally if you wish; there are few places on Formentera where nudism raises eyebrows, and these two are certainly not included.

Just off the point, separated by a strait that can be forged at low tide, is **Espalmador ❿**, a privately owned, lamb chop-shaped islet with an idyllic lagoon (a favourite haunt of the Spanish Royal Family) and an unofficial mud-bath from which the adventurous emerge daubed in sulphurous grey clay. The beach is better visited before or after the midday invasion of speedboats and daytrippers from Ibiza.

Punta Pedrera ⓫, an empty moonscape and the site of an old Arab quarry on the northern tip of the western coast, has rocky secluded platforms, caves and crystal-clear water, but hardly conforms to everybody's idea of beach bliss. Land was bought here for a millionaire's playground with a private heliport, but the plans floundered in the face of local opposition.

Further down the same coast, just south of Sant Francesc, lies **Cala Saona ⓬**, a small bay with fine sand and a deep beach. Here you will find more classic Mediterranean charms: layered rusty cliffs, pine-tree copses and a colony of French summer residents, some of whom play regular games of *boules* here in the evening. The beach is one of the most popular with Formenterans at weekends. From here, the desolate end of Cap de Berberia is easy to reach.

Island ends

The most peaceful parts of the island are inevitably those without beaches: the peninsulas at either end, like the snout and tail of the dolphin of Formentera.

Most people speed over **La Mola**, a geographically distinct limestone plateau, pausing only for a quick look at the lighthouse sitting high above sheer cliffs and the unexpected monument to Jules Verne, who set part of a novel here. **El Pilar ⓭**, a sleepy village with a whitewashed 18th-century church, two defunct windmills and a choice of bars is known for its traditional fiestas, complete with old courtship dances, singing and poetry. Make sure to visit the ceramicists, and the *merceria* next to Bar El Pilar which sells fine handmade woollen articles.

The coastline, honeycombed with caves, including the **Cova des Fum ⓮**, where a party of Viking raiders made off with Arab treasure having smoked out the defenders, can only be seen by boat. But you can walk up from **Es Caló** to the ruins of the 14th-century monastery at **Es Monestir** or go south through farmland towards **S'Estufador ⓯**, a rocky break in the cliffs with a handful of boat sheds and small slipway where you can swim with safety.

The snout of the dolphin, **Cap de Berberia**, has the most atmospheric cliff walks, splashed with pink when the *frígola*, or thyme, is in blossom. ❑

BELOW: isolated Cap de Berberia.

INSIGHT GUIDES

TRAVEL TIPS

Insight Guides portray destinations in depth, providing the complete picture and the top photography

Insight Pocket Guides focus on the best choices for places to see and things to do and include large fold-out maps

Insight Compact Guides' portability makes them the perfect books to carry with you for on-the-spot reference

Three types of guide for all types of travel

INSIGHT GUIDES Different people need different kinds of information. Some want *background information* to help them prepare for the trip. Others seek *personal recommendations* from someone who knows the destination well. And others look for *compactly presented data* for on-the-spot reference. With three carefully designed series, Insight Guides offer readers the perfect choice. Insight Guides will turn your visit into an experience.

The world's largest collection of visual travel guides

CONTENTS

Getting Acquainted

The Place

Situation: The Balearics, an archipelago of five islands (Mallorca, Menorca, Ibiza, Formentera and tiny Cabrera) lie off the northeastern coast of Spain. They are on the 39th and 40th North parallels, in the Balearic Sea (a part of the Mediterranean), and almost exactly on the Greenwich meridian. On the mainland of Spain, Barcelona and Valencia are the nearest principal cities, while on the northern coast of Africa, the closest city is Algiers.

Area: The archipelago covers a total surface area of 5,014 sq km (1,935 sq miles), 1,240 km (770 miles) of which is coastline. Mallorca is the largest island (3,640 sq km/1,405 sq miles).

Population: 800,000 (600,000 of whom live in Mallorca).

Language: Spanish and Catalan.

Religion: Catholic.

Time Zone: As part of Spain, the Balearics adhere to the time zones used by the continental EU countries. Between the months of October and May, this is GMT +1, but in summer one more hour is added. Dates of time changes are announced well in advance each year. Clocks go forward in spring, and back in autumn.

Currency: the *peseta* (written "pts"), scheduled to be replaced (by July 2002) by the pan-European euro.

Weights & Measures: Metric, as in the rest of Spain.

Electricity: 220 volts, using round, two-pronged plugs, so Britons will need an adaptor to use their appliances and North Americans an adaptor and transformer.

International Dialling Code: 34. The town code for Palma de Mallorca is 971.

Government/Economy

When General Franco died in 1975, Spain at last entered the modern world politically and economically. King Juan Carlos I has since guided the nation through a difficult transition, transforming it from a repressive military dictatorship into a parliamentary democracy, with himself as constitutional monarch.

On 29 December 1978, the new Spanish constitution rendered Spain a collection of 17 autonomous regions. Politically, the Balearic Islands form a *Comunidad Autónoma* within the Spanish state. All the islands together form a Spanish province, headed by the *Govern Balear*.

In recent history, the Balearic islands have undergone dramatic changes. Mass tourism has radically altered their infrastructure,

Public Holidays

Holidays vary depending on the region. The following is the official list issued by the *Boletín Oficial* of the Balearics, but see also page 299 for some of the major fiestas, which are celebrated with gusto in towns and villages. A booklet with a full listing of these is available at tourist offices in each island.

● **1 January** New Year's Day
● **6 January** Epiphany
● **March/April** Easter Thursday, Friday, and Monday
● **1 May** Labour Day
● **24 June** St John's Day
● **25 July** St James's Day
● **15 August** Assumption of the Virgin
● **12 October** Discovery of America Day
● **1 November** All Saints' Day
● **8 December** Immaculate Conception
● **25 December** Christmas Day
● **26 December** Gathering of the Virgin.

and in just 30 years their predominantly agrarian economy has become a service economy, with tourism accounting for two-thirds of the islands' gross domestic product.

Climate

The three main islands enjoy more or less the same temperate Mediterranean weather conditions, with the sun shining an average 59 percent of the time. The few local variations are caused by phenomena such as Mallorca's mountain ranges.

The Balearics' average high temperature is 21.2°C (70°F), the average low 13.8°C (57°F). Annual rainfall in Maó (Menorca) is 580 mm (23 in) a year, while that in Palma (Mallorca) reaches only 480 mm (19 in).

The best times to visit are spring and autumn, to avoid the baking heat of high summer.

Planning the Trip

Visas & Passports

Thanks to the importance of tourism, Spain puts few barriers in the way of visitors. A passport or similar travel document is all that is required for most tourists. However, for political or security reasons, and sometimes only to apply reciprocity, citizens of some countries must also have a valid visa stamped in their passport. Check with your travel agent.

Spain has ended the requirement to fill out landing cards for the Balearics, and there is no Immigration or Customs declaration form. Citizens of countries in the European Union normally walk through the National Police (Immigration) controls by showing only the front cover of their passport. Visitors who have a visa will normally have their passport stamped with the date of arrival. Applications for extensions of stay can be arranged, but cost time and money, and it is better to obtain a long-stay visa in the first place.

Money Matters

Spain's currency is the peseta. Notes are available in denominations of 10,000, 5,000, 2,000 and 1,000 pts, and coins to the value of 500, 200, 100, 50, 10, 5 and 1pts. Many shops already accept the euro, in anticipation of the planned introduction of this currency throughout the EU.

Cash and traveller's cheques

An unlimited amount of foreign currency and traveller's cheques may be brought into the Balearics. All banks and most hotels are authorised to buy foreign currency at the official rate of exchange (although bringing in lesser-known currencies may cause delay).

Though it's safer to carry most of your currency in traveller's cheques, it is also worth bringing a limited sum in US dollars or pounds sterling. If you can't find a place to cash cheques, there will usually be a shop or post office somewhere interested in exchanging pesetas for these currencies.

It is also a good idea to arrive with about 10,000 pts in 1,000 notes, which is sufficient to buy a drink or pay a taxi driver.

Credit Cards

The use of credit cards is widespread throughout Spain, and increasingly these are acceptable for most transactions. Most major cards are known and acceptable, especially Visa, BankAmeriCard and American Express.

Certain types of bank card can also be used to draw cash in pesetas from ATMs (cash machines) at banks. You will find that this is the most convenient and least expensive way of getting funds and many of the machines operate around the clock.

Bank Opening Hours

● **Winter** (mid-Sep to mid-June): Monday–Friday 8.30am–2.30pm Saturday 8.30am–1pm.
● **Summer** (mid-June to mid-Sep): Monday–Friday 8.30am–2.30pm

Health

Spain has few serious diseases apart from those you can contract in the States or the rest of Europe. Citizens of the US, Canada and United Kingdom do not need any immunisations to enter the country.

PRECAUTIONS

The most important health advice is to treat the sun with the respect it is due – even well-seasoned sunbathers can burn within minutes in Spain's summer sun. Always use a sunscreen product (current recommendations are that whatever your skin type you use a sun-protection factor of 15) and be especially careful with children, who don't know the danger, and who can dehydrate with often frightening speed. Drink plenty of non-alcoholic liquids and, if necessary, take salt pills with you.

Made in Spain

One final health note for anybody taking medication regularly; don't forget that if you have diarrhoea, your pill may not stay with you long enough to be effective. This is particularly worrying if the pill concerned is contraceptive, and could create a new dimension for the phrase "Made in Spain".

INSURANCE

British and EU residents are entitled to free medical treatment in Spain as long as they carry an E111 form (obtainable from post offices at home). Provision is not of the highest quality, however: medical staff may not even know what an E111 is, so you could have a battle on your hands obtaining free provision, plus you will have to pay for your own medicine.

It is therefore advisable to take out private medical insurance. You will have to pay for treatment when in Spain, so you must keep receipts for any bills or medicines you pay for to claim your money back. If you plan to do any watersports or mountaineering, you might have to pay a supplement to cover you for accidents.

Of course, general travel insurance is also recommended to cover you for everything from theft to flight cancellation.

What to Pack

Clothes

Dress is generally very casual on the Balearic Islands. Cotton tends to be more comfortable than

Tourist Offices

Australia
Spanish National Tourist Office
203 Castereagh Street,
Suite 21a, PO Box A-685,
Sydney, NSW.
Tel: 02 9264 7966.
Canada
Spanish National Tourist Office
102 Bloor Street West,
14th floor, Toronto, Ontario.
Tel: 416 916 3131.
UK
Spanish National Tourist Office
22 Manchester Square,
London SW1M 5AP.
Information: 0171-486 8077.
Brochures: 0891 669922.
US: New York
Spanish National Tourist Office
665 5th Avenue,
New York NY 10022.
Tel: 212 759 8822.
  Chicago
Water Tower Place,
Suite 915 East,
845 North Michigan Avenue,
Chicago, IL 60611.
Tel: 312 642 1992.
  Los Angeles
83 Wilshire Boulevard,
Suite 960, Beverly Hills,
Los Angeles, CA 90211.
Tel: 323 658 7188.
  Miami
1221 Brickell Avenue,
Suite 1850, Miami, FL 33131.
Tel: 305 358 1992.

synthetic materials in the heat, and shorts, T-shirts and sandals are the norm for tourists in summer (with swimsuits usually better confined to the resort or beach), though you should try to look respectable if you are visiting local churches.

Apart from high-society events, codes of dress for business and formal occasions are as elsewhere in Europe.

Essentials
Whatever time of year you visit the Balearic Islands, you will need sunglasses, a hat and sunscreen to protect you from the sun (though most brands are available locally).

Remember, too, to pack spares of essentials like glasses, contact lenses and dentures, as well as your prescribed medicine; plus a spare prescription from your doctor for replacement medicines; and a camera and/or camcorder (film of all sorts is sold in many outlets throughout the islands).

Getting There
BY AIR
The islands of Mallorca, Menorca and Ibiza have modern airports, and are served regularly by both scheduled and charter flights from a large choice of departure-points, mainly in Europe. The list of the carriers serving the Balearics includes: Iberia, SAS, Lufthansa, Luxair, British Airways, Caledonian, Swissair and Air France, among many others. There are special deals all year round from the UK, so check with your local travel agent well in advance.

Scheduled services operate from several Spanish mainland cities, and these are flown by both Iberia and Aviaco.

Visitors to the fourth largest Balearic island, Formentera, can make their connections in Ibiza, from where frequent passenger and car ferries cross to the port of La Savina. Ferries also operate to Formentera from Denia and Alicante on the Spanish mainland.

All-inclusive packages
The cheapest way to fly to the islands is usually on a package tour. Many all-inclusive packages are offered by tour operators and travel agents from points all over Europe, and seasonally from the US, Canada, Iceland and so on. Major European tour operators such as Thomson, TUI or Spies have appointed agents throughout the world, through whom it is possible to reserve a holiday and leave from the airport most suitable to you.

It is also possible to travel independently, choosing your own airline and hotel, and using taxis for your transfers. The price of independence can be high, though,

without the benefit of the airline-seat and hotel-room discounts that tour operators can negotiate. The savings available in buying a ready-assembled holiday do not mean you will be part of a regimented group, with a tour-guide waving a little flag, leading a long line of tired sightseers. The only time you need be with others is during the flight and on the bus transferring you to and from your hotel.

Delays
Expect bottlenecks and delays in the baggage halls of the three major airports on the islands, particularly in the summer high-season. As the majority of flights arriving are one-stop charter rather than multi-stop scheduled services, the incidence of lost or mishandled baggage is lower than at many airports.

Return visitors to Mallorca will find that Palma's Son Sant Juan airport has been renovated and enlarged. But in the summer more than 100,000 visitors are expected through the airport each day. Hold-ups are frequent due to the sheer number of flights, and air traffic control problems at Madrid airport also contribute to the delays; however, Spain's Ministry of Transport is trying to find a solution to the problem and has allocated funds to improve the system.

Transfers
The airports of the three largest islands are a short hop from the capitals. Buses leave every 15 minutes from each airport, taking you straight into the city centres. Taxis are also available and cost under £5.

Useful numbers
MAIN AIRPORTS:
• Son Sant Juan, Mallorca
Tel: 971 789099.
• Aeropuerto de Menorca.
Tel: 971 157000.
• Aeropuerto de Ibiza.
Tel: 971 302200.
AIRLINES:
Iberia. Tel: 971 789976.
British Airways. Tel: 971 787737.

BY SEA

Services are provided by convenient ferry routes, primarily from Barcelona and Valencia, with the highest frequency of services from the former. In summer, there are also services to Alcúdia, in Mallorca. Ferries operate from Alicante and Denia to Ibiza and Formentera. There are also regular inter-island ferries, and a fast hydrojet (two hours) runs between Palma and Ibiza.

All the ferries from Valencia and Barcelona carry cars, trucks, boat-trailers and so. Passengers can reserve a cabin for the eight to 10-hour trip, but the ordinary ticket entitles you to an airline-type seat in one of the lounges. Most ferries have restaurants and coffee shops and large bar-lounges (usually noisy with continuous TV).

The principal operator of these services is the Trasmediterranea, popularly known as La Tras. As with other ferry lines, La Tras has appointed agents throughout the world, with reservations available locally or through your own travel agent. Flebassa operates between Mallorca and Menorca twice daily. For further information about the above services contact:
Trasmediterranea Tel: 971 702300.
Flebassa Tel: 971 566454.

Trains to Spanish Ports
Services by rail, including sleepers and car-carriers, operate from all over continental Europe, feeding into either Valencia or Barcelona for transfer on to the ferry to the

Generally speaking, the longer you stay in the Balearics the more economically attractive driving becomes, particularly if you can get cheap lodgings, too. It also ensures independence and mobility during your stay.

Although Spain's roads are often criticised, particularly by Spaniards themselves, the truth is that the crowding during holidays and long weekends is due mainly to an enormous increase in the number of private cars over the last few years; road-building has simply not been able to keep pace with demand.

The regional and local governments, however, do a reasonable job of widening and improving existing roads, building new ones where possible, and creating by-passes around cities. Most main and secondary roads in the Balearics are in good condition, comparable to elsewhere in Europe.

Balearics. It is essential to make advance reservations.

In addition, a high-speed service (AVE) now functions between Sevilla and Madrid, and plans for a Madrid-Barcelona route are under way. You can also take the Talgo 200, which travels at 200 kph (125 mph), and operates throughout Spain.

Practical Tips

Business Hours

The islands have traditionally observed the noon-time siesta, with businesses and shops generally open from 8/9am to 1/1.30pm, and from 4/4.30pm to 7/7.30pm. As an exception, shops and businesses in Menorca tend to reopen after lunch at a later hour, around 5pm.

In certain sectors of business, these traditional hours are changing. For example, the big department stores such as El Corte Inglés and the out-of-town hypermarkets generally open all day, from 10am to 9pm, but close on Sundays.

Other businesses, related to firms in other countries and different time zones, will also sometimes have differing hours. Shops in resorts usually open all day every day in summer.

Also in summer, generally from June through to August, many government and professional offices are open only on weekday mornings.

Media

NEWSPAPERS
Spanish

There are several excellent Spanish-language newspapers published on the islands. Some of these are the *Diario de Ibiza*, *Diario de Mallorca*, *Ultima Hora* and *Diario Insular de Menorca*. In addition, all of the major mainland newspapers such as *El País*, *Vanguardia* and *Ya* are available at most kiosks.

International

Most newsstands also have today's (or at worst, yesterday's) *Figaro*,

Specialist Operators

The Spanish National Tourist Office (*see page 286*) provides a list of tour operators offering holidays in Spain. Here are some specialist agents:

● **Bird watching/painting courses**
Alternative Mallorca,
60 Steinbeck Road,
Leeds LS7 2PW.
Tel: 0113–278 6862.

● **Villa Holidays**
Magic of Spain,
227 Shepherd's Bush Road,
London W6 7AS.
Tel: 0181–748 7575.
● **Walking holidays**
Globespan, Colinton House,
10 West Mill Road,
Colinton Village,
Edinburgh EH13 0NX.
Tel: 0131–441 1388.

La Stampa, The Times, Daily Telegraph, Daily Express, Daily Mail and Sun, along with Die Telegraaf and other European and US papers, including the International Herald Tribune.

English Publications

• **Mallorca** English-speakers in Mallorca have their own peculiar love-hate relationship with the Majorca Daily Bulletin, otherwise known as the Daily Bee. Nobody publicly admits to buying the paper, but everybody seems to have read it, and many people quote from it. There is a useful listing of local and BBC radio, television and satellite programmes, and good sports coverage. World news sometimes appears with a delay of a day or so, as it often needs to be translated from the Spanish parent paper, Ultimattora. The paper appears six times per week.

Another English paper, The Reader, can be bought at several points on the island. Also a good read, it appears weekly and offers editorial comment, letters from readers, a good London Column, funnies from the world's press, advice to foreign residents, cartoons, recipes, coming events and some island satire.

• **Menorca** The annually published guide, Menorca 99 (2000 in the year 2000, and so on), is a useful holiday companion. Published by Noel Evisson, a Briton who lives locally, it has useful facts and

Public Toilets

The Govern Balear has recently installed public toilets on many streets throughout the islands (carry tissue with you as they rarely have paper). Also, every bar, café and restaurant has lavatories, which are considered public property by the Spanish, whether they are buying a drink there or not. They're referred to as los servicios or el lavabo, and signs are usually for Dones or Damas (Ladies) and Homes or Caballeros (Men).

Consulates

UNITED KINGDOM
• Plaça Mayor 3a, Palma.
Tel: 971 712445/716048.
• Isidor Macabich 45, 1st floor, Eivissa [Ibiza town]).
Tel: 971 301818.
UNITED STATES
Jaume III 26, Palma.
Tel: 971 722660.

figures for visitors and advertising. It is available free at convenient pick-up points on Menorca.

Another English publication in Menorca is the newsy and informative Roqueta, published (and largely produced by) Annette Bell. Roqueta comes out monthly from April to September, and there is one winter issue, in December. It is filled with useful information and articles about the island and its people. Many English-speaking non-resident home-owners subscribe.

• **Ibiza** There is a twice-monthly English paper, called Ibiza Now, published by Sally Wilson. Very informative for both residents and visitors, it is well-produced and worth buying.

TELEVISION

Spanish television gives good coverage of international news and sports, particularly events in which Spain is involved. Thus, there is good footage of tennis, football, basketball, golf, grass and roller-skate hockey, handball, water-polo and others.

To enjoy the many movies shown by Spanish television, it is possible to have receivers altered at moderate cost, to enable reception of the original soundtrack, whether in English or another language.

RADIO

Radio stations are varied in both quality and content, and more than one of the Spanish stations broadcast continuous music.

• **Mallorca** The English-speaking station in Palma, Mallorca (Radio

103.2 FM) is worth listening to, with a variety of local personalities presenting their own individual style of show. These include local news, music, interviews, quizzes and other items with advertising and are a good source of information about the island.

• **Menorca** For broadcasting schedules of Menorca's English radio programme, check the local English newspapers.

• **Ibiza** Two local stations carry about one hour a day of English broadcasting, one of which is on Radio Popular (89.1 FM). Ibiza Now publishes broadcasting schedules.

Postal Services

Nobody with genuinely urgent mail would place it in the Spanish postal system's care. Service is not so much just slow; it is unreliable, with a letter or package sometimes taking you by surprise by arriving within two days, but with an equal chance that it could take three weeks, or simply disappear.

Emergency steps have been taken, with the introduction of an Express mail service, with red-coloured mail boxes appearing alongside the regular yellow ones, but all this has done is to relegate anything put in the yellow boxes to a low priority.

Fortunately, the gap has been partially filled by the local motorcycle messenger services, the reliable national express companies such as SEUR, as well as international express companies such as DHL and FEDEX. Other competitors appear to cope with packages and urgent documents throughout Spain, and these include the railway system.

English-speaking residents in the islands regularly keep British postage stamps at home, and get their mail hand-carried by people travelling on the frequent services to the United Kingdom, where their delivery either within the UK or to other destinations is more reliable, and faster.

Postmen in Spain don't have to deliver packages regarded as being oversize. Packages and parcels are therefore dispatched to a central post office, and a collection slip sent to the addressee, who must present themselves with identification to collect the mail.

One of the results of the modernisation of post offices is the installation of what looks like bullet-proof glass on the counters, making it hard to communicate with the person on the other side. Among the saving graces that the old-style post office had, despite all its faults, was the possibility of talking in a relaxed way with the staff, who for the most part are helpful and good-humoured, but are now fenced off from the public.

When posting anything on the islands, place your name and address on the reverse side of envelopes or parcels, preceded by the word *Remitente* ("sender"). The Spanish post office will not open undeliverable mail in order to obtain a return address.

Telecommunications

TELEPHONE
The telephone service works reasonably, with public coin-phones throughout the islands. The local telephone directory (a single book for all the islands), on the other hand, is frustrating, as you need to know the precise town or *pueblo*

in which someone lives before you can find his or her name. A person may live in the municipality of Calvià, but his number be listed under Portals Nous.

Useful Numbers

● **Directory enquiries** 003
● **International operator** (Europe) 008
● **International operator** (elsewhere) 005

FAX
The main post offices usually have public fax services, but on business days there is often a queue, with messengers from different companies sending messages to various parts of the world. They will accept incoming messages only if the recipient is actually present.

Alternatively, Palma has an excellent business services office, with English-speaking staff who will help you find numbers, place your call, send your telex or fax, and hold any incoming messages. It charges either a membership fee or a temporary resident fee, on top of which you pay for the metered phone or fax service:
Network Business Communications Avenida Joan Miró, 149, 07015 Palma de Mallorca.
Tel: 971 403903.

Fax: 971 400216.
Email: network@atlas-iap.es

Business Travellers
With its own distinctive laws and regulations, Spain has a business environment where expert assistance is needed to start a business or to buy a property.

PROFESSIONAL HELP
A good first step is to call on the Spanish consulate, or, if there is one, the Chamber of Commerce, to explain your intentions. They will usually provide guidance.

Secondly, try to obtain copies of magazines such as *Balearic Homes and Living, New Projects* or *Lookout*, aimed at English-speaking people living or intending to live in Spain. These magazines' addresses are listed under *Further Reading*.

During a first exploratory visit, it is a good idea to have a temporary base, using the offices of a recommended lawyer or one of the business service organisations (*see Telecommunications, above*) and an introduction to the manager of one of the English-speaking banks in order to get a local briefing on conditions. Eventually, to start the process of obtaining permits and business licences, you would be advised to use the services of a

Local Tourist Offices

Mallorca
Consellería de Turismo de Baleares, Montenegro 5, Palma.
Tel: 971 176191
Fax: 971 176185.
Good for information on all islands.
Palma Municipal Tourist Office (OIT), Santo Domindo 11, Palma.
Tel: 971 724090.
Fax: 971 720240.
Also in Plaça Espanya (tel: 971 711527) or at the airport (tel: 971 260803).

Other municipalities, such as Calvià, have their own local offices, some seasonal, mounted on trailers in tourist areas.

Menorca
Oficina de información turística, Plaça Explanada 40, Maó.
Tel: 971 363790.
At airport. Tel: 971 157115.
Consell Insular de Menorca, Camí del Castell 28, Maó.
Tel: 971 351515.

Ibiza
Tourist Office (Consell de Ibiza), Passeig de Vara de Rey 13, Eivissa.
Tel: 971 392484.
Municipality of Santa Eulália, Ricardo Riquer Wallis, Santa Eivissa.
Tel: 971 330728.

Formentara
Oficina de Turismo, Port of Sa Savina, at the ferry terminal.
Tel: 971 322057.

For more information, try these useful Internet addresses:
● **www.bitel.es/calvià.mallorca** – a multilingual guide to the busy resorts in the Clavià district, including Palma Nova, Magalluf and Santa Ponça.
● **www.mallorcaweb.com** – a multilingual Mallorca-based directory. Includes information on beaches, restaurants, places to stay and cultural events.

gestoría, who specialises in preparing and delivering official documents, and overcoming bureaucratic hurdles.

BUYING PROPERTY

For property purchases in the islands, use only the services of a an estate agent with an API accreditation (College of Real Estate Agents). Many have English-speaking staff to advise you of the legal requirements, such as those affecting the transfer of funds to Spain and so on.

Travelling with Kids

The Spanish love children and take very good care of their own. Most restaurants are child-friendly, especially at lunchtime. For a fun day out, try one of Mallorca's many water amusement parks, featuring water chutes, paddling pools and playgrounds. These include:

Aquapark, between Cala Figuera and Magalluf.

Hidropark, in the Port d'Alcúdia.

Aqua City-Park, between Palma and S'Arenal.

Aqualandia, between Palma and Inca.

Marineland, off the Palma-Peguera motorway.

Winter brings seasonal visits by circuses and fairs, and big clubs run special out-of-season afternoon sessions for the young, generally on Saturdays and Sundays.

Gay Travellers

The islands of Mallorca and Ibiza have, in recent years, proved to be an extremely agreeable environment for gay men and women, who have found the freedom to live or holiday in peace there.

On the two islands, there are all sorts of businesses run by gays, ranging from hostals and restaurants to bars, discos and nightclubs. Ibiza has an especial concentration of such businesses, most of which are in the town of Eivissa (Ibiza). In Palma, the focus of nightlife action around the Plaça

Gomila is also the centre of gay bars and discos. For a list of gay venues see Nightlife (page 302).

Disabled Travellers

As in the rest of Spain, the Govern Balear has become more aware of the need for facilities for travellers with disabilities. As a result, hoteliers, architects and airports have now made these facilities a priority. In addition, the beaches in Magalluf, Palma Nova, Illetas, Santa Ponça and Peguera have introduced amphibious wheelchairs, which can be used free of charge.

People with mobility difficulty who intend visiting the islands need only advise their travel agent or airline, and will find that conditions and provisions in airports and hotels, at least, should be similar to those elsewhere. The municipal transport authority EMT provides special bus services for wheelchairs and the severely handicapped. For information in Mallorca, tel: 971 295700.

Security and Crime

As with any busy resort, there is a great deal of visitor-related crime in the islands. Many foreign criminals target places like the Balearics

Tipping

Although the locals often leave close to nothing, it is usual to tip waiters an extra 10 percent. Hotel porters should be given 100–200 pesetas for each piece of luggage they carry, whereas those at airports have fixed rates. It is also courteous to tip hairdressers, chambermaids and room service attendants at least 100 pesetas, and the same goes for tour guides and the bus drivers on excursions and round trips. With taxis, round off the sum to the next 100 pesetas and they will thank you effusively. When paying for drinks in cash, it is usual to leave 50–100 pesetas on the counter.

Emergencies

- **Any emergency** 112
- **Police** (Policía Nacional) 091
- **Fire Service** (Bomberos) Palma: 080. Elsewhere: 085
- **Ambulance** Palma: 971 200102 Maó (Men.): 971 361180 Ciutadella (Men.): 971 381993 Ibiza: 971 301214

during the summer. In addition, the islands have their own home-grown criminals who prey on local citizens and visitors alike.

Then there are the steeply rising numbers of people who have become dependent on stupefying drugs and who depend on crime to pay for their habits. The tourist is an easy target.

While you are in the Balearics, it is advisable not to wear jewellery, not to carry cash or valuables and to make use of the hotel safe rather than leaving valuables in your room.

If you are mugged, there is little point in resisting, and criminals may be armed. It is best not to get into a discussion, and simply hand over what you have. See above for numbers to call if you are involved in or are a witness to a crime.

If you must carry a hand or shoulder bag, avoid walking near the kerb, as much of the bag snatching on the islands is carried out by two people on a motorcycle, one driving and one snatching. The other preferred place to snatch and run is at busy road junctions, when the average pedestrian is distracted by looking at the traffic or traffic lights.

Medical Treatment

Spain has a Social Security service, with hospitals in all major towns. In addition, there are privately run clinics in many places.

Mallorca has a large Social Security hospital, on the edge of Palma. There are also large clinics in and around Palma, most of which are associated with one or another private patients' insurance plan.

Health Warning

Alcoholic drinks in the islands are much the same as anywhere, but beware the dangers of *garrafa*. This is the Catalan word for demijohn and refers to the practice of bulk-buying cheap liquor and using it to refill brand-name bottles.

Not all *garrafa* is bad for you, but there is no doubt that a lot of it will give you a headache, and in some cases it can affect your eyes and other functions. Don't be taken in by people who say this is a trick practised only in small bars or poor areas. Some of the most popular bars and clubs do it, and charge at least as high a price as for the real brand you think you're getting.

The Spanish Red Cross operates a clinic in Palma and, in common with other clinics, runs its own ambulance service.

Dotted around the various resorts, there are also medical centres, some of them quite small, where routine and emergency treatment can be obtained, or where first-aid can be applied prior to transfer to a specialised hospital. In the Palma area there are medical practices run by foreign doctors, most of them English-speaking.

Useful Numbers

• **Clínica Femenía**, tel: 971 452323. This is the hospital used by most foreigners. Staff speak fluent English and some of the nurses are English. Relatives and friends can even enjoy a swim in the pool.
• **Clínica Miramar**, tel: 971 450212.
• **Son Dureta**, tel: 971 175000.

Religious Services

Catholic churches are located in all towns throughout the islands and in the neighbourhoods of larger cities. There are also temples and churches for other religious or spiritual beliefs.

Mallorca

Anglican Church, Nuñez de Balboa, Palma. Tel: 971 737279.
Baptist Mission, Aragón 24, Palma. Tel: 971 462805.
Jewish Synagogue, Monseñor Palmer 3, Palma. Tel: 971 738686.
Mormon Church, Marqués de la Cenia 35, Palma. Tel: 971 450743.

For more information, call the Anglican Church, which has a complete list of other religious services on the island.

Menorca

English-speaking services are usually held at the **Church of Santa Margarita**, in Carrer Stuart, Villacarlos. Times are posted in several places around the island, and certainly in the English Library, Carrer Deiá 2, Maó.

Ibiza

English-speaking services are held by the Resident Chaplain, Joe Yates-Round. Tel: 971 343383
There is a Jewish Cultural Group in Florabunda, Santa Eulália.

Getting Around

Orientation

The best way to appreciate downtown areas is to explore on foot, with the help of a good map. Any bookshop will have a good choice, but among the clearest are those produced by Firestone locally and those issued by the Spanish National Tourist Office. In addition, there are published walking-tour guides of the local countryside.

Place Names

The authorities are in the process of changing all place names in the Balearics so that they conform to the correct spellings in the Balearic variants of Catalan. In this book, we have given the updated local form of place names, but note that as you travel around you may find that local signs have not necessarily been changed yet. This book is ahead of the times!

By Bus/Coach

Most routes begin in Palma, but smaller villages are also connected with one another. There are far fewer buses during the winter season (1 November until 30 April), when some of the lines cease operations entirely.
Mallorca Almost all buses begin their journeys from Palma's Plaça Espanya or on surrounding streets.
Menorca Buses do not operate within Maó. But there are two main stations in the city with buses going to other towns, depending on the destination: at José María Cuadrado 7 and on Plaça de la Explanada.

Ibiza The main bus station is at Isidor Macabich 42.

Formentera Buses go from Autocares Pay, Can Xicu Lluquinet, San Ferran.

By Train

Mallorca has two railway lines, both starting at the Plaça Espanya in Palma. The state-run FEVE railway (tel: 971 752245) connects Palma with Inca 20 times a day, stopping at Marratxí, Santa María del Camí, Consell, Alaró, Binissalem and Lloseta.

The electric Palma-Sóller railway is said to be one of the most profitable trains in Spain. The service's first-class carriages are equipped with leather seats, mahogany panelling and brass fittings, and travellers can enjoy a splendid view of the passing landscape from the little platform between carriages.

From Sóller, the journey can be continued on the famous old tram known as the Orange Express, which takes passengers through groves of aromatic citrus fruits to the port of Sóller 5km (3 miles) from the centre.

Driving

Having a car on the islands enables you to reach a lot of attractions in inaccessible corners of the country. There are few roads on the islands, so you should drive with particular care in busy holiday periods, especially on the mountain roads.

In Mallorca, perhaps the best way to cover the ground is to follow the island's natural features, driving from Palma towards Andratx and on to Valldemossa, Deià and Sóller.

In Menorca, Ibiza and Formentera, the distances are even shorter than in Mallorca, allowing drivers to cover each island in a single day.

Car Hire

Among Spanish provinces, the Balearics have the highest number of registered road vehicles per capita. This indicates the good health of the local economy, but also the great number of self-drive car hire outlets.

The easiest and fastest way to hire a car is at the airports upon arrival, where you'll find branches of Atesa, Avis, Hertz and Europcar. Mallorcan companies provide airport pick-up services, too, and it's worth comparing prices.

Rules of the road

Most foreign driving licences are accepted in the Balearics.

Driving is on the right in the islands, and seatbelts are obligatory both in the front and back of cars. As in most of Spain, main roads have a top speed-limit of 100 kph (62 mph), urban roads 60 kph (37 mph) and motorways 120 kph (75 mph). The police levy heavy on-the-spot fines for both speeding and not wearing your seatbelt.

Parking

Parking in the cities has become difficult due to the excess of cars. ORA tickets, which are available at tobacco shops (*estanco*), enable you to park for up to 90 minutes for a reasonable price. In Palma, the best option is to park in one of the private car parks in the centre and then walk. In towns, many entrances have a *Vado Permanente* (No Parking) sign, accompanied by a validatory police permit number. Parking in front of such a sign can mean a fine, and a trip to the car pound to retrieve a car that has been towed away.

Taxis

Taxis in and around the cities are cheap compared to other European countries, except for cross-island trips, which are very dear. The official prices are posted at all cab ranks, but make sure you confirm them with the driver. There are several taxi ranks, but the easiest option is to hail taxis on the street.

Cab firms to phone on the islands include:
Mallorca Tel: 971 401414.
Menorca Tel: 971 367111.
Ibiza Tel: 971 301794.

Where to Stay

Choosing a Hotel

Spanish authorities categorise visitor accommodation as follows:
H – Hotel
HR – Residence hotel
HA – Apartment hotel
RA – Residential apartment
M – Motel
Hs – Hostel
P – *Pension*
HsR – Residence hostal

These abbreviations appear on a sign at the door of places to stay. The letter R indicates that the establishment does not have a restaurant, although it may offer breakfast or a cafeteria service.

Apartamentos Turisticos (AT) are awarded one, two or three "keys", a grading that appears on the sign at the entrance. Hotels, on the other hand, are graded by stars – from the budget-priced one-star through to the high-priced five-star deluxe. Hostels and *Pensions* are graded three, two or one stars.

An excellent book, *Hoteles, Campings, Apartamentos – Baleares*, which is published by Spain's tourism ministry, covers all the accommodation on offer on the islands. You can contact the Secretaria General de Turismo at María de Molina 50, 28006 Madrid for details.

The listings below are divided by island. In each case, the list begins with the main town, followed by other towns which are listed in alphabetical order. When a town has more than one hotel, these are listed in order of comfort, beginning with the most expensive.

Hotels in Mallorca

PALMA

Son Vida Sheraton Hotel
Raixa 2, Urbanización Son Vida.
Tel: 971 790000.
Fax: 971 790017.
Considered to be one of the best hotels in Palma, it offers breathtaking views of the city and its bay, as well as luxuriously decorated rooms, a golf course, tennis courts, swimming pools, a sauna and Turkish baths, among many other facilities. **$$$$**

Valparaíso Palace
Francisco Vidal 23, La Bonanova.
Tel: 971 400411.
Fax: 971 405904.
Overlooking Palma, views of the harbour and bay, set in lush gardens. Indoor and outdoor pools, separate health clubs for men and women. Clients can enjoy cocktails in the Conde Duque piano bar. The Normandía restaurant offers stunning views of the bay and delicious food. **$$$$**

Meliá Victoria
Avda Joan Miró 21.
Tel: 971 734342.
Fax: 971 450824.
Reigning over the Palma harbour front, the Meliá Victoria has its main entrance close to the nightlife around Plaça Gomila, and its lower, harbour exit leads directly to the centre of the night's activities on the Passeig Marítimo. **$$$$**

Bellver Sol
Gabriel Roca 11.
Tel: 971 738008.
Fax: 971 731451.
Faces out over the harbour front, close to the centre of town. Well-equipped rooms, large dining room with a lavish buffet breakfast. When making a reservation, ask for a room with a view of the Club Náutico. Don't forget to try their marvellous cocktails. **$$$**

Sol Palas Atenea
Passeig Ingeniero Gabriel Roca 29.
Tel: 971 281400.
Fax: 971 451989.
A modern building overlooking the harbour, the Palas Atenea is a good address if you are travelling on business. The hotel complex

Price Guide

For a standard double room:
$$$$ = over 20,000 pesetas
$$$ = 15–20,000 pesetas
$$ 15,000 pesetas
$ = under 8,000 pesetas

includes a garden, two pools, a sauna, massage parlour, Jacuzzi, two bars and a restaurant. The reception organises sightseeing excursions round the island. **$$$**

Uto Palma
Avda. Joan Miró 303.
Tel: 971 401211.
Fax: 971 401250.
Located at the sea's edge in Cala Mayor, the Uto has two pools, a gymnasium and sauna, seaside terraces and gardens, and is near to all the Cala Mayor action. Ideal for families with children. **$$$**

Costa Azul
Passeig Marítimo 7.
Tel: 971 731940.
Fax: 971 731971.
Although only a two-star hotel, the Costa Azul is listed as an old favourite with families and business travellers over the years. **$$**

Jaime III Sol
Passeig de Mallorca 14.
Tel: 971 725943.
Fax: 971 725946.
Set in the elegant part of town and near the waterfront, this comfortable hotel is close to all the downtown area of Palma. The bar Sol is one of the meeting points for the locals. **$$**

Staying in a Monastery

Travellers seeking peace may want to spend a couple of nights in one of the many monasteries in Mallorca, set in magical surroundings. Two of the best are:

Lluc Monastery
Lluc. Tel: 971 517025.
This is still one of the most visited areas of the island. The monastery offers different types of rooms, those on the second floor being the most in demand.

Saratoga
Passeig de Mallorca 6.
Tel: 971 727240.
Fax: 971 727312.
The Saratoga is convenient for the business traveller on a tight budget, close enough to be able to walk to most lawyers, banks, businesses and shops downtown. **$$**

Borne
Sant Jaime 3.
Tel: 971 725943.
Fax: 971 725946.
The exceptional structure of the building and its courtyard make this hotel one of the most attractive in Palma. Recently renovated, it offers beautifully decorated rooms and is in the centre of town. **$**

Hostal Monleón
La Rambla 3.
Tel: 971 715317.
Old building in the centre of town, clean and comfortable, and very cheap. **$**

OUTSIDE PALMA

It would be impossible to list all the Mallorcan hotels worthy of mention outside Palma, so the following list is a selection of some of the best and most interesting.

Banyalbufar

Son Net Hotel
Tel: 971 147000.
Fax: 971 147001.
Opened in June 1998, this is probably Mallorca's top hotel. It is set deep in the mountains, surrounded by lavish gardens, and every room is individually decorated

Prices are very reasonable. Make sure you make reservations in advance.

Santa Lucía
Manacor del Valle.
Tel: 971 501877.
Surrounded by ghost towns and the Tramuntana mountain, this sacred place offers exceptional accommodation. From here travellers can plan a thousand and one excursions.

and has its own terrace. Exclusive, and so is the price. **$$$$**

Costa de Calvià
Hotel Son Caliu
Urbanización San Caliu.
Tel: 971 682200.
Fax: 971 683720
Exotic gardens surround the swimming pool. Panoramic view from the rooms. Facilities include indoor pool aimed at off-season clients. **$$$**

Deià
La Residencia
Son Canals.
Tel: 971 639011.
Fax: 971 639333.
With its individually designed and decorated rooms, this is quiet luxury in a hill town that is home to artists and poets. Facilities include a large, oval swimming pool, tennis courts and transportation to a private beach and lush gardens. One of the most luxurious rural hotels in Spain, its restaurant, El Olivo, is famous for excellent cuisine. A 45-minute drive from Palma. **$$$$**
Costa d'Or
Llucalcari, Deià.
Tel: 971 639025.
Fax: 971 609347.
Overlooking both the mountains and the sea, this charming hotel's facilities include a swimming pool and terrace with views of the breathtaking coastline. A 10-minute walk through the pines will take you to a small, rocky beach. You need

Price Guide

For a standard double room:
$$$$ = over 20,000 pesetas
$$$ = 15–20,000 pesetas
$$ 15,000 pesetas
$ = under 8,000 pesetas

to make reservations well in advance. **$$**

Illetas
Bonanza Playa
Carretera de Illetas.
Tel: 971 401112.
Fax: 971 404050.
Built into a cliff at the sea's edge, the hotel's lobby area is at street level on the top floor, with rooms and extensive facilities below. Family run with repeat clients year after year. **$$$**
Meliá del Mar
Paseo de Illetas 7.
Tel: 971 402511.
Fax: 971 405852.
Only a few metres separate the hotel from the sea. Surrounded by beautiful botanical gardens, facilities include a swimming pool and tennis courts along the coastline. **$$$**

Orient
L'Hermitage
Tel: 971 180303.
Fax: 971 180411.
Housed in a converted 17th-century mansion, this fine hotel is set at the foot of the mountain with magical surroundings. Excellent

restaurant and marvellous exotic gardens. **$$$$**

Paguera
The Villamil
Boulevard de Paguera.
Tel: 971 686050.
Fax: 971 686815.
A member of the Trust House Forte chain, about 30 minutes from Palma. Overlooks the beach, and has gardens and sun-terraces to relax in. **$$$**

Playa de Formentor
Hotel Formentor
Tel: 971 865300.
Fax: 971 865155.
Overlooking the beach and surrounded by pines and gardens, this peaceful traditional hotel has housed celebrities such as Winston Churchill and Agatha Christie. Excellent cuisine. **$$$$$**

Valldemossa
Can Marió
Uetam 8.
Tel: 971 612122.
Fax: 971 616029.
This is one of the most charming small hotels on the island. Set in the heart of the village, once the home of Chopin and George Sand, it is the perfect place for a peaceful couple of days. Only a 30-minute drive from Palma. **$**

Hotels in Menorca

Most hotels are seasonal, open only from May until October.

Maó
Port Mahón Hotel
Passeig Marítimo.
Tel: 971 362600.
Fax: 971 351051.
The Port Mahón overlooks the fjord-like port, once the Mediterranean base for Nelson's Royal Navy. Quiet, almost sedate, it makes a good base for a business or holiday visit. Facilities include an outdoor swimming pool. **$$$**
Sant Ignasi
Carretera a Cala Morell.
Tel: 971 359393.
Fax: 971 480537.

Finca Holidays

This is the new chic term for the old-fashioned farm holiday.
Fincas are the former estates on Mallorca, many of which have given up farming for good and have restored their buildings, adding swimming pools and sanitation, in order to rent out their rooms to tourists. Most *fincas* are set in beautiful surroundings and are comfortably furnished, with an open fire, clay pots in the kitchen and old

ploughs and pitchforks leaning against the stone walls.
Holidays can be booked either as a full package (including flight, transfer or rental car) from travel agents in the UK or via central reservations at:
Tel: 971 706004.
Fax: 971 470971.
Also available is a booklet obtainable on the Internet at: fincas/agrotourism/country house hotels, or call 971 721508.

Royal Holidays

A series of magnificent hotels with special character have joined forces under the name Reis de Mallorca (Kings of Mallorca). For more information, a booklet, *Reis de Mallorca*, lists 18 of these top hotels. Tel: 971 770737.

Eighteenth-century *finca* on the outskirts of Maó, surrounded by palm trees. Quiet luxury. Rooms on the ground floor have private gardens. **$$$**

Hotel del Almirante
Crta. Villacarlos, near Maó.
Tel: 971 362700.
Fax: 971 362704.
A typically Georgian-style mansion which belonged to British Admiral Collingwood and whose ghost, according to the legend, still lives in room number seven. Good views of Maó harbour, hacienda-style accommodation around a swimming pool. Open May to October. **$$**

Apartamentos Royal
Carmen 131.
Tel: 971 369534.
Fax: 971 351305.
A tourist apartment with a two-key grading. Central and convenient to downtown. Pool, gardens and bar cafeteria. **$$**

Capri
San Sebastian 8.
Tel: 971 361400.
Fax: 971 350853.
Ideal for business travellers, right in the centre of town. **$$**

Ciutadella
Almirante Farragut
Avda. de los Delfines
Tel: 971 388000.
Fax: 971 388107.
A very large hotel, built on a promontory over the sea, with a small beach on one side. In summer, tour operators from all over Europe keep the Farragut fully booked. **$$$**

Esmeralda
Passeig de San Nicolás 171.
Tel: 971 380250.
Fax: 971 380258.

With beautiful views of the harbour, the hotel's facilities include a swimming pool, garden and tennis courts. **$$**

Hotels in Ibiza

Although there are city-centre hotels in Eivissa (Ibiza town), the level of activity and noise is high. As distances around the island are relatively short, it is best to stay outside the city and make trips into town for shopping or nightlife. Most hotels are seasonal, open only from May until October.

Es Cubells
Les Jardins de Palerm
Apdo 62, San Jose.
Tel: 971 800318.
Fax: 971 800453.
Les Jardins (five minutes' drive from Es Cubells) is unclassifiable, although listed as a *pension*. Self-described as "a little piece of Paradise", it is the ideal hideaway for lovers or honeymooners, and children aren't encouraged. The 10-room retreat is operated by jack-of-all-trades René Wilhelm, a Swiss former Formula III driver, decorator, fashion designer, boutique owner and more. There is an excellent *nouvelle cuisine* restaurant, as well as a pool and gardens. **$$**

Platja d'en Bossa
Hotel Torre del Mar
Tel: 971 303050.
Fax: 971 304060.
One of the island's best hotels, with rooms looking out to sea. **$$$**

Sant Miquel
Hotel Hacienda Na Xamena
Tel: 971 334500.
Fax: 971 334606.
The most exclusive and luxurious hotel on the island, Na Xamena belongs to the prestigious *Relais et Châteaux* chain. Excellent facilities and restaurant. **$$$$**

Santa Eulália
Ca's Catalá
Carrer del Sol.
Tel: 971 331006.
Fax: 971 339268.

Camping

● **MALLORCA**
The main official campsite in Mallorca is in the northern part of the island.
Platja Blava, Ctra. de Artà, 23km (14 miles) from Alcúdia.
Tel: 971 537511.
Near a sandy beach with crystal-clear waters. Tennis courts, hot-water showers and bicycle rental. Very well organised.

● **MENORCA**
There are two main campsites in Menorca. It is advisable to make reservations beforehand.
Son Bou Platja, Ctra. Alaior-Torre Soli Nou, 5km (3 miles) from Alaior.
Tel: 971 372605.
Fax: 971 372605.
Facilities include hot-water showers. First rate.
S'Astalaia, Ctra Cala Galdana, 4km (2 miles) from Ferreires.
Tel: 971 374232.
Open all year. Third rate.

● **IBIZA**
The best campsite in Ibiza is:
Camping Es Can, Es Can.
Tel: 971 332117. First rate.

Classified as a Residence Hostal, the Ca's Catalá is owned and run by Kim and Jill Brown (he is Canadian and she British), and offers 12 pleasantly furnished single and double rooms, a pool and garden. Breakfast only is served, but non-residents drop in for this and also for mid-morning coffee and pastries. A very nice, tucked-away in-town home from home. **$$**

Sant Antoni
Hotel Nautilus
Port des Torrent.
Tel: 971 340400.
Fax: 971 340462.
Right on the sea, with excellent facilities including a pool. **$$$**

Hotel Pike's
Camí de Sa Vorera.
Tel: 971 343511.
This rambling converted farmhouse in a peaceful countryside setting has long been a favourite rock star

haunt: Julio Iglesias and George Michael, for example, rate it no less than the "best' and "greatest" hotel in the world. Run by genial Australian Tony Pike, it has 26 idiosyncratically decorated rooms and suites, plus a sports centre with pool, spa, Jacuzzi and tennis court. **$$$$**

Hotels in Formentera

In addition to the places listed below, there are other hotels, apartments and hostels scattered around the coast near to or on beaches. The largest grouping of such places is around Cala Pujols, Es Caló and along Mitjorn beach.

Playa de Mitjorn
Hotel Club Formentera Playa
Tel: 971 328000.
Fax: 971 328035.
Near the beach, with two swimming pools and tennis courts. **$$$**
Hotel Club La Mola
Tel: 971 327069.
Fax: 971 327000.
Good facilities, located right on the beach. **$$$**
Hotel Costa Azul
Tel: 971 328042. **$**

Playa Es Pujols
Hostal Rocaplana
S'Espalmador 41.
Tel: 971 328335.
Fax: 971 328401.
Overlooks the beach, friendly and helpful service. **$**

Where to Eat

Choosing a Restaurant

Regional food in Spain can be as varied as the wine and it is worth keeping an eye open for the specialities of each region.
Restaurants in the Balearics come in all shapes, sizes and standards, some with owner-chefs offering fresh and imaginative food; some a standard menu with a high content of frozen ingredients; some with a good ambience but poor food, some with awful decor but a great menu. In general, however, restaurants that stay open all year usually score better on service and food than seasonal or beach establishments, which by necessity offer less at a higher cost as they have to live for 12 months on six to seven months' income.
The answer to the question "what to eat?" is "everything". If it is served by professionals, whether it is local, Oriental or French, it should be good. Wherever you are, there'll be a choice of restaurants nearby, and the distance to other towns is never great.

Mallorca Restaurants

SPANISH/SEAFOOD
Calvià
Es Comell
Ctra. de Son Font.
Tel: 971 670180.
Friendly pub atmosphere, with owner David mixing drinks at the cosy bar. International cuisine. **$$**

Deià
Bens d'Avall
Urbanización Costa Deià, Muleta, between Sóller and Deià.
Tel: 971 632381.
French cooking with fresh produce

from the fertile valley of Sóller. Excellent fish. **$$$**

Inca
Celler Ca'n Amer
Miguel Durán 39.
Tel: 971 501261.
Excellent home-cooking with a touch of class. **$$$**

Price Guide

The approximate cost per person, including house wine, is coded in the following way:
$$$ = over 5,000 pesetas
$$ = 2,500–4,500 pesetas
$ = less than 2,500 pesetas

Palma
Koldo Royo
Passeig Marítimo 3.
Tel: 971 457021.
Koldo is one the most admired chefs among gourmets. Exquisite Basque cuisine, with views of Palma Bay. Closed Saturday lunch and all day Sunday. **$$$**
Porto Pi
Avda. Joan Miró 174.
Tel: 971 400087.
Creative gourmet Basque cuisine. Impeccable service. One of King Juan Carlos' favourites. Closed Saturday lunch and Sunday. **$$$**
Rififi
Avda. Joan Miró 182.
Tel: 971 402035.
One of the best seafood restaurants on the island and much favoured by celebrities. The service, perhaps not surprisingly, is excellent. Closed Tuesday. **$$$**
Casa Gallega
Carrer Pueyo 4.
Tel: 971 721141.
Although *tapas* is the house speciality, eating the more expensive lunch or dinner in the rustic upstairs dining room is highly recommended. Try their delicious lobster soup. **$$$**
Diplomatic
Palau Reial 5.
Tel: 971 726482.
Dressy restaurant serving traditional cuisine; busy lunchtime weekdays. **$$$**

Palma's Bars and Cafés

The following small eateries are great for coffee and snacks.
• **Bar Bosch**, Plaça Juan Carlos I. A meeting place for locals, business people and tourists in the heart of the city. Large terrace and excellent toasted sandwiches.

Es Parlament
Conquistador 11.
Tel: 971 726026.
One of the most aristocratic restaurants in town, best known for its excellent paella. **$$$**

Bodega Santurce
Concepción 34.
Tel: 971 710801.
Basque food in this family-run hole in the wall. Open lunchtime only. No reservations required. Uncomfortable seating, but great value. **$$**

Port d'Andratx
Layn
Almirante Riera 19.
Tel: 971 623011.
Great seafood with views of Andratx Bay. Don't be surprised if you bump into Claudia Schiffer. **$$$**

Valldemossa
Can Marió
Uetam 8.
Tel: 971 612122.
One of the best home-cooking restaurants on the island. Great service and even better prices. **$**

ITALIAN
Palma
La Fontana
Industria 6.
Tel: 971 451666.
Near downtown shopping. Specialities include *antipasti* and meat dishes. **$$**
Don Peppone
Bayarte 14.
Tel: 971 454242.
Great home-made pasta. **$**

FRENCH
Palma
Le Bistrot
Teodoro Llorente 6.
Tel: 971 287175.

• **Café Lìrico**, Avda. Maura 6. Popular with intellectuals and artists, this beautiful old building has a large terrace, pool table and great sandwiches. A local favourite.
• **Club de Mar**, Passeig Marítimo. Meeting point for the jet set.

One of the most select French menus in town. **$$$**
La Casita
Avda. Joan Miró 68.
Tel: 971 737557.
Unpretentious, imaginative French cooking in a cosy atmosphere. Small, with one, genial waiter. **$$**

ASIAN
Palma
Shangri-La
Passeig Marítimo 1.
Tel: 971 452575.
Luxurious Chinese by harbour. **$$$**
Shogun
Camilo José Cela 14.
Tel: 971 735748.
One of the best Japanese restaurants in Palma. Good service, sushi and *sukiyaki* a speciality. **$$$**
Chino Mandarìn
Avda. Joan Miró 17.
Tel: 971 738136.
The first Chinese restaurant that opened in Palma. Several generations have enjoyed their exquisite duck crêpes. **$$**
Gran Dragón
Ruiz de Alda 5.
Tel: 971 280200. Or
Avda. Joan Miró 146.
Tel: 971 701717.

Coffee Houses

Mallorca
• Forn del Santo Cristo, Pelaires 2, Palma.
• Can Francesc, Orfila 4, Palma.
• La Tetera, Carrer Temple, Pollença.
Menorca
• The Mad Hatter, Maó Harbour, near the aquarium.
• The Tea Pot, Stuart 4, Villacarlos.

One of the most popular Chinese restaurants in Palma. Open every day, all year round. **$$**

Portals Nous
The Crazy Dolphin
The Roundabout, near Marineland.
Tel: 971 676645.
One of the few places with Indonesian food. Impeccable service. **$$**

Palma Nova
Gran Dragûn
Tel: 971 681338.
Branch of the much-loved and respected Palma Chinese. **$$**

VEGETARIAN
Palma
Bon Lloc
Moral 7.
Tel: 971 718617.
Rustic atmosphere in the old part of town. **$**

Menorca Restaurants

Cala Torret
Pizzería Sienna
Italian. **$$**

Ciutadella
Cas Quintu
Plaça Alfonso III 4.
Tel: 971 381002.
Menorcan and other dishes. **$$**
Casa Manolo
Marina 117.
Tel: 971 380003.
In the port, with terrace, air-conditioning and magnificent views. Seafood. **$$**

Es Castell
Rocamar
Cala Fonduco 32.
Tel: 971 365601.
Seafood, in the port. **$$**

Fornells
Es Pla
Pasaje des Pla.
Tel: 971 376655.
By the harbour, this is the best of the waterside restaurants for fresh fish and seafood risotto. Marvellous views of the small port. One of King Juan Carlos' favourites. **$$$**

Price Guide

The approximate cost per person, including house wine, is coded in the following way:
$$$ = over 5,000 pesetas
$$ = 2,500–4,500 pesetas
$ = less than 2,500 pesetas

Maó
Club Marítimo
Muelle del Levante 287.
Tel: 971 364226.
Imaginative food. Sea views. $$$
Pilar
Cardona y Orfila 61.
Tel: 971 366817.
Local cuisine. Evenings only. $$
Il Porto
Maó harbour.
Tel: 971 368222.
Italian. $

Torret
Pan y Vino
Tel: 971 150322.
Small, atmospheric restaurant popular with expats. $

Ibiza Restaurants

Eivissa (Ibiza town)
S'Oficina
Avda. de Espanya 6.
Tel: 971 300016.
One of the best representatives of Basque cuisine on the island. Closed on Sundays. $$$
El Olivo
Plaça de Vila 7.
Tel: 971 300680.
Excellent quality. Closed on Monday and November to March. $$$
Chez Françoise
Plaça del Parque 5.
Tel: 971 391919.
French cooking. Relaxed and very select atmosphere. $$$
Mesón de Paco
Avda. Bartolomé Rosselló 15.
Tel: 971 314242.
Ibiçenco cooking in a cosy atmosphere. $$
Sa Soca
Ctra. Eivissa, Sant Josep, 18km (11 miles) from Eivissa.
Tel: 971 341620.
Ibiçenco cooking. $$

San Miguel
Hotel Hacienda Na Xamena.
Tel: 971 334500.
Known worldwide for its excellent international cuisine and its views of the coast and mountains. $$$

Sant Sosep
Ca na Joana
Ctra. Sant Sosep, 10km (6 miles).
Tel: 971 800158.
International and *Ibiçenco* cooking. Excellent and imaginative cuisine. In summer opens only at midday. $$$

Santa Eulália
Le Bistrot
Passeig Marítimo 82.
Tel: 971 330655.
Fresh fish and seafood looking out on to the busy street. Great atmosphere in the evenings. $$$
Pinocho
D'enmig 18.
Tel: 971 310176.
Italian food, from pasta to home-made pizza. $$

Drinking Notes

The islands are excellent if you like a drink or two. Not only are they notable for the colossal number of bars, but also for their variety. There are cocktail bars, piano bars, disco bars, bar-cafés, bar-restaurants, cabaret bars, casino bars, beach bars, *bodegas* (cellars), gay bars, roof-top bars, youth bars and even bars in the hospitals. Drinking is civilised. In all but the busiest bars and some on the beaches, the waiter or barman runs a tab, not asking for payment with each drink.

Lunchtime drinking, particularly in a *bodega*, can be very enjoyable, sipping a sherry or other aperitif before eating. For during the meal Balearic-grown wines are available in great variety, from a strong Binissalem red, great with strong, highly spiced island food, to a sparkling white or rosé (*vino de aguja*) to accompany lighter food. Mainland Spanish wines are also on most menus.

Favourite liqueurs are the islands' anis-based *herbes* or, from

Beach Eating

On the largest Balearic islands, the advent of summer means the reopening of the many and varied beach restaurants and bars, commonly called *chiringuitos*. You'll find even the smallest and most remote coves have a *chiringuito*, dishing up grilled sardines, squid and other delicacies. Of course, most also serve chicken and chips, and hamburgers. Having obtained a permit from the local municipality to run the catering on the beach, a *chiringuito* operator will probably have the concession for *tumbonas* (beach beds) and possibly pedal-boats as well.

the mainland, an interesting combination of anis and juniper berries called *Pacharán*. Most visitor-oriented bars serve *sangría*, a cold punch containing red wine, liqueurs, clear lemonade, spices, slices or chunks of mixed fruit, and sugar to taste; everyone you meet says they make the best recipe.

Be sure of what you are drinking, however, as not all bottled liquors are what they seem to be from the label (*see Health Warning, page 291*). For a list of bars, turn to *Nightlife (page 300)*.

Culture

Classical Music

A varied programme of classical music concerts results from initiatives taken by government, business and private bodies. There are visiting soloists, orchestras and chamber groups, while the Pollença Summer festival is a major international musical event.

MALLORCA

The **Centro Cultural Sa Nostra** (tel: 971 725210) in Palma offers concerts on Fridays. In the municipal museum, La Cartuja, in Valldemossa piano concerts are held in the mornings, which include a visit to the monk cell occupied by Chopin and George Sand.

The major annual event to try and see in Mallorca is the traditional summer performance by the **Capella Mallorquina**. This takes place, usually on the third Sunday in July, in the Torrent de Pareis natural amphitheatre – a magnificent setting in which to enjoy a leading mixed choir.

Concerts of various types are also held in Palma's **Teatro Principal**, the Auditorium's main hall (on the harbour-front) or the smaller Sala Mozart, plus other venues (details are printed in local papers, including the *Majorca Daily Bulletin*, or ask the tourist office).

It is also worth asking about open-air concerts, which abound in town and village plazas, football grounds and bullrings. In summer, visitors can enjoy concerts held at Son Marroig, Sa Foradada, Deià, once the residence of the Archduke Luis Salvador – classical music with spectacular views of the sea, and if you are lucky, of the sunset in an outstanding location.

MENORCA

Has its own programme of concerts, announced in the press and on posters.

IBIZA

The island is visited by travelling groups and orchestras, but is more famous for holding spectacular pop concerts in various locations, notably in the Privilege nightclub.

In summer the International Festival of Classical Music offers concerts in Eivissa town hall and in the Centro Cultural in Sant Carles de Peralta.

Art

Art lovers may like to investigate the following art galleries while in Mallorca:

Palma
Agora, Pedro Dezcallar y Net 4
Tel: 971 712530
Altair, San Jaime 23
Tel: 971 716282
Art Fama, Centro Comercial Los Geranios. Tel: 971 721307
Bearn, Concepción 6
Tel: 971 722837
Ferran Cano, Paz 3
Tel: 971 714067
Jaime III, Avda. Jaime III
Tel: 971 710836
Maneu Punt d'Art, Cecilio Metelo 6
Tel: 971 721342
Lluc Flux, Rivera 4
Tel: 971 719090
Fundación La Caixa, Plaça Weyler 3
Tel: 971 720111

Pollença
Centro Cultural Guillem Cifre de Colonya
Tel: 971 530015.

Deià
Galería de Arte "Sa Tafona",
Hotel La Residencia
Tel: 971 639011.

Valldemossa
Museo Municipal Cartuja de Valldemossa
Tel: 971 612106.

Fiestas

If you can, try to get to a fiesta during your stay. Each island has several, celebrating saints' days and religious occasions. Steeped in centuries of tradition, they are spectacular events with bonfires, fireworks, horse parades, processions carrying icons and folk dancing. Many include age-old rituals, such as herding animals

Diary of Events

5 January The Three Magi Procession, Palma, Mallorca.
16–17 January St Anthony's fiesta throughout Mallorca.
17 January Quirky and colourful *Processó d'els Tres Trocs* (Procession of the Three Knocks) in Ciutadella, Menorca.
19 January St Stephen's fiesta in Pollença, Mallorca.
February *Vuelta ciclista*, one of Mallorca's biggest cycle races.
March Clay goods fair at Marratxí (Mallorca).
April *Mostra de Cuina Mallorquina*, culinary week, specialising in home-grown cooking, in Palma.
Good Friday Processions everywhere, two of the best of which are the night *devallaments* in Sineu and Pollença, Mallorca.
1 May Agricultural show in Sineu, Mallorca.
9 May Brave Women of Sóller festival in Sóller, Mallorca.
June Palma book fair.
23–4 June St John's (Sant Juan) Fiesta in Cuitadella, Menorca.
July *Cala Ratjada* summer festival of classical music (Mallorca).
August Chopin Festival at Valldemossa, Mallorca.
September Procession of the Beata in Santa Margalida, Mallorca (first Sunday).
October Alcúdia cattle and crafts festival, Mallorca.
November Craft fair, Inca, Mallorca.
16 December Patron saints procession in Palma, Mallorca.
• Local tourist offices have a complete list of events.

through the streets, or parading the town dressed in animal skins. In January the youths of Pollença, Mallorca, compete over the *pi de Sant Antoni*, a greased pole with a cock at the top. At the Feast of St Stephen (January) a procession is led by *cavallets*, or dancers dressed as horses and imitating the animals' trot.

Cinema

Despite the growing popularity of watching films on video at home, there are still queues at the many cinemas to see first-run movies. One can also enjoy the various cinema festivals held at the **Centro Cultural Sa Nostra** and the **Fundación La Caixa** in Palma. Cinemas such as the **Renoir** show films in their original language with subtitles. Listings are published daily in the press.

Ballet

Various Spanish and international ballets visit the islands, principally Mallorca, where the usual venue is the Auditorium in Palma.

Opera

Touring opera companies visit the islands, principally Mallorca. Spanish light opera (*zarzuela*) companies frequently appear at Palma's Teatro Principal.

Theatre

Spanish plays (mainly comedies) are staged frequently at Palma's Teatro Principal or the Auditorium, and some of these visit Menorca and Ibiza. In winter, expats, mainly British, produce plays for their own community. Among the most active are the two theatre groups in Santa Eulália, Ibiza.

Nightlife

The Balearic Islands have a plethora of bars and nightclubs. However, visitors should bear in mind that as in all resort areas bars often trade for a season only, to be replaced by new owners. Naturally, the "in" places also come and go. The best areas to explore at night in Palma are, and most probably always will be, La Lonja, Passeig Marítimo, Plaça Gomila and Puerto Portals. Stroll around any of these and you're bound to find the right place to suit your mood. New bars open every other week, but here is a list of the best and most stable places – perhaps it could also be said to be a list of survivors.

Pubs and Bars

PALMA

Abaco
Sant Juan 1.
Cocktails and a decadent baroque atmosphere, with classical music and rose petals falling from the ceiling at midnight. Truly one of the most unusual bars in Mallorca. No jeans.

Admiral's Bar
Passeig Marítimo 35.
Right on the harbour. Elegant and a bit dressy, with excellent cocktails and service.

Africa Bar
Teniente Mulet 17, near Plaça Gomila.
The Africa Bar is popular all year round with English-speaking residents. Owner Maureen McLaughlin keeps things going with memory-lane music, raffles, stuffed animals all over the walls, and a swear-box to help keep it all clean.

Agua
Jaime Ferrer 6 (La Lonja).
Drinks and lively music.

Bar Bellver
Plaça Gomila 10.
Principal bar on the plaza. Bernat and his professional staff have one of the top summer places to drink.

La Bodeguita del Medio
Vallesca 18.
A replica of the Bodeguita del Medio in Havana. Their speciality is the *mojito*, a rum cocktail served with freshly crushed mint leaves, immortalised by Hemingway.

Bar Bosch
Plaça Pio XII.
Opposite C&A department store, across from the tortoise fountain in the Borne, this is the favourite downtown sidewalk café.

Bar Chotis
Carrer de Nigul, Plaça Gomila.
Tucked away in an alley next to La Cocina, Chotis is for the young. Run by Bert and Maruja, and offering a choice of good draught beers, it helps if you like to play space invader machines.

Club de Mar Bar
Club de Mar marina, on Avda Gabriel Roca, Passeig Marítimo.
Very busy with locally based yacht people and visiting boaties. Outside terrace, and reasonable prices.

Duksa
Passeig Mallorca 10, downtown.
Close to the main shopping area, with both indoor and terrace tables for watching the passing scene.

Dylans
Avda. Joan Miró, opposite the Hotel Borenco.
Music bar, mainly for the young, playing rock and jazz. At the back, there's a huge patio and pool table.

Hogan's
Monseñor Palmer (facing the port).
A bit of Ireland in Palma. Guinness, Kilkenny and good music.

Made in Brasil
Passeig Marítimo 27.
Authentic Brazilian music and cocktails, with lambada and samba lessons available. Made in Brasil gets very lively at weekends.

Bar Marìtimo
Passeig Marítimo 1.
Has a large outdoor terrace.

Minim
Right on Plaça Gomila.
One of the most popular bars with

young people; the clients overflow into the square and block traffic, but it is all good-natured fun. Next door is Tito's disco. Weekends only.

La Oficina
Passeig Mallorca 26.
A bar used mainly by local business people but owner Tony welcomes visitors for coffee, aperitifs or snacks. Pavement tables.

El Patio
Plaça Gomila.
Formerly a famous restaurant, El Patio is now a stylish club for teenagers and students.

La Pollila
Avda. Joan Miró 55, near Plaça Gomila.
Popular with the young. Passers-by can't miss the loud music and strange-smelling smoke issuing from windows and door.

Rustic Bar
Plaça Mediterráneo.
Run by the people from the next-door Hostal Terramar, the bar appeals to local English youth, and has a downstairs pool table. Music is 60s and 70s.

Totem
Avda. Joan Miró 47, near Plaça Gomila.
This is a topless bar. Prices of drinks increase in proportion to the degree of interest shown in the staff. Many other topless bars exist in the area, but are not listed due to lack of space.

Trago Loco
Robert Graves 13.
For stay-up-lates. Music and videos till sun-up.

Es Trui
Plaça Gomila.
Popular with a younger crowd who like their background music right in the foreground. Pleasant decor and a nice owner.

Wellies
At the superb Puerto Portals marina, just outside Palma. Wellies is not cheap, the service is disorganised, yet the best location in the marina ensures it is always full of action. There is a great choice of other bars and restaurants within the marina, which are not listed due to lack of space. The best move is to go there and walk around.

Las Verjas
Plaça Mediterráneo, tucked away in a corner next to the Tai-Pan Chinese restaurant, in the Plaça Gomila area. Drink the bottled beer and go accompanied, preferably by a local.

Live Music in Palma

American Country
Passeig Marítimo 1.
American food, drink and music. Country and western, tex-mex and hamburgers.

Banderas
Puerto Portals 79-81.
Friendly staff and the authentic ambience of a live-music venue.

Bluesville
Ma d'es Moro 3.
Jazz and blues every night. Shows begin around 11pm.

Waikiki
Plaça Mediterráneo.
Until the early hours. Owner Laval, from Mauritius, serves exotic all-night cocktails.

MENORCA
Ciutadella
Box
A renovated palace in the centre of town with a large terrace.
El Mosquito
Salsa.
La Torre de Papel
Camí de Maó 46.
A hip, busy café-bar with a bookshop at the front.

Maó
Akelarre
On the waterfront.
Late-night music.
Icaro
On the waterfront.
Late-night music.
Sa Sinia
San Josep 49.
Live music.
Sí
Virgen de Gracia 16.
Good atmosphere and drinks.

Villacarlos
Georgetown Cocktail Bar
Calapadera 4.

IBIZA
In Eivissa (Ibiza town) the preferred bars are those facing the harbour, or along the main square of Vara de Rey. Pleasant bars with a nautical tone can also be found in Botafoch, the marina near Talamanca beach. The "in" thing is to go to a rave until sunrise; they're usually held on one of Ibiza's many sandy beaches or up in the mountains.

Santa Eulália
Anita's Bar
Doubles as bar and post office. Try their delicious *herbes* drink.
Fred's Bar
In the main square, next to the Guardia Civil. Living off its former reputation and its great location, but the service is off-hand.
Grumpy's Pub and Bistro
Sant Juan 3. Tel: 971 332175.
HQ of the local cricket fraternity.
Bar Miramar
Sant Juan 27.
Tel: 971 331272.
Noisy pub and restaurant run by Eddie and Rosie from Britain.
Pomelo
Camino de la Iglesia.
Tel: 971 330474.
Popular uptown meeting place.
Top Hat
Isidoro Macabith.

Sant Antoni
Café del Mar
Not far from the harbour jetty.
New Manhattan
Carrer Soledad.
San Francisco
Near Carrer Soledad.

Gay Venues
PALMA
Capri is a bar with a sun-terrace, along the road toward the Apartsuit building. The only bar in this category to open in the mornings, go here for coffee and croissant at breakfast-time, when host Basilio dispenses sympathy for tough tales from the previous night, along with aspirin, if required.
The Ivy House, Plaça Gomila area, is run by host, Paco. Very white,

Greek-style decor, tasteful and well-furnished with comfortable seating. **Gigolo**, also nicely decorated and with a large rear patio. Offers late-night shows, professionally staged. Hetero couples are often turned away at the door .
La Yedra Long a meeting place for international travellers. Near several other gay bars, including Gigolo.
Milord, near The Ivy House.
Querelle, across the street from Gigolo, has the same door policy and stages late-night shows, with host Marcos to welcome guests.
Sombrero, all on its own on Avenida Joan Miró, welcomes lesbians.
Status, just up the street from Querelle, past Plaça Gomila, is tucked away down the stairs next to the Pesebre Restaurant, and has Pepe and Bernardo as hosts.

EIVISSA

As in Palma, the gay bars in Ibiza town are pretty much neighbours, clustered around the foot of Dalt Vila. The best are:
Anfora Disco, San Carlos 1.
Angelo's, Alfonso XII 11.
Bronx, Bulevar, Ibiza.
Incognito, Santa Lucia.
Mouvi Bar, Mayor 34.
Napoleon, Santa Lucia 21.
Why Not?, Plaça del Puerto.
   Es Caballet Beach, out via the airport road toward the Salinas salt-flats, is recognised as a gay beach.

Nightclubs

MALLORCA

Arenal & Can Pastilla area
Bolero, Laud 32.
Joy Palace, Misión San Gabriel.
Makiavelo, Padre Bartolomé Salvà 3.
Riu Palace. One of the biggest and best-known of the many discos along Platja de Palma, between Can Pastilla and s'Arenal.
Zorba's, Avda. Son Rigo 4.

Cala Mayor area
La Sirena. One of the oldest discos on the island. Latest music.

Port d'Alcúdia area
Menta. Beautiful people congregate

around the swimming pool until dawn. Great music.

Palma
Bésame Mucho, Avda. Joan Miró 3. Perfect for a romantic evening. Slow dancing to live music. No fee.
Club de Mar. One of the most select discos in town.
Tito's Palace, Plaça Gomila. One of the most modern and exclusive discos in Europe.
Pacha, Passeig Marítimo. Beautiful people.

Palma Nova, Magalluf & Paguera area
BCM. Possibly the largest disco in Europe.

MENORCA
Jaleo, in San Luis. Beautiful people.
Cueva d'en Xeroi, Cala d'En Porter. Scores extra points for its original location – inside a large cave on the cliff face above the beach. Open nightly 10pm to dawn.
Adagio's, in Ciutadella.
Jazz Cava, in Maó centre. A casino turned into a disco. Live music.
Flinstones, San Jorge 10, Villacarlos.

Enjoying a Flutter

Casinos Both Mallorca and Ibiza have modern casinos. Mallorca's is 10 minutes from Palma, and apart from a gaming room, has a major dinner-show, sports centre and beach club, plus an excellent restaurant. Ibiza's casino is close to Eivissa and the marina, with a restaurant and entertainment.
   Residents and tourists are required to show identification to get into casinos. In the case of non-residents, a passport is essential. Much underground gambling takes place on the islands, usually in privately-run clandestine card-games, but these are unlikely to be seen by visitors.

Lotteries There are several lotteries available to the public, including the visitor. Among these

IBIZA
The island has some of the best and extravagant discos in the world. The action doesn't start until around 3am, when everything is possible as long as you are willing to stay up all night. Following is a list of the largest and most popular in Eivissa (Ibiza town):
Privilege, on Carrer Sant Rafael.
Pach, on Passeig Marítimo.
El Divino, on Passeig Marítimo.
Space, on the Platja d'En Bossa. Opens when the other discos close, at dawn.
   Other discos (smaller in size but more cosy) are:
Amnesia, on Carrer San Rafael.
El Dome, on Alfonso XII. Eccentric and pink.

FORMENTERA
The quietest island when it comes to nightlife, Formentera has no large discos. But there are plenty of small bars and cafés along the narrow stretch of land, and the Hotel La Mola is a good option for dancing or having a drink.

is the daily pool run by the blind peoples' benevolent society, ONCE; a weekly national lottery; a weekly "primitiva" lottery (not unlike the National Lottery in the UK, won with a combination of numbers); a football and horse-racing pool; and regional lotteries such as Catalonia's two weekly lotteries.
   Large tax-free prizes of 300 to 400 million pesetas are not unknown, and the national lottery holds a giant lottery at Christmas, named El Niño after the baby Jesus, and another draw known as El Gordo, "The Fat One", in which huge amounts are won.

Slot machines The Spanish are avid gamblers; slot-machine annual revenues here are the highest in Europe.

Sport

Participant Sports

All three main islands have golf, tennis, scuba, horseriding, soccer, squash, windsurfing and other popular sports available for visitors to enjoy. Formentera, with its location and beaches, tends to specialise in windsurfing and watersports, including underwater.

Hang-gliding, go-karting and other activities, including several fun water parks are also available. On the islands there are 38 tennis clubs, over 10 golf courses, innumerable soccer and sports grounds, and a large number of other organised sports.

The following list details various sporting bodies in the Balearics, but for more information contact the local tourist office in Palma.

Golf
The following are two of Mallorca's most prestigious golf courses.
Capdepera Golf
Carretera Artà-Capdepera, km 3.5
Tel: 971 818500.
Open 7am–7pm. Has a golf school and a restaurant.
Club de Golf Santa Ponça
In Torrenova, the busy headland bordering Palma Nova and Magalluf.
Pula Golf
Carretera Son Servera-Capdepera, km 3.
Tel: 971 817034.
Son Vida Club de Golf. Tel: 971210. In the exclusive *urbanización* of Son Vida, 5km (3 miles) northwest of Palma.

Tennis/Squash
Mallorca Tennis Club, Mestre d'Aixa, Palma. Tel: 971 738473.
Elite Club, Avda. Joan Miró 334, Palma. Tel: 971 402080.

Horseriding
Rancho Colorado, El Arenal, Mallorca. Tel: 971 264595.
Horse Riding School, Bunyola, Mallorca. Tel: 971 613157.

Water-skiing
Ski Club Calanova, Son Ferrer, Calvià, Mallorca. Tel: 971 100320.

Parachuting
Real Aeroclub de Baleares, Marratxí. Tel: 971 600114.

Hang-gliding
Club Parapente Mallorca. Tel. 971 891366.

Scuba
Tritón. Tel: 971 466125.
Unidad Costa Norte, Calvià, Mallorca. Tel: 971 102676.

Outdoor Activities

Hiking and Climbing
Hiking and climbing holidays on the islands are increasingly popular. Simple hikes in the flatter parts of the island can be undertaken alone, but guides are essential up in the Serra de Tramuntana, where walkers face differences in height of up to 1,000m (3,328ft). The major dangers are sudden rainstorms and deep ravines.

There are a number of interesting hiking excursions, one of which goes from Valldemossa in Mallorca to the Puig del Teix – a six-hour walk that takes hikers to the top of the mountain with a panoramic view of Deià and the Mediterranean coast. For more information, contact one of the many tourist offices in Palma.

For information on mountain climbing, call GEM on 971 711314.

Cycling
Cyclists will encounter all levels of difficulty in Mallorca. The flat stretches of coast in the north, the nature reserve of Albufera at Alcúdia, and the island's flat interior present no trouble. The northwest coast, however, has marvellously steep parts for the particularly ambitious cyclist.

Every kind of bicycle, including mountain bikes (and even Harley-Davidson motorcycles), can be hired at the resorts. In Ibiza and Formentera, cycling is highly recommended, and presents no trouble even for the unfit because of their flatter geography.

Birdwatching
Mallorca has a huge variety of wildlife, mainly on its neighbouring uninhabited islet of Dragonera, and in the Albufera nature reserve, in Alcúdia. Contact GOB (tel: 971 721105) for more information.

Spectator Sports

Spaniards are avid football fans. During the winter soccer season there are games all over the islands on Sundays, and even the smaller villages have teams.

Tennis tournaments, horse-racing, car and motorcycle races, sailing regattas, handball, basketball, billiards and other competitions all have either paid or gratis entry for spectators. Bull-fighting does not have a popular following on the islands. although there are bull rings in Palma and Muro, Mallorca.

The high point of the sailing season in Mallorca is the Copa del Rey (King's Cup) in August.

Shopping

What to Buy

All the islands produce good leatherware, with footwear factories in Mallorca and Menorca, and nicely designed leather clothing available everywhere.

Mallorca has artificial pearl and glass-blowing factories.

Menorca has a well-developed costume jewellery industry, and also produces excellent cheeses and gin.

Ibiza is known for its Ad Lib fashion label, an attractive mix-and-match approach to fashion, and also has a large cottage industry in hippie crafts and jewellery. The three main islands have branches or franchises known internationally, including Benetton, Bally, Loewe, Charles Jourdan and so on.

Locally produced pottery and ceramics (particularly cooking vessels) are a good buy on all islands, and there is a choice of good embroidery and basketwork.

Reasonably priced paintings by local artists are also worth looking at, and these can be seen in galleries, or at lower prices in the flea and hippie markets.

Shopping Hours

Shops Most shops are open 9.30am–1.30pm and 4.30–8pm on weekdays, and usually open mornings only on Saturdays, although a number do stay open all day Saturday.

Supermarkets The multiple stores and hypermarkets do not close at lunchtime, and usually open from 10am to 9pm Monday to Saturday.

Shopping Areas

Palma has the largest choice of areas, with its Avenida Jaime III, Passeig Mallorca, Passeig Marítimo, Avenida Sindicato, Plaça Mayor, Via Roma and the Saturday flea-market.

There are multiple stores, such as C&A and El Corte Inglés, and large super and hyper-markets, both in and out of town. In the city, there are covered markets for groceries, meat and seafood, all well worth a visit, although parking nearby can be difficult.

Markets & Antiques

A list of suppliers for speciality shopping, such as antiques, embroidery, jewellery and so on is issued by the local government and distributed through tourist information offices and hotels. In the high season, most resorts have a good choice of shops open, often till late at night.

Menorca has good shopping in Maó, with most of the same variety of outlets as in Palma. Good buys in artisan-work can be found all over Ibiza. This is particularly the case at the Wednesday Hippy Market at Punta Arabi, near Santa Eulália. Each town has its own market, with typical products of the area. Normally these take place in the town plaza in the mornings. Following is a list of the most interesting markets.

PALMA
Antiques
Juan de Juan
Arabí 5.
Filled with old junk. If you are lucky, you may find an object of value.
Palau Real
Carrer Palau Real.
Sells antiques but with a modern design. Very interesting pieces.

Markets
El Rastro Palmesano (Flee Market)
Avda. Alomar Villalonga.
Every Saturday, the streets are filled with second-hand and new clothes, shoes, antiques, old books

and so on. Get there early if you want to find anything worth taking back with you.
Mercado del Olivar
Near Plaça Espanya.
A beautiful old market full of arches, which sells fresh fish, vegetables and fruit. Try the *tapas* with a cold beer in one of the five bars.

OUTSIDE PALMA
Markets
Monday: Calviá, Manacor, Monturi, Lloret.
Tuesday: Alcúdia, Artà, Can Picafort.
Wednesday: Andraxt, Capdepera, Llucmajor.
Thursday: Ariany, Campos, Can Pastilla, Inca, Llucmajor.
Friday: Alaró (afternoon), Algaida, Binissalem, Can Picafort (afternoon), María de la Salut.
Saturday: S'Arenal, Buger, Bunyola, Cala Ratjada, Campanet, Campos, Costix, Esporlas, Sóller.
Sunday: Alcúdia, s'Arenal, Felanitx, Llucmajor, Muro, Sa Pobla, Pollença.

MENORCA
Markets
Ciutadella: Fri, Sat am
Maó: Tue, Sat am
San Luis: Mon, Wed am
Villacarlos: Mon, Wed am

IBIZA
Markets
Eivissa (Bahamas Complex): Sat pm, in summer only.
San Miguel: Thurs pm
Sant Antoni (Sa Tanca): Fri, all day in summer.
Santa Eulália (Punta Arabi): Wed all day.

Language

The Local Language

Although Spanish (or Castillian) is the national language, the Balearic people also use a vernacular language, which in Mallorca is known as Mallorquin, in Menorca Menorquin, and in Ibiza Ibiçenco (Eivissenc). All three languages, which are local variants of Catalan, are similar in vocabulary, with component words having their origin in Italian, Latin, French, Portuguese and Arabic. A visitor with knowledge of a Latin or Romance-based language can manage to understand much of what is being said.

In his book *Majorca Observed*, Robert Graves states that Mallorquin is as ancient a language as English and more pure than Catalan or Provençal, its two closest relatives.

While local people speak Spanish and everybody in the tourist business is fairly fluent in English, you may find the following small list of Catalan words and expressions useful. Pronunciation is phonetic, so that most words are spoken as spelt, usually with the stress on the penultimate syllable, unless an accent indicates otherwise.

Signs on main roads are in Spanish and Mallorquin.

Common Words and Phrases

good morning	*bon día*
good afternoon	*bona tarde*
good night	*bona nit*
see you later	*fins després*
thank you	*grácies*
today	*avui*
excuse me	*perdó/escolti*
please	*per favor*

luggage	*equipatje*
you're welcome	*de rés*
it's all right	*está be*
now	*ara*
do you speak English?	
	parla el ingles?
how much is that?	*que val?*

On the Street

where?	*on?*
open	*obert*
closed	*tancat*
left	*esquerra*
right	*dreta*
straight ahead	*tot dret*
beach	*platja*
bill/check	*sa conta*
newspaper	*periódic*
post office	*correus*
square	*plaça*
stamp	*segell*
street	*carrer*
urgent	*urgent*
water	*aigua*

At the Hotel

bed	*llit*
change	*canvi*
doctor	*metge*
a room	*una habitació*
soap	*sabó*
towel	*tovallola*
two people	*dues personas*

Further Reading

Bookshops

Books on the Balearics can be found at principal bookshops, such as the Librería Fondeville, Arabí 14, Palma; Librería Ereso, Carrer Peraires 1, Palma; and Island Books, Isidoro Macabich, Santa Eulália, Ibiza. La Foradada Press publishes a series of books on Mallorca (some in English), available at bookshops and kiosks.

Throughout the islands, there are second-hand book-exchanges and libraries specialising in English. Further reading material includes:

General Background

Insiders and Outsiders, Paradise and Reality in Mallorca by Jackie Brown (Berghan Books). This is an interesting account of how the population of a small village has gained full advantage from the economic opportunities opened up by foreign investment, without losing the meaning and value of their culture.
Majorca Observed by Robert Graves and illustrated by Paul Hogarth (Foradada Press).
The Spaniard and the Seven Deadly Sins by Fernando Diaz-Plajas (Pan Books).
Wild Olives by William Graves (Hutchinson). Robert Graves' son's account of growing up in Deià and his troubled relationship with his father.

Flora and Fauna

Birdwatching in Mallorca by Ken Stoba (Cicerone Press). A useful catalogue of Mallorcan birdlife and birdwatching sites.
Butterflies of the Province by Honor Tracy (Methuen).
Menorca by John and Margaret Goulding (Windrush). This general

guide has detailed information on the island's flora and fauna.

Specialist Guides

Entrée to Mallorca by Patricia Fenn (Quiller Press). Enthusiastic restaurant guide.
Landscapes of Mallorca by Valerie Crespi-Green (by Sunflower Books).
Trekking in Spain by Marc Dubin (Lonely Planet). This trekking guide has a detailed chapter on hikes in the Serra de Tramuntana in Mallorca.
Walking in Mallorca by June Parker (Cicerone Press).

Travel Accounts

A Winter in Majorca by George Sands (Valldemossa Editions, Mallorca). George Sand's famously scathing account of her brief stay on the island in 1838–9, accompanied by her lover, Frédéric Chopin, translated and with comments by Robert Graves.
Jogging Round Majorca by Gordon West (Black Swan). Delightful, whimsical account of a journey round an unspoilt island by Gordon West and his wife Mary in the 1920s.
Not Part of the Package by Paul Richardson (Pan Books). An entertaining "alternative" travel book about a year on Ibiza.

Magazines

Balearic Homes and Living. Published by Edificio Neptuna, Plaza Mediterráneo, 07015 Palma de Mallorca.
Lookout. Published by Puebla Lucia, Fuengirola, 29640 Malaga.
New Projects. Published by Editora Inmobiliaria Balear, Julian Alvarez 12a–2, Palma de Mallorca.

Other Insight Guides

Europe is comprehensively covered by the 400 titles in Apa Publications' three series of guidebooks which embrace the world.

Insight Guides

This series provides the reader with a full cultural background and top-quality photography. Titles which highlight Spanish destinations include: Spain, Northern Spain, Catalonia, Barcelona, Madrid, Southern Spain, Gran Canaria and Tenerife.

Pocket Guides

Apa Publications also publishes Insight Pocket Guides, written by local hosts and containing tailormade itineraries to help users get the most out of a place during a short stay. Each title also has a pull-out map. Spanish destinations in the series include: Madrid, Barcelona, Granada and Seville, Costa Blanca, Costa del Sol, Ibiza, Mallorca, Tenerife and Gran Canaria.

Compact Guides

To complete all the needs of travellers, Insight Compact Guides, in essence mini encyclopaedias, give you the facts about a destination in a very digestible form, supported by maps and colour photographs. Titles in the series include Mallorca, Barcelona, Costa Brava, Gran Canaria and Tenerife.

ART & PHOTO CREDITS

Ajuntament de Palma 33
L.J. Barbadillo 198/199, 202T, 203, 221
Peter Bargh/Mark Azavedo Photo Library 123
Alfredo Caliz/Cover 95, 124, 127
Agustin Catalan/Cover 77
Agustin/Rabal/Cover 78
Juan Costa/Cover 79, 249
Luis Davilla/Cover 97
Andrew Eames 22, 216
Glyn Genin 23, 24, 30, 47, 48, 78, 85, 90, 91, 143, 145T, 147T, 147L, 147R, 148T, 148, 149T, 150, 152, 153T, 161, 164T, 164, 165, 167, 168T, 169T, 169, 170, 171, 172, 173T, 173, 176, 177, 178T, 178, 179, 183, 184, 185T, 187, 189T, 189, 190T, 190L, 190R, 192T, 192, 193, 194T, 195T, 196
Doug Goodman 125, 158/159, 231
Juame Gual 21, 25, 57, 67, 70, 106, 132/133, 166, 191, 202, 254
Wolfgang Huppertz/Agenda 35, 72
Michael Kottmeier/Agenda 154, 168, 182
Oliver Krist 56
Melba Levick 251T
Llenas/Cover 151
Mike Mockler 102, 103, 107
Trevor Moore/Mark Azavedo Photo Library 142
Don Murray 1, 12/13, 16/17, 19, 37, 42, 43, 44, 45, 46, 64, 73, 82, 88, 98, 110/111, 112, 114, 116, 118, 119, 140/141, 186,

188, 197, 200, 201, 213, 230, 274, 275
Museo de Mallorca 28, 29, 31, 34
Museo Diocesano, Palma 27, 39, 41
Kim Naylor 32, 36, 115, 136, 194
Angel Ortega/Naturpress 105
Walter Obiol 80/81, 117
Roberto Olivas/Naturpress 146, 149, 153, 174/175, 227
Jose R. Platon/Cover 215
G. P. Reichelt/Apa Archive 62/63
A. Rodriguez-Llenas/Cover 94
Spectrum 83
Bill Wassman 2/3, 6/7, 8/9, 10/11, 14, 18, 20, 26, 38, 40, 49, 50/51, 52/53, 54, 55, 58, 59, 65, 66, 69/69, 71, 74/75, 84, 86/87, 89, 92/93, 96, 99, 100/101, 104, 113, 120/121, 122, 126, 128/129, 130/131, 134, 135, 145, 155, 160, 180/181, 185, 195, 206/207, 208/209, 210, 212, 216T, 218T, 218, 219, 220, 221T, 222T, 222, 223, 224, 225, 226, 228/229, 232T, 232, 233, 234, 235, 236T, 236, 237, 238T, 238, 239, 240/241, 242/243, 246, 247, 249T, 250, 252T, 252, 253T, 253, 255, 256, 257T, 257, 258, 259, 260/261, 262, 263, 264, 265T, 265, 266T, 266L, 266R, 267, 268, 269, 270/271, 272/273, 275, 277T, 277, 278T, 278, 279, 280
Betty Luton White 4/5

Cartographic Editor **Zoë Goodwin**
Production **Stuart A Everitt**
Design Consultants
Carlotta Junger, Graham Mitchener
Picture Research **Hilary Genin, Monica Allende**

Picture Spreads

Pages 60/61
Top row, left to right: Michael Kottmeier/Agenda; Quim Llenas/Cover; Joan Costa/Cover; Carlos Agustin
Bottom row, left to right: Carlos Agustin, Bill Wassman, Spectrum, Doug Goodman
Pages 108/109
Top row, left to right:
J. Barbadillo/Naturpress,
J.L. González Grande/Naturpress,
L.J. Barbadillo/Naturpress
Centre row, right: L.J. Barbadillo
Bottom row, left to right:
J Barbadillo/Naturpress,
J.L. González Grande/Naturpress,
J.L. González Grande/Naturpress,
L.J. Barbadillo/Naturpress
Pages 156/157
Top row, left to right: Glyn Genin, Private Archive, Associated Press Photos, Paris, Galerie Bischofberger
Bottom row, left to right: Glyn Genin, Roberto Olivas/Naturpress, Glyn Genin, Topham Picturepoint
Pages 204/205
Top row, left to right: Glyn Genin, Roberto Olivas/Naturpress, Don Murray, Glyn Genin
Bottom row, left to right: Kim Naylor, Glyn Genin, Don Murray, Wolfgang Huppertz/Agenda

Map Production Berndtson & Berndtson Productions
© 1999 Apa Publications GmbH & Co. Verlag KG (Singapore branch)

Index

Numbers in italics refer to photographs

The World of Insight Guides

400 books in three complementary series cover every major destination in every continent.

Insight Guides

Alaska
Alsace
Amazon Wildlife
American Southwest
Amsterdam
Argentina
Atlanta
Athens
Australia
Austria
Bahamas
Bali
Baltic States
Bangkok
Barbados
Barcelona
Bay of Naples
Beijing
Belgium
Belize
Berlin
Bermuda
Boston
Brazil
Brittany
Brussels
Budapest
Buenos Aires
Burgundy
Burma (Myanmar)
Cairo
Calcutta
California
Canada
Caribbean
Catalonia
Channel Islands
Chicago
Chile
China
Cologne
Continental Europe
Corsica
Costa Rica
Crete
Crossing America
Cuba
Cyprus
Czech & Slovak Republics
Delhi, Jaipur, Agra
Denmark
Dresden
Dublin
Düsseldorf
East African Wildlife
East Asia
Eastern Europe
Ecuador
Edinburgh
Egypt
Finland
Florence
Florida
France
Frankfurt
French Riviera
Gambia & Senegal
Germany
Glasgow

Gran Canaria
Great Barrier Reef
Great Britain
Greece
Greek Islands
Hamburg
Hawaii
Hong Kong
Hungary
Iceland
India
India's Western Himalaya
Indian Wildlife
Indonesia
Ireland
Israel
Istanbul
Italy
Jamaica
Japan
Java
Jerusalem
Jordan
Kathmandu
Kenya
Korea
Lisbon
Loire Valley
London
Los Angeles
Madeira
Madrid
Malaysia
Mallorca & Ibiza
Malta
Marine Life in the South
  China Sea
Melbourne
Mexico
Mexico City
Miami
Montreal
Morocco
Moscow
Munich
Namibia
Native America
Nepal
Netherlands
New England
New Orleans
New York City
New York State
New Zealand
Nile
Normandy
Northern California
Northern Spain
Norway
Oman & the UAE
Oxford
Old South
Pacific Northwest
Pakistan
Paris
Peru
Philadelphia
Philippines
Poland
Portugal
Prague

Provence
Puerto Rico
Rajasthan
Rhine
Rio de Janeiro
Rockies
Rome
Russia
St Petersburg
San Francisco
Sardinia
Scotland
Seattle
Sicily
Singapore
South Africa
South America
South Asia
South India
South Tyrol
Southeast Asia
Southeast Asia Wildlife
Southern California
Southern Spain
Spain
Sri Lanka
Sweden
Switzerland
Sydney
Taiwan
Tenerife
Texas
Thailand
Tokyo
Trinidad & Tobago
Tunisia
Turkey
Turkish Coast
Tuscany
Umbria
US National Parks East
US National Parks West
Vancouver
Venezuela
Venice
Vienna
Vietnam
Wales
Washington DC
Waterways of Europe
Wild West
Yemen

Insight Pocket Guides

Aegean Islands★
Algarve★
Alsace
Amsterdam★
Athens★
Atlanta★
Bahamas★
Baja Peninsula★
Bali★
Bali Bird Walks
Bangkok★
Barbados★
Barcelona★
Bavaria★
Beijing★
Berlin★

Bermuda★
Bhutan★
Boston★
British Columbia★
Brittany★
Brussels★
Budapest &
  Surroundings★
Canton★
Chiang Mai★
Chicago★
Corsica★
Costa Blanca★
Costa Brava★
Costa del Sol/Marbella★
Costa Rica★
Crete★
Denmark★
Fiji★
Florence★
Florida★
Florida Keys★
French Riviera★
Gran Canaria★
Hawaii★
Hong Kong★
Hungary
Ibiza★
Ireland★
Ireland's Southwest★
Israel★
Istanbul★
Jakarta★
Jamaica★
Kathmandu Bikes &
  Hikes★
Kenya★
Kuala Lumpur★
Lisbon★
Loire Valley★
London★
Macau
Madrid★
Malacca
Maldives
Mallorca★
Malta★
Mexico City★
Miami★
Milan★
Montreal★
Morocco★
Moscow
Munich★
Nepal★
New Delhi
New Orleans★
New York City★
New Zealand★
Northern California★
Oslo/Bergen★
Paris★
Penang★
Phuket★
Prague★
Provence★
Puerto Rico★
Quebec★
Rhodes★
Rome★
Sabah★

St Petersburg★
San Francisco★
Sardinia
Scotland★
Seville★
Seychelles★
Sicily★
Sikkim
Singapore★
Southeast England
Southern California★
Southern Spain★
Sri Lanka★
Sydney★
Tenerife★
Thailand★
Tibet★
Toronto★
Tunisia★
Turkish Coast★
Tuscany★
Venice★
Vienna★
Vietnam★
Yogyakarta★
Yucatan Peninsula★

★ = Insight Pocket Guides
with Pull out Maps

Insight Compact Guides

Algarve
Amsterdam
Bahamas
Bali
Bangkok
Barbados
Barcelona
Beijing
Belgium
Berlin
Brittany
Brussels
Budapest
Burgundy
Copenhagen
Costa Brava
Costa Rica
Crete
Cyprus
Czech Republic
Denmark
Dominican Republic
Dublin
Egypt
Finland
Florence
Gran Canaria
Greece
Holland
Hong Kong
Ireland
Israel
Italian Lakes
Italian Riviera
Jamaica
Jerusalem
Lisbon
Madeira
Mallorca
Malta

Milan
Moscow
Munich
Normandy
Norway
Paris
Poland
Portugal
Prague
Provence
Rhodes
Rome
St Petersburg
Salzburg
Singapore
Switzerland
Sydney
Tenerife
Thailand
Turkey
Turkish Coast
Tuscany
UK regional titles:
  Bath & Surroundings
  Cambridge & East
    Anglia
  Cornwall
  Cotswolds
  Devon & Exmoor
  Edinburgh
  Lake District
  London
  New Forest
  North York Moors
  Northumbria
  Oxford
  Peak District
  Scotland
  Scottish Highlands
  Shakespeare Country
  Snowdonia
  South Downs
  York
  Yorkshire Dales
USA regional titles:
  Boston
  Cape Cod
  Chicago
  Florida
  Florida Keys
  Hawaii: Maui
  Hawaii: Oahu
  Las Vegas
  Los Angeles
  Martha's Vineyard &
    Nantucket
  New York
  San Francisco
  Washington D.C.
Venice
Vienna
West of Ireland